# CYBORG SELVES

# Ashgate Science and Religion Series

*Series Editors:*

Roger Trigg, *Emeritus Professor, University of Warwick, and Academic Director of the Centre for the Study of Religion in Public Life, Kellogg College, Oxford*

J. Wentzel van Huyssteen, *Princeton Theological Seminary, USA*

Science and religion have often been thought to be at loggerheads but much contemporary work in this flourishing interdisciplinary field suggests this is far from the case. The *Ashgate Science and Religion Series* presents exciting new work to advance interdisciplinary study, research and debate across key themes in science and religion, exploring the philosophical relations between the physical and social sciences on the one hand and religious belief on the other. Contemporary issues in philosophy and theology are debated, as are prevailing cultural assumptions arising from the 'post-modernist' distaste for many forms of reasoning. The series enables leading international authors from a range of different disciplinary perspectives to apply the insights of the various sciences, theology and philosophy and look at the relations between the different disciplines and the rational connections that can be made between them. These accessible, stimulating new contributions to key topics across science and religion will appeal particularly to individual academics and researchers, graduates, postgraduates and upper-undergraduate students.

*Other titles in the series:*

*The Cognitive Science of Religion*
James A. Van Slyke
978-1-4094-2123-8 (hbk)

*Science and Faith within Reason*
*Reality, Creation, Life and Design*
Edited by Jaume Navarro
978-1-4094-2608-0 (hbk)

*Naturalism, Theism and the Cognitive Study of Religion*
*Religion Explained?*
Aku Visala
978-1-4094-2426-0 (hbk)

# Cyborg Selves
A Theological Anthropology of the Posthuman

JEANINE THWEATT-BATES
*New Brunswick Theological Seminary, USA*

ASHGATE

© Jeanine Thweatt-Bates 2012

All rights reserved. No part of this publication may be reproduced, stored in a retrieval system or transmitted in any form or by any means, electronic, mechanical, photocopying, recording or otherwise without the prior permission of the publisher.

Jeanine Thweatt-Bates has asserted her right under the Copyright, Designs and Patents Act, 1988, to be identified as the author of this work.

Published by
Ashgate Publishing Limited
Wey Court East
Union Road
Farnham
Surrey, GU9 7PT
England

Ashgate Publishing Company
Suite 420
101 Cherry Street
Burlington
VT 05401-4405
USA

www.ashgate.com

**British Library Cataloguing in Publication Data**
Thweatt-Bates, Jeanine.
 Cyborg selves : a theological anthropology of the
 posthuman. – (Ashgate science and religion series)
 1. Theological anthropology. 2. Human body–Religious
 aspects. 3. Technology–Religious aspects.
 I. Title II. Series
 202.2-dc23

**Library of Congress Cataloging-in-Publication Data**
Thweatt-Bates, Jeanine.
 Cyborg selves : a theological anthropology of the posthuman / Jeanine Thweatt-Bates.
   p. cm. – (Ashgate science and religion series)
 Includes bibliographical references and index.
 ISBN 978-1-4094-2141-2 (hbk) – ISBN 978-1-4094-2142-9 (ebk)
 1. Theological anthropology. 2. Philosophical anthropology. 3. Human evolution. 4. Human beings–Forecasting. 5. Cyborgs. I. Title.
 BL256.T55 2012
 233–dc23

2011050161

ISBN 9781409421412 (hbk)
ISBN 9781409421429 (ebk)

Printed and bound in Great Britain by the
MPG Books Group, UK

# Contents

| | |
|---|---|
| *List of Figures and Table* | *vii* |
| *Foreword by Wes Sherman* | *ix* |
| *Preface* | *xi* |
| Introduction: Theology and the Posthuman | 1 |
| 1   The Cyborg Manifesto | 15 |
| 2   The Transhumanist Manifesto | 41 |
| 3   Post-Anthropologies | 67 |
| 4   Theological Anthropologies | 109 |
| 5   Constructing a Theological Post-Anthropology | 135 |
| 6   Christology and the Posthuman | 175 |
| *Bibliography* | *193* |
| *Index* | *205* |

*Dedicated to my daughters*

# List of Figures and Table

**Figures**

I.1 Dinosaur Comics, "Dudes! Why are there no cyborgs yet?" By kind permission of Ryan North, qwantz.com — 2

1.1 Dinosaur Comics, "YOU ARE PROBABLY A CYBORG RIGHT NOW. are you aware??" By kind permission of Ryan North, qwantz.com — 21

1.2 Lynn Randolph, in the collection of Donna Haraway, "The Laboratory/The Passion of the OncoMouse," oil on masonite, 10" x 7" (1994). Reproduced with permission — 31

1.3 Lynn Randolph, "Cyborg," oil on canvas, 36" x 28" (1989). Reproduced with permission — 35

**Table**

3.1 Key differences between the cyborg and upload — 68

# Foreword

I was raised to think of the "self" as an accumulation of actions and thoughts over the course of a life. The word "self" like the word "soul" are signifiers that help bring definition to this life. Objects, like a painting, act in a similar way. A painting then becomes a stand-in for humanity and the artist. Literature, a painting, a building, a dance, a country: by themselves these will inevitably fail us, but where one of these things can only carry us so far the others can fill the void that we are trying to define. Walt Whitman in *Song of Myself* wrote, when words and the idea of living and dying could no longer be defined by him, "I sound my barbaric yawp over the roofs of the world." Whitman was left with a moan. When this great poem and his attempts to define his life could no longer be defined by words, he sounded a guttural yawp.

I was asked to paint a painting for Jeanine by her husband Brent to celebrate and mark her Doctorate degree. I was glad to do so because that is what I do; I paint paintings. The thing that became interesting about this commission for me, and the genesis of it, was our conversations about the cyborg and how science fiction uses this object to extend the idea of the human race or self. Through a number of conversations with Jen and Brent the central question "where is the self located" became important to me. Because of this I began asking my studio classes where they found themselves. When assigned to draw or paint a self-portrait, I would ask them where did they find themselves, in the mirror or in the body they were trying to depict?

As for myself, I was reminded of E.H. Gombrich's introduction to *The Story of Art*, where he argues that art objects are really more about the artist than the objects they make. I began to reflect on this idea as I painted *Cyborg*. I have often thought about my paintings as a place that holds my thoughts and, when completed, holding a part of myself; art is not a decoration but a declaration stated by the artist. I see the body of my work as living on separately from myself, acting as a stand-in for me, holding my thoughts in place. The question then is where does the self reside?

We have a sense of personal space. We often associate it with the body but we also use external things to define the self, be it a home, a painting, or our physical body. It is in the combination of these objects that we start to understand the self and these objects give us some kind of tangible idea of ourselves. I paint in an attempt to understand myself, and this life. I also collect art to fill the gaps where my own work seems to fail me. I use my art and my collection in a way that can help bring a tangible sense to the things I can't yet express. I like to think of my paintings, and art in general, as defining ourselves and lighting the way as we get closer to the idea of the self.

Wes Sherman
February 2011

# Preface

As I begin this sentence, a wakeful cry from down the hall interrupts me: my second child has decided to insert herself into this composition process once again. During the course of this project, I have given birth to two daughters. Experiencing this not once, but twice, while inhabiting the sometimes harmonious, sometimes discordant narratives of cyborg feminism and natural childbirth—this, more than anything else, has kept the fact of cyborg embodiment firmly in view. Never has the confusion of material and ontological boundaries between bodies, between self and other, been more clearly evident to me than in the physical state of pregnancy. I am grateful for the constant reminders of my children that I am not a floating head, regardless of how many times I might get lost in the text.

Others have contributed, knowingly and unknowingly, to the conception, research, writing, and revising of this book: Sarah Hinlicky Wilson and Andrew Wilson, who send me links to every article on cyborgs they come across; Lisa Powell, Anna Mercedes and Richard R. Bohannon II, Kenneth Reynhout, Jennifer Bayne, and Amy Michelle deBaets, whose own interests and research have not deterred them from contributing valuable critiques and insights; Raymond Bonwell and the marvelous participants in the Science for Ministry Institute; members and contributors of the American Academy of Religion Transhumanism and Religion Session; James Hughes, for his willingness to converse at length, and his good humor in confronting my ire over artificial wombs; Wentzel van Huyssteen, who has been superlatively supportive and encouraging, and whose work within the religion and science field on both methodology and the topic of human uniqueness provides the framework for this investigation into the posthuman and theological anthropology; Sarah Lloyd, my editor; Ira Lester Hays, still my favorite cyborg; and Christ's Church for Brooklyn, which, however scattered we may have become, is still my spiritual home. I must also add a note of appreciation to New Brunswick Theological Seminary, a community which in many ways embodies the Christian cyborg ideal these pages seek to express, and which has been a welcoming and stimulating community of learning for me.

A special note of gratitude goes to Wes Sherman, whose painting "Cyborg," commissioned by my spouse, graces our home and the cover of this book. Wes's abstract paintings are often commentary and interpretation of other artists' images; this, in recognition of her contributions to Haraway's cyborg discourse, he painted in dialogue with Lynn Randolph's cyborg imagery, in particular, her "Sky Walker Biding Thru," 58" x 46", oil on canvas (1994). In Wes's version, the female figure of Lynn's painting is transformed into a dark, multidimensional posthuman figure, perhaps archetypically feminine in its curvature but juxtaposed to a sharply angled, glossy triangular shape and framed by a silvery background evocative of classic 1950s shells of robots or starships, creating ripples of earthy overtones in the shifting connections between self and environment, as she moves out into her unknown future. Wes's image is earthy and technological, and beautiful to contemplate.

Finally, for the inspiration to renegotiate my own categorical identities, which the most formative relationships in my life have given me, I am truly grateful: to my husband, my parents, my sisters, and my daughters.

Jeanine Thweatt-Bates
June 30, 2011

# Introduction: Theology and the Posthuman

The questions voiced by T-rex and Utahraptor are ubiquitous in musings regarding what we might call our posthuman future. Why isn't it here yet? Or maybe it already is. Won't it be scary? Or maybe it will be brilliant. When it finally arrives, will we have brought it on ourselves? Or maybe it is simply the next phase of an inexorable deterministic evolutionary process. What counts as human, and what counts as posthuman? Are people with artificial organs cyborgs, or, "are claims of cyborgnicity lies until you can see incandescent red eyes?"

It may seem strange to propose that Christian theologians should ponder the concept of the posthuman, but it hardly seems strange to suggest that Christian theologians should concern themselves with what it means to be human. Theological anthropology, a view of what it means to be human with reference to the God of the scriptures, whom Christians believe created the universe and everything in it, is at the very heart of the Christian tradition. In pondering the posthuman, we are once again pondering the question of what it means to be human, in relation to God.

## Defining the Posthuman

What is the "posthuman"? One answer is simply that nobody knows; theologian Brent Waters writes that this "question is impossible to answer definitively because no such creature yet exists, and there is little consensus among those who speculate on its emergence."[1] While this is true, we can say that the term posthuman has emerged as a way to describe a new and growing appreciation for the plasticity and flexibility of "human nature" spurred by discoveries in biotechnology and virtual, information and communication technologies. Posthuman has become a way of naming the unknown, possible, (perhaps) future, altered identity of human beings, as we incorporate various technologies into our human bodies and selves. It therefore functions as an umbrella term, covering a span of related concepts: genetically enhanced persons, artificial persons or androids, uploaded consciousnesses, cyborgs and chimeras (mechanical or genetic hybrids). Thus, the posthuman is not any one particular thing; it is an act of projection, of speculation about who we are as human beings, and who we might become.

---

[1] Brent Waters, *From Human to Posthuman: Christian Theology and Technology in a Postmodern World* (Burlington, VT, 2006), p. 50.

Figure I.1    Dinosaur Comics, "Dudes! Why are there no cyborgs yet?"
By kind permission of Ryan North, qwantz.com

Waters is therefore right to insist that there is no definitive answer to the question, "what is a posthuman," in the sense that this would presuppose a single, univocal answer. Posthuman is not singular; posthuman is inevitably plural. It is therefore misleading to speak casually of "the" posthuman, as if humanity were subject to a steady techno-evolutionary progress to a universally agreed upon and clearly evident particular posthuman end. But this plurality is not simply a consequence of the fact that, at this point in time, the posthuman remains mostly speculative. Rather, plurality is built into the very concept of posthumanity. The plasticity of human nature which engenders posthuman speculation regarding humanity's future selves also ensures that whatever possible forms that future may take, uniformity is hardly to be expected and certainly not guaranteed.

One way of approaching the posthuman is to presume that it is an emerging or imminent future reality, one which human beings carry the responsibility for constructing and which carries no guarantees of success. Such an approach gives rise to an unavoidable ambiguity in our anticipation of our posthuman future. How human will this future be, or how post-? This question of continuity and discontinuity with the human as we now conceive of it is part of the fascination the posthuman holds for us, and yet another source of disagreement. Intuitively, we place various conceptions of the posthuman on a continuum, with the post*human* on one end, the *post*human on the other. And it is hardly surprising that for most the former seems inevitably to be the more benign, exciting, reasonable, and warranted, while the latter seems dangerous, rash, incomprehensible, and disgusting.

There is, then, in addition to its inherent plurality, a disturbing ambivalence to the posthuman. It is both liberating and oppressive in its multiple possibilities. Technological advances make promises of better health, elimination of genetically heritable disease, longer lifespans, and perhaps even enhanced capabilities, but at the same time can also represent an invasion of bodily integrity, as well as economic and political exploitation and oppression. And, given the plurality represented by the posthuman, it seems possible that both the promises and the threats will manifest themselves in equal measure. This, in a sense, forms the core of posthuman discourse: the exploration of these manifold possible alternatives and the hard work of evaluating which possibilities are most likely, most beneficial, or most suspect, and the even harder work of identifying what criteria are available and appropriate for the making of such judgments.

This points us to yet another function of posthuman discourse. The concept of the posthuman also functions as a way of critically interrogating the concept of human nature itself: is there any such thing as human nature, and if so, is it the kind of universal, essential, inherent and immutable quality it has previously been presumed to be? What concept of the human informs our concept of the posthuman? What evaluation of human nature and the human condition is expressed in our longing for, or our horror of, the possibility of the posthuman? What is the "human" we want to construct our posthuman future in continuity with? This investigation into "what it means to be human" thus morphs into a question about "what counts as human" (and therefore, posthuman). The first is an investigation into a given, asking questions about what it means to inhabit the ontological category of human; the second presumes that the category itself, the boundaries that define it, is constructed—and therefore a matter requiring conscious and conscientious deliberation. This shift, from inquiry into the given ontological category to inquiry into the constructed ontological category of the human, is one effect of the disquieting presence of the posthuman.

### Terminal(ogical) Confusion

This inherent plurality of possibility is sufficient explanation for the existing lack of consensus regarding the posthuman. The posthuman might mean the termination of humanity as we know it, through either annihilation or salvific transformation, or it might mean, as some indeed argue, something we already in fact are. This plurality also results, unsurprisingly, in a certain amount of terminological confusion and imprecision in discussions of the posthuman.

In theological discussions, the term posthuman is most often used specifically with reference to transhumanism. Transhumanism is an organized international movement, which, while diverse, is unified in its advocacy of technology to ameliorate, and perhaps even to transcend, the limitations of the human condition into a state of existence which is "better than well."[2] The term "transhuman" originated with the futurist F.M. Esfandiary (also known as FM-2030) as shorthand for "transitional human," and refers to "an intermediary form between the human and the posthuman"; transhumanists therefore are humans who "wish to follow life paths which would, sooner or later, require growing into posthuman persons."[3] Oliver Krueger observes that "posthumanism" is often incorrectly conflated with "transhumanism," but idiosyncratically reserves "transhumanism" to refer to the movement begun by F.M. Esfandiary, and uses "posthumanism" to refer specifically to the ideas of Marvin Minsky, Hans Moravec, and Ray Kurzweil, asserting that "in no way do they refer to the early transhumanists such as Esfandiary."[4]

However, as Noel Castree and Catharine Nash point out, this is not the only way the term posthuman is currently used: "Accounts of a posthuman present or imminent posthuman future may be framed by either an anti-humanist celebration of this shift or by humanist concern about the apparent fracturing of the human subject ... Critical posthumanism names an approach that is alert to the ways in which the category human is evoked even in those accounts which celebrate its erosion."[5] For Nash and Castree, then, the single term posthuman may signal any one of these conceptually distinct posthuman constructions—humanist, anti-humanist, or critical constructions.

Cary Wolfe has recently made a further conceptual distinction between the terms "posthuman" and "posthuman*ism*." If the term posthuman is defined as the end goal of transhumanism, achieved by "escaping or repressing not just [humanity's] animal origins in nature, the biological and the evolutionary, but more generally by transcending the bonds of materiality and embodiment altogether," then, Wolfe writes, "posthumanism in my sense isn't posthuman at all."[6] Wolfe's posthumanism, in contrast, opposes the fantasies of disembodiment and autonomy evident in the transhumanist posthuman vision.

---

[2] "Better than well" was the motto of the World Transhumanist Association, now known as "Humanity+" (see www.humanityplus.org/learn/about-us).

[3] N. Bostrom, "The Transhumanist FAQ: A General Introduction," The World Transhumanist Association, http://humanityplus.org/learn/transhumanist-faq/. While Bostrom is the primary author and editor of the current 2.0 version, the creation of the original document was a collaborative effort involving numerous contributors (acknowledgments can be found at the above URL).

[4] Oliver Krueger, "Gnosis in Cyberspace? Body, Mind and Progress in Posthumanism," *Journal of Evolution and Technology* 14/2 (2005).

[5] N. Castree and C. Nash, "Posthuman Geographies," *Social & Cultural Geography* 7/4 (2006): pp. 501–2.

[6] Cary Wolfe, *What Is Posthumanism?* (Minneapolis, MN, 2010), p. xv. Wolfe observes that the term can be traced through two separate "genealogies," one which originates with Michel Foucault and one which can be traced back to the Macy conferences in cybernetics (p. xii).

So, "posthuman" as it is currently used may sometimes refer to transhumanist ideas of the posthuman future, in a sort of humanism-plus. It may also refer to anti-human constructions within what Stephen Garner characterizes as "narratives of apprehension," as in, for example, *Star Trek: The Next Generation*'s "Borg," or Arnold Schwarzenegger's "Terminator."[7] Or, in what Nash and Castree call "critical posthumanism," the word posthuman may signal yet another construction entirely, one best symbolized by the figure of the feminist cyborg. In this usage, the term refers to the pursuit of an alternative to philosophical humanism: posthumanism in Cary Wolfe's sense.

Thus, along with many others, I view "posthuman" as an open term without any single accepted definition, and indeed, a term with multiple and even mutually exclusive competing definitions. In this book, I argue that these multiple and competing notions of the posthuman currently crystallize around two distinct promising visions, cyborgs and uploads.

The cyborg is a feminist posthuman construction, birthed in the landmark essay referred to in shorthand as the "A Cyborg Manifesto," by Donna J. Haraway, first published in *The Socialist Review* in 1985.[8] The ensuing body of literature commenting and critiquing that original essay, and subsequent works by Haraway, constitute one distinct posthuman discourse, in which the hybrid embodiment of the cyborg serves as a symbol for the ontological kinship of the human with the nonhuman. The uploaded consciousness is a transhumanist construction, proposed as a desirable but still theoretical possibility for shedding the problematic biological body for a virtual existence or a more durable artificial body.[9] In this text, then, "posthuman" functions as a generic term with no specific content, while "cyborg" refers specifically to Haraway's posthuman construction, and "upload" to a specific transhumanist posthuman construction.

One of the major goals of this book is therefore to convince you of the differences between these two major posthuman constructions, in the hope of clarifying what is currently a rather muddled interdisciplinary conversation in theology on the posthuman. The differences between these two posthuman constructions are significant, but currently, these differences generally go unremarked by theologians addressing the topic of the posthuman. This crucial mistake results not only in misreading these two posthuman discourses, but in corresponding misdirected theological responses to the posthuman. The consequences of such theological misreading of the posthuman is that theology's contribution to posthuman discourse, and its possible intervention in the construction of the posthuman, is

---

[7] For an excellent interpretation of the Star Trek narrative along these lines, see Elaine Graham, *Representations of the Post/Human: Monsters, Aliens and Others in Popular Culture* (New Brunswick, NJ, 2002).

[8] Donna J. Haraway, "A Cyborg Manifesto: Science, Technology and Socialist-Feminism in the Late Twentieth Century," in *Simians, Cyborgs and Women: The Reinvention of Nature* (New York, 1991).

[9] Bostrom, "The Transhumanist FAQ."

fatally weakened. If, as N. Katherine Hayles contends, we are at a crucial historical juncture with regard to our emerging posthuman future, such that we bear a moral responsibility in the visioning and construction of our future selves, the stakes are high; theologians must know precisely what is at stake in order to contribute helpfully to the process of fashioning a faithful posthuman future.

## Transversing

Thus, one of the immediate challenges of interdisciplinary engagement between theology and the posthuman is the complexity of the posthuman discourse itself, and the bifurcation of posthuman discourse into two distinct posthuman constructions, the cyborg and the upload. Further, the different epistemological presumptions at work in each of these posthuman discourses means that the interdisciplinary methodological challenges for engaging the cyborg and the upload are significantly different. Thus as theologians engage the posthuman, identifying precisely which posthuman construction is under consideration and specifying the interdisciplinary conversation partners is a crucial prerequisite.

Transhumanists characterize their movement as a continuation of Enlightenment rational humanism; Haraway, in contrast, is a feminist theorist and historian and philosopher of science. The epistemological differences between these two posthuman discourses require careful methodological attention from theologians wishing to engage in interdisciplinary conversation with the posthuman.[10] J. Wentzel van Huyssteen's "postfoundationalism," however, provides an apt approach for an interdisciplinary theological dialogue with the posthuman in both its manifestations.

By naming his approach "postfoundationalism," van Huyssteen signals that he seeks to negotiate a middle way between foundationalist notions of a single universal rationality, and nonfoundationalist notions of multiple, incommensurable rationalities. The means by which van Huyssteen proposes to split the difference between foundationalism and nonfoundationalism is to define human rationality in a way that recognizes the plurality of epistemic communities, disciplines, and specific forms of rationality, but simultaneously posits an inclusive notion of "shared resources of rationality," which enables communication across academic disciplines and specific epistemic communities. This affirms "the epistemically crucial role of interpreted experience," while at the same time it enables the human knower to reach "beyond the confines of the local community, group, or culture, toward plausible forms of transcommunal and interdisciplinary conversation."[11]

---

[10] A more detailed comparison of the differing epistemologies of these posthuman discourses is offered in Chapter 3.

[11] J. Wentzel van Huyssteen, *The Shaping of Rationality: Toward Interdisciplinarity in Theology and Science* (Grand Rapids, MI, 1999), pp. 8–9.

This is particularly important for theologians, as van Huyssteen makes the case for the necessity of interdisciplinary engagement between theology and the sciences. The notion of postfoundational rationality implies that theology "can no longer be excluded from the broader epistemological endeavor," but also constitutes "the final and decisive move beyond fideist strategies that claim theology's 'internal logic' or self-authenticating notions of divine revelation as a basis for disciplinary integrity."[12] Just as rarefied and specialized forms of scientific reasoning are an expression of the basic rationality that defines us as a species, so are the rarefied and specialized forms of theological reasoning. This creates an epistemological equivalency, of some sort, between theology and the sciences, as each are defined as distinct forms of human rationality. This is a bonus and a burden for theology as a discipline; while it rebuts charges of inherent irrationality that persist as a result of the Enlightenment faith versus reason split, it also closes firmly shut the escape hatch of fideism, obligating theologians to engage with other expressions of human rationality faithfully.

Van Huyssteen picks up Calvin Schrag's metaphor of transversality to elucidate the process of interdisciplinary dialogue, in the sense of "extending over, lying across, and intersecting."[13] This metaphor refers not only to the way certain problems or concepts may intersect or overlap across disciplines, but also to the way in which human rationality itself is "a lying across, extending over, and intersection of various forms of discourse, thought, and action."[14] Thus, "the important thing in this notion of transversal rationality is discovering the shared resources of reason precisely in our very pluralist beliefs or practices, and then locating the claims of reason in the transversal connection of rationality between groups, discourses, or reasoning strategies."[15] These interdisciplinary and transcommunal encounters, in other words, take place "within the transversal spaces between disciplines," and it is in these transversal spaces where human rationality, in the broadest sense, is to be found.[16]

This metaphor emphasizes once more the important insight of postfoundationalism that rationality is expressed variously and specifically within the plurality of our epistemic communities, but is not exclusively contained within them. Pragmatically, this requires of us that as we encounter one another in interdisciplinary and transcommunal dialogue, that we begin with the presumption that each participant is rational, and in more than one sense. It is easy enough to attribute rationality to each person in a radically postmodern sense, according to her

---

[12] Ibid., pp. 12–13.

[13] Calvin Schrag, *The Resources of Rationality: A Response to the Postmodern Challenge* (Bloomington, IN, 1992), pp. 148–79, van Huyssteen, *The Shaping of Rationality*, p. 20.

[14] J. Wentzel van Huyssteen, *Alone in the World? Human Uniqueness in Science and Theology*, The Gifford Lectures (Grand Rapids, MI, 2006), p. 21.

[15] Ibid.

[16] Ibid., p. 9.

own communal standards and resources. Such an acknowledgment can take place even in the face of ultimately judging those communal epistemic standards to be lacking; the problem of incommensurability therefore remains. Thus, the second sense in which postfoundational interdisciplinary dialogue requires recognition of rationality is the much broader sense in which one affirms the rationality of all participants, not simply according to the standards of their discrete disciplines and epistemic communities, but in the transversal sense, which makes it desirable, possible, and ultimately necessary, to step out of those communities in a common quest for a larger intelligibility. In this sense, only a refusal to dialogue is an expression of irrationality.

For this interdisciplinary project, the discipline of theology transversally intersects with multiple dialogue partners on a topic which is already inherently interdisciplinary. The "posthuman" is an area of philosophical, speculative, cultural, and metaphorical construction which emerges as the result of transversal connections with the sciences, including genetics, nanotechnology, medical and pharmaceutical and information technologies, and artificial intelligence (AI). The posthuman's dwelling place, in other words, is precisely that interstitial, transversal space in which human rationality exercises its quest for intelligibility. As theology also enters this transversal posthuman space, theological notions of what it means to be human become part of the posthuman dialogue and, perhaps, theologians, too, will participate in the construction of the posthuman.

*With Transhumanists*

One specific obstacle to successful interdisciplinary conversation on the posthuman is the apparent mutual animosity between Christian theologians and transhumanists. Interdisciplinary engagement between transhumanism and Christian theology seems to have begun with an invitation from the Templeton Oxford Summer Seminars in Christianity and the Sciences to the World Transhumanist Association president, Nick Bostrom, for an informal conversation on the ideals and values of transhumanism. Heidi Campbell and Mark Walker describe the event as "uneven, with new highs and lows set in terms of dialogue between faith and transhumanism," and describe the "nadir" of the August 2004 conference:

> At this point several transhumanists turned the conversation to the question of how to manipulate persons of faith in a manner that they might overcome their ignorance, and so help swell the numbers of transhumanists … But what was painfully embarrassing for some participating in the conference was the suggestion that persons of faith are weak-minded.[17]

---

[17] Heidi Campbell and Mark Walker, "Religion and Transhumanism: Introducing a Conversation," *Journal of Evolution and Technology* 14/2 (2005): pp. i–iv.

Though, as Campbell and Walker are quick to point out, many transhumanists do not view transhumanism to exclude persons of faith, the presumption that religious belief is by definition irrational and that the practice of religion is irreconcilable with transhumanism, or any other scientifically literate worldview, predominates.[18] Alternatively, a minority position argues for the possible convergence of religious faiths and transhumanism, but presumes that religious traditions and theologies must radically adapt to conform to tranhumanist views.

This is unsurprising insofar as transhumanism claims a philosophical continuity with the Enlightenment and rational humanism; these attitudes can be traced directly back to Enlightenment attitudes regarding the split between faith and reason.[19] Yet it clearly presents a challenge in the context of interdisciplinary engagement between transhumanism and theology, for it leaves transhumanism with no motivation for interdisciplinary conversation with theology, and theologians who wish to engage transhumanism are burdened with the prerequisite task of making the case for their own rationality before beginning to address substantive matters of mutual interest.

One contributing factor may be the relative self-isolation of the transhumanist movement until the recent deliberate moves toward popularizing and mainstreaming transhumanism. This has, perhaps, insulated the development of transhumanist thought from the increasingly sophisticated critiques of modernist, foundationalist, scientific philosophies being voiced from various quarters, including philosophy of science. In this sense, then, these recent moves to bring transhumanism into mainstream Western culture may also potentially open up transhumanism itself in a transversal sense, creating a willingness for interdisciplinary exchange that reaches beyond the boundaries of the sciences well-represented within transhumanism to incorporate the insights of other disciplines, including theology.

This hopeful move within transhumanism toward a more public dialogue with both allies and critics, exemplified in the branch of the movement calling itself democratic transhumanism or technoprogressivism, is mirrored in the call toward an interdisciplinary, public theology by J. Wentzel van Huyssteen. What should be potentially attractive to the transhumanists about van Huyssteen's interdisciplinary proposal is the centrality of the concept of rationality, not only as the key to bridging the different disciplinary domains, but as what "ultimately defines us as a species."[20] Van Huyssteen's repudiation of nonfoundationalist,

---

[18] Ibid., p. iv. See for example the empirical data gathered by William S. Bainbridge, "The Transhuman Heresy," *The Journal of Evolution and Technology* 14/2 (2005). Bainbridge suggests that "historical and theoretical considerations suggest that the power of traditional religions is directly threatened by transhumanism, so the sacred monopolies can be predicted to try to suppress it" (p. 91).

[19] Bostrom, "The Transhumanist FAQ." This philosophical heritage of the movement is traced in more detail in Chapter 2 and Chapter 3.

[20] van Huyssteen, *The Shaping of Rationality*, p. 2. This early statement should of course be interpreted in the context of the later and more programmatic work on human

postmodern relativism and the related theological strategy of fideistic withdrawal into privatized religious discourse, in favor of an interdisciplinary and public theology, should function as a reassurance that a postfoundationalist theology is at least interested in being rational, even if there remains subsequent disagreement on what that means. Moreover, van Huyssteen's respect for scientific knowledge is such that, though disputing the "lingering imperialism of scientific rationality," he can write, "the selection of scientific reflection as possibly our best available and clearest example of the cognitive dimension of rationality at work is indeed justified."[21] Even further, van Huyssteen goes so far as to say, "the rationality of theology, first of all, is definitively shaped by its location in the living context of interdisciplinary reflection; secondly, this interdisciplinary context is—epistemologically at least—significantly shaped by the dominant presence and influence of scientific rationality in our culture."[22]

In order to make good on this potential, however, the participants in this academic and philosophical interdisciplinary engagement must learn to resist the temptation to over-generalize. The overview of transhumanism as a movement offered in Chapter 2, defining the major branches of the movement and each branch's characteristic philosophical, technological, and teleological differences, is my attempt to avoid the easy mistake of generalizing too freely with regard to the transhumanist movement. Underscoring the diversity and complexity of the transhumanist movement must go hand in hand with any attempt to characterize the movement as a whole, as evident even in the transhumanists' own efforts to define their core values and goals. This does not outlaw all attempts at characterizing the movement, but the difficulty of this challenge is not to be underestimated, and even efforts undertaken in good faith may occasionally fail.[23]

What is needed, therefore, is a healthy specificity in the identification of conversation partners, topics of mutual concern, and desired outcomes for the exchange. Concretely, this requires theologians to become familiar enough with the complex terrain of transhumanism to be able to identify its internal tensions,

---

uniqueness: van Huyssteen, *Alone in the World?*

[21] J. Wentzel van Huyssteen, "Postfoundationalism in Theology and Science," in J. Wentzel van Huyssteen and Niels H. Gregersen (eds), *Rethinking Theology and Science: Six Models for the Current Dialogue* (Grand Rapids, MI, 1998), p. 36. On this point, van Huyssteen has been criticized by Mikael Stenmark for covertly privileging scientific knowledge despite his overt emphasis on the importance of everyday rationality, the importance of which Stenmark wishes to underscore. See Mikael Stenmark, *How to Relate Science and Religion: A Multidimensional Model* (Grand Rapids, MI, 2004), pp. 82–103.

[22] van Huyssteen, *The Shaping of Rationality*, p. 6.

[23] See, for example, the disappointing exchange between Lutheran theologian Ted Peters and transhumanist Russell Blackford. Russell Blackford, "Trite Truths About Technology: A Reply to Ted Peters," *The Global Spiral* 9/9 (2009), www.metanexus.net/magazine/tabid/68/id/10681/Default.aspx, Ted Peters, "Transhumanism and the Posthuman Future: Will Technological Progress Get Us There?," *The Global Spiral* 9/3 (2008), http://metanexus.net/magazine/tabid/68/id/10546/Default.aspx.

disagreements, and differences, accurately attribute individual views, and understand which points of view are being represented. Appreciation of the political and social complexities of transhumanism is more than simply a requirement for an academic exchange; as transhumanism continues to evolve and define itself as a movement, engagement with its allies and critics may prove to be formative for its future. Katherine Hayles wrote in 1999 that "the best possible time to contest for what the posthuman means is now," which may be even more true now, a decade or so later, with the emergence of distinct strands of transhumanism, including "democratic transhumanism" or "technoprogressivism."[24] It may be that critical and thoughtful theological engagements may influence the internal politics of transhumanism in demonstrating that the technoprogressive elements prove the most productive in interdisciplinary engagement; and it may be that herein lies the most promising site for collective construction of the posthuman.[25]

## With Cyborgs

In contrast to the epistemological assumptions of transhumanism, Donna Haraway's proposal of "situated knowledges" converges intriguingly with van Huyssteen's postfoundationalism. It is not merely coincidental that van Huyssteen's postfoundationalism is closer to Haraway's notion of situated knowledges than the transhumanists' notion of rationality, as both thinkers begin with a critique of modernist philosophy of science and foundationalism.[26] Both van Huyssteen and Haraway seek to negotiate an epistemically responsible middle way between the temptations of Enlightenment objectivism and radical postmodern relativism. In doing so, both thinkers emphasize the importance of the social and historical embeddedness of the embodied human knower, communal accountability, hermeneutics, and a critical realism that grants an independence to the natural world and other creatures. There are thus fewer immediate methodological

---

[24] N.K. Hayles, *How We Became Posthuman: Virtual Bodies in Cybernetics, Literature, and Informatics* (Chicago, IL, 1999), p. 291.

[25] My sanguinity regarding democratic transhumanism/technoprogressivism as the most promising form of transhumanism is tempered by the points of view offered by former transhumanists and critics Justice de Thezier and Dale Carrico (see Dale Carrico, "Superlative Summary," http://amormundi.blogspot.com/2007/10/superlative-summary.html, Justice de Thezier, "Mute: Why Reimaginative Democrats Should Ignore the Siren Songs of a Posthuman Future," *Re-public*, www.re-public.gr/en/?p=660).

[26] Moreover, this convergence stands as a specific example of the way in which feminist philosophies of science have informed philosophies of science at work within the religion and science dialogue within Christian theology. See J. Jeanine Thweatt-Bates, "Feminism, Religion and Science," in James Haag, Michael L. Spezio, and Gregory R. Peterson (eds), *The Routledge Companion for Religion and Science* (New York, 2011).

obstacles to the engagement of Haraway's cyborg discourse by theology than there are in the engagement of the transhuman.[27]

However, properly understanding the cyborg means acknowledging this unnatural figure's repudiation of commonly held notions of God-ordained natural givens. Haraway's suspicion of religious metanarrative and, particularly, a suspicion of the Christian tradition, folds together the biblical narrative of God with the cultural narrative of Nature—both of which she positions the cyborg to strongly challenge. Thus the challenge for Christian theology, in engaging the cyborg, is not to demonstrate its rationality, as it is with transhumanism, but to demonstrate its capability for inclusivity and beneficence for all humans, posthumans, and nonhumans who together inhabit God's creation. It is, in fact, precisely this emphasis that emerges in theological dialogue with the cyborg as found in the work of Anne Kull, Elaine Graham, and other ecotheological appropriations of the cyborg.

It is, again, van Huyssteen's postfoundationalist rationality, and the quest for intelligibility at the heart of it, that answers this challenge. This quest for intelligibility is what motivates each of us to look beyond the boundaries of our own communities, and seek to understand the others, not as adversaries, but as rational agents in their own right. This broad inclusivity, built into the very notion of postfoundational rationality, is the key to disarming the suspicions of the cyborg with regard to the Christian tradition and its practitioners.

To return to van Huyssteen's claim that just this sort of rationality is at the heart of what it means to be human, we may discover that what it means to be human is, in other words, to willingly locate oneself in the interstitial, transversal, out-of-bounds spaces where interdisciplinary dialogue happens and the posthumans dwell. On our well-marked epistemic maps with their firm disciplinary boundaries, these are the spaces labeled "there be dragons"; fear of the monstrous is, after all, justification for staying within our safe and well-fortified boundaries, and the cyborg is often a figure of the monstrous.[28] But it may be that we in fact discover, as we enter those dangerous monster-infested spaces, that to be human is to be cyborg.

## Overview of Structure

The structure of this book roughly follows van Huyssteen's movement of interdisciplinary engagement, starting with a survey of the posthuman, moving to transversal engagement on the specific issue of theological anthropology, and

---

[27] Further and more detailed discussion of Haraway's epistemology can be found in Chapter 1 and Chapter 3.

[28] Donna J. Haraway, "The Promises of Monsters: A Regenerative Politics for Inappropriate/D Others," in Lawrence Grossberg, Cary Nelson, and Paula Treichler (eds), *Cultural Studies* (New York, 1992).

ending with a return to an intradisciplinary theological locus, Christology. The first two chapters offer an introductory survey of the posthuman discourse generated by Donna Haraway's figure of the cyborg (Chapter 1), and the posthuman discourse of transhumanism (Chapter 2). These opening chapters mirror each other in structure and provide the necessary background information for a more detailed comparison of the specific posthuman anthropologies embedded within each of them.

Chapter 3, the longest chapter, moves to an analysis and comparison of the (post) anthropologies implicit in both the cyborg and transhumanist upload, focusing specifically on the topics of embodiment, gender, epistemology, and kinship with the nonhuman. Chapter 4 turns to Christian theological anthropology, focusing on the notion of humanity as created in *imago dei*, as well as other significant aspects of Christian theological anthropology, such as belief in human uniqueness, notions of sin, and formulations of agency. Chapter 5, another lengthy chapter, offers a constructive proposal for a "theological post-anthropology," emphasizing posthuman subjectivity and relationality, multiple embodiments, and hybridity as its key components. Finally, Chapter 6, "Christology and the Posthuman," is a brief gesture toward addressing the systematic theological questions raised regarding the locus of Christology, and offers a notion of the "cyborg Christ" as a way of incorporating the anthropological insights of the posthuman into Christology.

# Chapter 1
# The Cyborg Manifesto

Posthuman discourse has crystallized around two very different possibilities: Donna Haraway's cyborg, and transhumanist "uploads." These two visions mark a bifurcation of posthuman possibility and employ radically differing philosophical and ethical commitments. Mapping the contrast between these two competing posthuman visions provides both an entry into the posthuman discourse as well as illuminating the issues at stake.

The image of the cyborg comes to the fore in discussion of the posthuman because it is such a potent symbol of the difference effected by technology between the human and the posthuman. In the figure of the cyborg, the human is physically intertwined with the nonhuman, the organic with the mechanical. The cyborg, therefore, has become the symbol of the posthuman *par excellence*, for it wears its differences visibly, literally engrafted into the skin.

Feminist theorist Donna Haraway's work on the symbol of the cyborg has proved (to use a doubly ironic term) seminal, as Haraway's landmark essay, "A Cyborg Manifesto," has become a reference point for discussions of the posthuman.[1] Even as she herself has moved on from the figure of the cyborg and distanced herself from the term posthuman, the philosophical and ethical issues she identifies in the "Manifesto" have been taken up by other scholars, making this essay indispensable for entry into the posthuman discussion.

In "A Cyborg Manifesto," Haraway builds on a critique of feminist essentialism, in which the identity of woman qua woman is assumed to be naturally given, self-evident, and unchanging. She points out that challenging patriarchal and colonial essentializing tendencies eventually leads to the conclusion that *all* claims of identity based on a natural or organic standpoint are suspect. This is her reason for choosing the cyborg as a feminist symbol; identifying herself as "cyborg" is Haraway's symbolic shorthand for the rejection of any attempt to define human identity on the basis of "nature." This basic stance is the key critique of Haraway's posthuman discourse on human nature, a deliberate breakdown of the dichotomy between nature and technology.

---

[1] Donna J. Haraway, "A Cyborg Manifesto: Science, Technology and Socialist-Feminism in the Late Twentieth Century," in *Simians, Cyborgs and Women: The Reinvention of Nature* (New York, 1991).

## Neither Fish nor Fowl

A cyborg is a hybrid figure: neither wholly organic nor solely mechanical, the cyborg is both simultaneously, straddling these taken-for-granted ontological and social categories. It is this hybrid aspect of cyborg existence that holds simultaneously so much threat and promise. Human beings construct social categories as a way of ordering our coexistence, and often experience the transgression of the boundaries of those categories as the threat of primordial chaos unleashing itself into our lives. And yet, those who find themselves outside the clean definitions of those social categories experience the transgression of them as a promise of liberation.

Haraway identifies three "breached boundaries" represented by the cyborg: human/animal, organism/machine, and (as subset of the second) physical/nonphysical. These identified boundaries constitute the defining content of "human nature," and therefore the breaching of them constitutes the challenge of posthuman to the concept of human nature.

Haraway states matter-of-factly that "by the late twentieth century in United States scientific culture, the boundary between human and animal is thoroughly breached."[2] Yet, as her brief remarks make clear, it is not so much the advent of the cyborg, or even the science and technologies which make it possible, which has initiated this breach. Rather, it is simply the cumulative result of continuing biological research into evolutionary theory over the last 200 years. Haraway remarks that "the last beachheads of uniqueness have been polluted if not turned into amusement parks—language, tool use, social behaviour, mental events, nothing really convincingly settles the separation of human and animal."[3] Many people, she claims, are no longer invested in such a stark separation of human and nonhuman animal, and yet, of course, there is also a strong resistance to evolutionary theory. This is particularly evident within U.S. culture, with its recurrent legal battles over the inclusion of creationism alongside evolutionary theory in standard biology textbooks, prompting an acerbic line from Haraway that "teaching modern Christian creationism should be fought as a form of child abuse."[4] The human/nonhuman animal boundary is as actively defended as it is breached, and the policing of it, of course, is the direct result of the tacit realization of its fragility.

The human/animal boundary breach is symbolized by the cyborg's posthuman cousin, the chimera. A classic Greek mythical ontological category, the chimera is now redefined as a genetic mixture of two animal species, and represents the ultimate blurring of classificatory species boundaries. Beginning with the human/animal boundary may seem tangential, but it is important, because it sets the stage conceptually for the erasure of boundaries more obviously represented by the cyborg. Haraway sees technology as effecting the same breach as evolutionary

---

[2] Ibid., p. 151.
[3] Ibid.
[4] Ibid., p. 152.

theory, though in perhaps a more spectacular and emotionally forceful way, in genetic engineering as well as more obviously mechanical cyborg technologies.[5]

Haraway's terminology in fact slips a bit at this point: "By the late twentieth century, our time, a mythic time, we are all chimeras, theorized and fabricated hybrids of machine and organism; in short, we are cyborgs."[6] Chimera and cyborg, as representatives of the posthuman, seem to be used in a roughly equivalent manner, thus explaining why Haraway places the cyborg at the human/animal boundary. In later works, in fact, cyborgs are treated as a subset of transspecies crossing, and characterized as "junior siblings in the much bigger, queer family of companion species."[7] What is significant in these figures, the cyborg included, is the "trans": whether between organisms, or between organism and machine, or between genders, the boundaries that we commonly use to mark human identity and human nature have been crossed.

The second breached boundary identified by Haraway is organism and machine.[8] As the chimera symbolizes the transgression of the human/animal boundary, here, the cyborg is the result of the breached human/machine boundary, a (con)fusion of organic life and mechanical object. Despite our instinct to classify the cyborg an inhabitant of the imaginative worlds of science fiction, literal cyborgs abound: simple medical devices such as pacemakers, and more complicated medical devices such as prostheses or the ECMO, join the organic human body to create an integrated system in which organic functions are regulated, restored, or replaced.[9] These integrations may not be quite the "seamless" ones we envision for the future, but they nonetheless meet the basic criterion of melding together, in some sense, the organic human body with mechanical devices. "Modern medicine," Haraway writes, "is full of cyborgs, of couplings between organism and machine, each conceived as coded devices."[10]

---

[5] Donna J. Haraway, "Femaleman©_Meets_Oncomouse™. Mice into Wormholes: A Technoscience Fugue in Two Parts," in *Modest_Witness@Second Millennium. Femaleman©_Meets_Oncomouse™* (New York, 1997), p. 60.

[6] Haraway, "A Cyborg Manifesto," p. 150.

[7] Donna J. Haraway, *The Haraway Reader* (New York, 2004), p. 300.

[8] Haraway, "A Cyborg Manifesto," p. 152. Haraway draws the boundary between all organic life and machine, rather than between human and machine. However, as the concern of this section is to elucidate the transgression of the boundary marked by the posthuman, I will speak of the human/machine boundary.

[9] ECMO is an acronym for "extracorporeal membrane oxygenation," a medical device which performs respiratory and blood pumping/scrubbing functions externally from the body. Advances in prosthetics have also begun to push boundaries with new human/machine interfaces. See, for example, Leigh R. Hochberg, Mijail D. Serruya, Gerhard M. Fries, Jon A. Mukand, Maryam Saleh, Abraham H. Caplan, Almut Branner, David Chen, Richard D. Penn, and John P. Donahue, "Neuronal Ensemble Control of Prosthetic Devices by a Human with Tetraplegia," *Nature* 442 (2006).

[10] Haraway, "A Cyborg Manifesto," p. 150.

This conception of both the organic and the mechanical as "coded devices" is the gateway through which the merging of the mechanical and the organic is accomplished. The term "cyborg" was coined in 1960 by Manfred Clynes and Nathan Kline, to refer to their concept of a mechanically enhanced or altered human being who could survive extraterrestrial environments. Their proposal, presented first at the Psychophysiological Aspects of Space Flight Symposium and later published in the journal *Astronautics*, defined cyborgs simply as "self-regulating man-machine systems."[11] This cybernetic description of both mechanical and organic entities as self-regulating systems of information is the crucial conceptual move which enables the envisioning of a system which is part organic and part mechanical, functioning smoothly as one unit. The example given of such a system, the original cyborg, is a mouse attached to a Rose osmotic pump.

The inherited Western philosophical, social, and legal emphasis on the centrality of individual autonomy and freedom for distinctive human identity means that the boundary between "Man and Machine" marks out the difference between human beings as determiners and machines as determined; that is, human beings as agents and machines as acted upon. N.K. Hayles argues that the notion of an autonomous self, with a will clearly distinguishable from the wills of others, is subverted in the posthuman.[12] She offers the narrative example of the film *Robocop*: "We have only to recall Robocop's memory flashes that interfere with his programmed directives to understand how the distributed cognition of the posthuman complicates individual agency."[13] Thus to blur this boundary casts doubt on one important articulation of human uniqueness, free will. In Haraway's descriptive summation, "Our machines are disturbingly lively, and we ourselves frighteningly inert."[14]

Yet, as philosopher and cognitive scientist Andy Clark observes, the original 1960 vision of the cyborg was formulated precisely to *liberate* the human agent by allowing machine control to create additional layers of homeostatic functioning. Clynes and Kline write, "If man [sic] in space, in addition to flying his vehicle, must continuously be checking on things and making adjustments merely to keep himself alive, he becomes a slave to the machine. The purpose of the Cyborg ... is to provide an organizational system in which such robot-like problems were taken care of automatically, leaving man free to explore, to create, to think and to feel."[15] Thus, ironically, though the goal of Clynes and Kline's cyborg proposal was actually an enhanced freedom for the human person, the means by which they

---

[11] Manfred Clynes and Nathan Kline, "Cyborgs and Space," *Astronautics* (1960): p. 30.

[12] N.K. Hayles, *How We Became Posthuman: Virtual Bodies in Cybernetics, Literature, and Informatics* (Chicago, IL, 1999), pp. 3–4.

[13] Ibid., p. 4.

[14] Haraway, "A Cyborg Manifesto," p. 152.

[15] Andy Clark, *Natural-Born Cyborgs: Minds, Technologies, and the Future of Human Intelligence* (Oxford, 2003), p. 32, Clynes and Kline, "Cyborgs and Space," p. 30.

sought to secure the freedom from bodily distractions now seems to potentially threaten the autonomy of will which they presume.

This ironic contradiction at the heart of the original cyborg proposal is traced out in Chris H. Gray's analysis of the coping mechanisms of "medical cyborgs," individuals either temporarily or permanently dependent on machines to perform bodily functions for their survival, which explores the ways that this confusion of ontological and bodily boundaries affects the psyche. For individuals whose personal survival depends upon medical machinery, the question of breached boundaries is not a theoretical one, but a practical and pressing one. The additional freedom bought through the incorporation of technological devices with the damaged organic body is one which many come to take for granted, viewing the functioning of their mechanical and organic parts as one undifferentiated unit. At the same time, many also simultaneously experience acute psychological stress at the necessary redefinition of the self so as to include mechanical elements, and their dependence upon them, as a part of identity. This dependence is the flip side of their liberation; granted new freedoms, medical cyborgs are aware that this liberation is the result of a dependence on mechanism that cannot be ignored or denied.[16]

Thus what we see is that in conceiving our bodies as "coded devices" of information that can be, and sometimes indeed are, joined with mechanical devices, we invite both a subversion of our notions of autonomy, free will, and individual agency while at the same time opening up new potential freedoms and new manifestations of agency. Haraway asserts that "technological determination is only one ideological space opened up by the reconceptions of machine and organism as coded texts through which we engage in the play of reading and writing the world."[17] Haraway's cyborg, at least potentially, gains agency rather than losing it, as a result of the new possibilities, alternatives, and alliances opened up by the breach of the human/machine boundary.

As a subset of the breakdown of the boundary between organism and machine, Haraway sees an implied breakdown of the physical and nonphysical. This is not, as one might think, a commentary on materiality and spirituality. Rather, as Haraway's brief comments make clear, this is a way of describing how our machines and technologies have become in an important sense "invisible." In many ways, unlike the conscious struggle to renegotiate bodily boundaries vis-à-vis the integration of medical devices described above, the human–machine interface has become so simple, habitual, and ubiquitous that we scarcely notice our daily dependence on technologies for communication, transportation, and the supply of basic human needs. Haraway writes, "Our best machines are made of sunshine; they are all light and clean because they are nothing but signals, electromagnetic

---

[16] Chris H. Gray, "Medical Cyborgs: Artificial Organs and the Quest for the Posthuman," in Chris H. Gray (ed.), *Technohistory* (Malabar, FL, 1996).

[17] Haraway, "A Cyborg Manifesto," p. 152.

waves, a section of a spectrum, and these machines are eminently portable, mobile ... People are nowhere near so fluid, being both material and opaque."[18]

Andy Clark observes that it is these literally invisible (virtual, wireless) technologies which affect us most profoundly, because they are so transparent in usage. The efficacy of such technologies lies precisely in their invisibility, in the way that they integrate themselves into our daily lives and habits and shape our patterns of thought and relationship, without our conscious notice of them. Improvements in such technologies can mean expanded capabilities, but also often mean improvements in the user interface, making the device in question more user-friendly by requiring less conscious attention and fewer acquired skills in order to be effective. That is to say, technological improvement often translates into increased invisibility.

Clark views this aspect of technology with equanimity, for humanity's new technologies, especially the invisible and virtual ones, are in his view simply the extension of *Homo faber*'s adaptive strategy of integrating self and environment in more intelligent and efficient ways. In this sense, Clark argues, human beings are now, and in fact always have been, "natural-born cyborgs." Our "posthuman" future is therefore nothing more or less than a simply human future; the posthuman, according to Clark, is inevitable and yet completely continuous with our past and present human selves. Clark's images of the cyborg as "natural-born" are therefore not the alien images of a literal bodily hybridity, but images which strike one as simply very human: a student texting on a cell phone, or listening to an iPod.[19]

Alexander Chislenko's coinage "fyborg," for "functional cyborg," emphasizes this continuum between the literal cyborgization of the flesh and the extended notion of cyborgs as human beings functionally integrated with their surrounding environment and technologies. As T-rex observes to Utahraptor, we're surrounded by cybernetic systems in the most mundane of settings, and they represent nothing more than the gradual improvement of our integration of self and environment. Whether this is labeled fyborg, cyborg, posthuman, or simply human, our evolution as a species can be described as an ongoing adaptive process of refining our integration of self and environment through tool use and technologies. The distinction between externally and internally located technologies, from this perspective, seems increasingly irrelevant.[20]

---

[18] Ibid., p. 153.

[19] For an exploration of the posthuman within the field of musicology see Justin D. Burton, "Ipod People: Experiencing Music with New Music Technology" (PhD Dissertation, Rutgers, The State University of New Jersey, 2009).

[20] For a dissenting point of view on the distinction between cyborgs and fyborgs and the relative importance of the boundary of the flesh, see Gregory Stock, *Redesigning Humans: Choosing Our Genes, Changing Our Future* (New York, 2002), pp. 24–6. Stock suggests that fyborgization offers greater flexibility and less inherent risk than literal cyborgism.

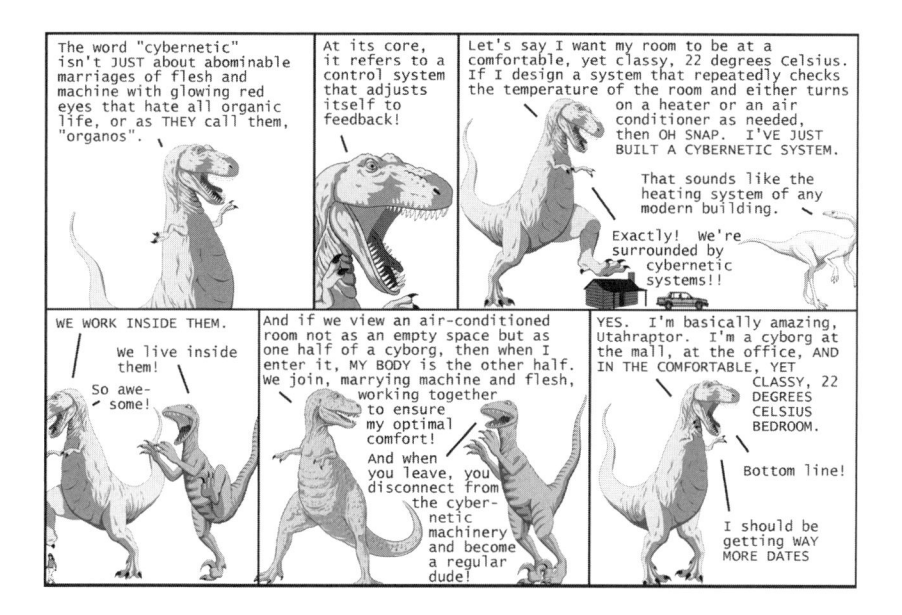

Figure 1.1  Dinosaur Comics, "YOU ARE PROBABLY A CYBORG RIGHT NOW. are you aware??" By kind permission of Ryan North, qwantz.com

Thus, N. Katherine Hayles writes, "Whether or not interventions have been made on the body, new models of subjectivity emerging from such fields as cognitive science and artificial life imply that even a biologically unaltered *Homo sapiens* counts as posthuman."[21] For both Hayles and Clark, it is technologies which, consciously or unconsciously, redefine our concept of ourselves, our capabilities, and the ways in which we interact with each other that promise a posthuman future. This reconfiguration of human subjectivity through the increasing integration of self and environment makes this technological–biological merger an ontological, not merely practical, matter. Clark's thesis of "extended minds," in which he argues that human cognition has always, but now increasingly, depends upon environmental scaffolding through various technologies, also then implies an "extended self," that is, a posthuman self whose boundaries include nonbiological components.[22]

Why do these "breached boundaries" matter? And why is it that Haraway can celebrate the breach of these boundaries, while others perceive only ontological threat?

Philosopher Peter Morriss argues that our conceptual categories, such as "cleanliness" or "food," function to organize our daily lives in a strong but mostly

---

[21]  Hayles, *How We Became Posthuman*, p. 4.

[22]  Andy Clark and David Chalmers, "The Extended Mind," *Analysis* 58/1 (1998).

invisible manner. It is only when something apparently anomalous occurs that we become aware of the boundaries governing our categorical concepts of food and not-food, or clean and not-clean.[23] Jeffrey Stout makes the same point in *Ethics After Babel*, discussing the concept of "moral abominations," using the illustrative example of "cabbits." Stout notes that his young daughter regularly confused cats with rabbits, not yet having learned to distinguish them as different categorical kinds—and therefore was unlikely not only to feel disgust, but even to notice anything anomalous in the cabbit. Stout concludes, "So it is not the cabbit-in-itself or the cabbit as immediately given to the senses that offends. The offense one takes depends upon the concepts one brings to the scene."[24] A moral abomination, then, in Stout's analysis, is "anomalous or ambiguous with respect to some system of concepts."[25]

Stout further notes that the intensity of moral disgust generated by abominations depends upon the presence, social significance, and sharpness of conceptual distinctions.[26] This is an important observation, for it explains why the cabbit remains merely a repugnant curiosity, whereas bestiality or cannibalism arouses deep feelings of horror and disgust; the conceptual line between cats and rabbits is less significant to us humans than the conceptual line between humans and other animals. This also explains why the image of the cyborg often arouses intense fear and disgust, for it visually and conceptually transgresses the same ontological boundary cannibalism or bestiality does; it threatens the distinction between human and nonhuman.

The logic of moral disgust is clearly operative in dialogue regarding the posthuman, as exemplified in Leon Kass's invocation of the "wisdom of repugnance." Kass offers repugnance, or what Stout calls moral disgust, as "the emotional expression of deep wisdom, beyond reason's power to fully articulate it."[27] Arguing for an absolute ban on the pursuit of human cloning, Kass categorizes cloning alongside incest, bestiality, and cannibalism, suggesting that like these acts—which arouse horror and disgust in the way that they violate the ontological boundary of human and nonhuman—cloning, too, violates this boundary at the

---

[23] Peter Morriss, "Blurred Boundaries," *Inquiry* 40/3 (1997): p. 264. Morriss, Jeffrey Stout, and Donna Haraway all draw upon Mary Douglas's work on taboo and pollution concepts.

[24] Jeffrey Stout, *Ethics after Babel: The Languages of Morals and Their Discontents* (Boston, MA, 1988), p. 148. Stout's topic of investigation in this essay is the categorization of homosexuality as "moral abomination," and thus investigates the categorical boundary of gender. A theological exploration of the connection between the notion of the ontological distinctiveness of the genders, the notion of "abomination" and the connection of misogyny to homophobia can be found in William S. Johnson, *A Time to Embrace: Same-Gender Relationships in Religion, Law and Politics* (Grand Rapids, MI, 2006).

[25] Stout, *Ethics after Babel*.

[26] Ibid.

[27] Leon Kass, "The Wisdom of Repugnance," *New Republic* 216/22 (1997).

expense of valuing human dignity and identity, by making human children into "artifacts." This is, Kass claims, "profoundly dehumanizing."[28]

For this reason, cyborgs and other posthuman hybrids are often seen as figures of the monstrous, moral abominations resulting from the transgression of ontological boundaries. Just as a common ancestry with nonhuman animals seems to threaten the ontological distinctiveness of humanity, so too can the technological innovation of the cyborg, as it presumes an ontological kinship with the nonhuman machine. Elaine Graham writes, "Just as monsters of the past marked out the moral and topographical limits of their day, so today other similar strange and alien creatures enable us to gauge the implications of the crossing of technological boundaries."[29] Representations of the posthuman, then, are also often "narratives of apprehension," in the phrase of Stephen Garner, stories which present the posthuman as monstrous and definitively anti-human.[30]

Graham's analysis of the posthuman figure of the Borg in the 1990s TV series *Star Trek: The Next Generation*, provides an iconic example of the monstrous posthuman. The Borg is portrayed as a collective consciousness, with multiple, basically identical, organic bodies fully integrated with cybernetic prostheses and utterly lacking individual differentiation. Visually, the Borg's technology seems to pierce the flesh in painful, invasive entry points along the body; the collective will of the Borg swamps the individual will just as invasively as its mechanical prostheses pierce the flesh. The Borg's capture of Captain Picard, who represents the very best of humanity, is therefore the ultimate threat: the extinction and of human identity and individuality at the hands of impersonal mechanical political or technological systems.[31] The Borg is technology that does not offer augmentation of the human self, a route to grander self-actualization, but the annihilation of the self and a threat to the taken-for-granted qualities of "individualism, self-determination and physical integrity."[32] Ironically, the goal of the original cyborg vision of Clynes and Kline—technological enhancement to allow space exploration without biological vulnerability—becomes the horrifying element of the *Star Trek* Borg. For Clynes and Kline, technological enhancement was a means of liberating the human agent, a means of increasing his (*his*, because this is a vision of man-in-space) freedom to explore, create, think, and feel. These activities define the truly and essentially human; keeping the body alive is robotic drudgework to be delegated to someone/

---

[28] Ibid.

[29] Elaine Graham, *Representations of the Post/Human: Monsters, Aliens and Others in Popular Culture* (New Brunswick, NJ, 2002), p. 39.

[30] Stephen Garner, "Transhumanism and the *Imago Dei*: Narratives of Apprehension and Hope" (PhD Dissertation, The University of Auckland, 2006).

[31] Graham, *Representations of the Post/Human*, p. 145. For an exploration of posthuman themes within science fiction literature, see Daniel Dinello, *Technophobia!: Science Fiction Visions of Posthumanity* (Austin, TX, 2005).

[32] Graham, *Representations of the Post/Human*, p. 147.

thing else.[33] In the Borg narrative, however, these essentially human qualities and capabilities are precisely what is threatened by the technological enhancement the Borg, for it comes packaged with a networked consciousness and collective will that overrides the individual member.

So what we see in *Star Trek: The Next Generation* narrative, Graham suggests, is a secular humanist vision, which defines the human in terms of autonomy, self-determination, rationality, subjectivity, emotional capacity, and universal dignity. The posthuman in this narrative world is a technological creature whose superiorities come paired with some crucial lack that compromises or even abolishes its original humanity. At its worst, the posthuman is the opposite of these human qualities—the technological anti-human Borg; at its best, as in the figure of Lieutenant Commander Data, it is an almost-human, missing one or more of these qualities, who can never be the real thing. In neither case is the posthuman at all desirable; instead, these stories tell us who and what we are by valorizing the qualities we see lacking or opposed in the posthuman mirror. What they tell us about who we are is often comically positive; humanity often comes off as the cosmic hero, incredibly and impossibly important, brave, clever, and good. At the same time, these narratives of apprehension warn us that our important, brave, clever, and good humanity is a fragile thing indeed, threatened by all sorts of encounters with the other, whether alien, technological, or even the less-good versions of ourselves.

Further, these narratives of apprehension often valorize a feminized, natural "humanity" over a masculine, technological threat, as Vincent Gaine's analysis of James Cameron's SF oeuvre suggests.[34] Powerful male characters and masculine-coded power structures within the military-industrial complex provide the source for the technological existential threat, while resolution of the narrative comes through a corresponding valorization of the feminine. In these narratives of apprehension, "anxiety over the technological is displaced 'onto the figure of the woman or the idea of the feminine,' which must remain 'natural' in order to maintain the conservative role of women within male power structures."[35] Yet, as Gaine observes, the mechanical enhancements and replacements of the male body which appear in these films, making the technologized male body more powerful, also serve to destabilize the distinction between human and nonhuman, masculine and feminine.

This double function of monsters, simultaneously marking the existence and the fragility of the boundary between human and nonhuman, "both bolsters and denaturalizes talk about what it means to be human."[36] In demonstrating that the boundary between human and nonhuman can be observably breached in certain

---

[33] Clark, *Natural-Born Cyborgs*, p. 32. Clynes and Kline, "Cyborgs and Space," p. 30.

[34] Vincent M. Gaine, "The Emergence of Feminine Humanity from a Technologised Masculinity in the Films of James Cameron," *Journal of Technology, Theology & Religion* 2/4 (2011), www.techandreligion.com/Resources/Gaine%20JTTR.pdf.

[35] Ibid.

[36] Graham, *Representations of the Post/Human*, p. 39.

ways, the boundary becomes arbitrary and constructed, rather than a firm, taken-for-granted natural given. What counts as human, and therefore posthuman, becomes an active question, the answer to which remains to be determined. And it is precisely this aspect of the cyborg that Donna Haraway finds ontologically therapeutic, leading to her hopeful (though not optimistic) discourse, which regards the cyborg not as monstrous threat, but as a potentially ironic, subversive, and therefore liberating figure. The potential, ironic promise of the cyborg and other monstrous figures lies in the way they may prompt us to recognize our active construction of, and therefore ownership of, our human and nonhuman boundaries, rather than prompting the paranoid fortification of them in denial of the kinships that exist across them. The means of dismantling these categorical boundaries lie in the cyborg's hybrid embodiment itself, a body that interrogates the distinctions between nature and culture, human and nonhuman, male and female—self and other, in all of its variations.

Daniel Dinello suggests that science fiction typically paints a dark picture of technology, and it is certainly true that the narratives of apprehension seem to outweigh the narratives of hope.[37] However, Haraway cites the work of Joanna Russ, Samuel R. Delany, John Varley, James Tiptree Jr., Octavia E. Butler, Monique Wittig, and Vonda McIntyre as storytellers and theorists for cyborgs.[38] In these feminist SF narratives, cyborg figures emerge as heroic protagonists, characters whose defiance of categorical identities is the source of powerful action. Octavia E. Butler's *Xenogenesis* trilogy offers a complicated heroine in the figure of Lilith Iyapo, a racially and culturally hybrid figure who becomes the unwitting mother of a genetically modified generation of alien–human hybrids. Joanna Russ's *The Female Man* tells the story of four genetically identical women who each occupy a different possible universe, and whose uncertainties about their own identities, histories, and gender serve to interrogate, subvert, and liberate the others from their false certainties.

More recently, the as yet unfinished ArchAndroid project of musician Janelle Monáe, which she describes as "emotion picture," provides an example of this kind of liberatory and salvific posthuman narrative. Working within an existing tradition of musicians playing with futuristic themes, Monáe names Fritz Lang's *Metropolis*, Isaac Asimov, Octavia E. Butler, and Ray Kurzweil as inspirational sources; of Butler, she says, "*Wild Seed* was the book that inspired me … the fact that [Butler] defied race and gender … You appreciated her work for being a human being."[39] From Kurzweil's *The Singularity is Near*, she takes the promise of an imminent posthuman future as an occasion for urgent intervention—not

---

[37] Dinello, *Technophobia!*, p. 1.
[38] Haraway, "A Cyborg Manifesto," pp. 173–9.
[39] Gillian Andrews, "Janelle Monae Turns Rhythm and Blues into Science Fiction," *io9* (2010), http://io9.com/5592174/janelle-monae-turns-rhythm-and-blues-into-science-fiction. Butler's novel *Wild Seed* is also specifically cited by Haraway, "A Cyborg Manifesto," p. 247.

to bring it more quickly, nor to avoid it, but to prepare humanity for the ethical challenges this encounter with a new form of the Other represents.[40]

Monáe's performative "alter ego" and protagonist of the ArchAndroid narrative is 57821/Cindi Mayweather, an android who is transformed by the criminal and ontological trespass of loving (and being loved by) a human being, from enslaved artifact into the salvific ArchAndroid who will return to liberate the oppressed. Monáe's work, weaving as it does narrative, music, dance, visual art, videos, and episodic short film, offers multiple sites and modes of commentary on the ontological, political, historical, and social implications of the cyborg figure. The short film/music video "Many Moons," nominated for a Grammy in 2009, presents Cindi Mayweather as the main attraction at a techno-slave auction, simultaneously historically recapitulating the ontological divide of racism and slavery and the SF trope of intelligent machines as yet another iteration of humanity's oppression and slavery of the Other.[41]

In Monáe's ArchAndroid, in contrast to common strategies of narrative resolution, this android Other is neither rescued by her lover by honorary incorporation into the Human, nor initiates a vindictive genocide of the Human for the sake of defending the self. Rather, the return of the ArchAndroid is anticipated as a celebration of the triumph of kinship across boundaries. Monáe comments, "Will we teach our kids to fear the android? Will we treat the android inhumanely? Act superior? I want people to wrap their minds around that. I think that we need a mediator, if we're all gonna rewrite history, and not oppress the Other. The Archandroid, Cindi, is the mediator, between the mind and the hand. She's the mediator between the haves and the have-nots, the oppressed and the oppressor."[42] From the point of view of this Kansas-born African-American artist, then, the power of the posthuman figure lies precisely in the way she embodies the confusion of boundaries, in a way that resonates with the historically boundary transgressing bodies of the many forms of the human that have preceded the posthuman.

**(Mother?) Nature**

One way of describing the cyborg's defiance of these ontological boundaries is to call it "unnatural." The hybridity of the cyborg, as well as its manufactured, technological origin, defy the expectation of a single, given, biologically inherited "nature." In a larger sense, as well, cyborg hybridity also calls into question the concept of "Nature" as the determining origin of given biological natures.

---

[40] This moves Monáe's work, in my estimation, firmly out of the transhumanist and into the feminist cyborg discourse, despite her use of Kurzweil as source.

[41] Janelle Monáe, "Many Moons" (music video), www.jmonae.com/video/many-moons-official-video/.

[42] Andrews, "Janelle Monáe Turns Rhythm and Blues into Science Fiction."

Haraway writes that "Nature is a topic I cannot avoid."[43] As more than one scholar has noted, Haraway's scholarly work in the history and philosophy of science, beginning with *Primate Visions*, continuing through her work on technoscience and cyborgs and into her current work on interspecies relations, can be read as her nuanced, multi-leveled response to the question "what gets to count as nature?"[44] In *Primate Visions*, Haraway contests the way primatology "constructs reality and nature as settled, ordered in particular ways, and there to be discovered; as *always* having been there to be found and appropriately named by those with special vision."[45] Through detailed investigation of the work of pioneer primatologists Carl Akeley, Robert Yerkes, and others, Haraway demonstrates how the "nature" of primates was spoken, written, and literally assembled for display, resulting in a "natural world [which] is primarily an accomplishment of particular human work, a factual fiction."[46]

No less does Haraway resist the category of the natural when it appears within feminism. Haraway's choice of the cyborg as feminist icon is an answer to second-wave feminism's tendency toward a biological essentialist view of Woman as a universal, natural ideal. This is, from Haraway's perspective, simply an acceptance of the dominant masculine narrative. "In this plot," she writes, "women are imagined either better or worse off, but all agree that they have less selfhood, weaker individuation, more fusion to the oral, to Mother, less at stake in masculine autonomy."[47] The essentialist feminist presumes women are better off thus—but does not dispute the narrative itself, accepting and even valorizing that women are naturally excluded from the masculine virtues extolled in the patriarchal narrative. Impatient with this, Haraway argues for an alternative, in the form of a cyborg feminism: "But there is another route to having less at stake in masculine autonomy, a route that does not pass through Woman ... It passes through women and other present-tense, illegitimate cyborgs, not of Woman born, who refuse the ideological resources of victimization so as to have a real life."[48] In other words, recourse to the natural reverses, rather than subverts, patriarchal narrative; recourse to the unnatural, in the form of the cyborg, subverts both forms of essentialism, patriarchal and feminist. Thus, Haraway's famous concluding

---

[43] Donna J. Haraway, "A Game of Cat's Cradle: Science Studies, Feminist Theory, Cultural Studies," *Configurations* 2/1 (1994): pp. 59–60.

[44] Anne Kull, "A Theology of Technonature Based on Donna Haraway and Paul Tillich" (PhD Dissertation, Lutheran School of Theology, 2000), p. 108, Joseph Schneider, *Donna Haraway: Live Theory* (New York, 2005).

[45] Donna J. Haraway, "Monkeys, Aliens, and Women: Love, Science and Politics at the Intersection of Feminist Theory and Colonial Discourse," *Women's Studies International Forum* 12/3 (1989): p. 9.

[46] Schneider, *Donna Haraway*, p. 34.

[47] Haraway, "A Cyborg Manifesto," p. 177.

[48] Ibid.

line: "Though both are bound in the spiral dance, I would rather be a cyborg than a goddess."[49]

The actual existence of cyborgs belies the appeal to nature; it is "a problematic argument resting on an unconvincing biology."[50] This, however, is not the only problem; an appeal to Nature also means an appeal to a demonstrably historically oppressive category. Haraway writes, "I cannot help but hear in the biotechnology debates the unintended tones of fear of the alien and suspicion of the mixed. In the appeal to intrinsic natures, I hear a mystification of kind and purity akin to the doctrines of white racial hegemony and U.S. national integrity and purpose that so permeate North American culture and history."[51] Haraway's objection to appeals to ahistoric Nature are not only that concepts of nature are culturally constructed and historical rather than timeless and essential, but also that these historical, cultural concepts have not been morally neutral. Rather, they have been damaging and oppressive, employed to reinforce sexism, racism, homophobia, and other forms of infectious fear of the other.

At the same time, Haraway resists modern technoscience's opposite extreme of a "nature of no nature."[52] This perspective reads nature as a blank slate, infinitely malleable, and available as raw material for the meaning-giving activities of human beings. As Haraway points out, this is simply a reiteration of the old dualism of nature/culture, only without the transcendental—nature without the capital "N," but nonetheless equally available for human exploitation as infinite resource. "Thus, the new nature of no nature gives back the limpid image of the world as engineered and engineering, as artifactual, as the domain of design, strategy, choice, and intervention—*all without transcendental moves*. That is this world's sacred secular magic, just as it has been since the founding stories of the Scientific Revolution."[53]

This double refusal gives Haraway's stance on natural discourse a complexity often missed by those who wish to take up one or the other of her critiques. Looking for "a different relationship to nature besides reification and possession," Haraway's argument is that nature is constructed, but not solely by humans; the construction of nature is a project undertaken by human and nonhuman agents.[54] She writes,

> The actors are not all "us." If the world exists for us as "nature," this designates
> a kind of relationship, an achievement among many actors, not all of them

---

[49] Ibid., p. 181.

[50] Haraway, "Femaleman©_Meets_Oncomouse™," pp. 61–2.

[51] Ibid., pp. 60–1.

[52] Ibid., p. 102. Haraway borrows from Marilyn Strathern to define the "nature of no nature": it is "'nature enterprised-up,' where 'the natural, innate property and the artificial, cultural enhancement become one.'"

[53] Ibid., p. 108.

[54] Kull, "A Theology of Technonature," pp. 139–40.

human, not all of them organic, not all of them technological. In its scientific embodiments as well as in other forms, nature is made, but not entirely by humans; it is a co-construction among humans and non-humans. This is a very different vision of nature from the postmodernist observation that all the world is denatured and reproduced in images or replicated in copies. That specific kind of violent and reductive artifactualism, in the form of hyper-productionism actually practiced widely throughout the planet, becomes contestable in theory and other kinds of praxis, without recourse to a resurgent transcendental naturalism.[55]

Nature herself becomes a coyote trickster-figure, an active participant in humanity's technoscientific investigations and not at all the passive resource and recipient of human construction previously presumed.[56] In this way, Haraway maintains the importance of material reality as something to which our conceptual categories must conform—a redefined objectivity which becomes a necessary component of her cyborg arguments, for it is the observable, material existence of cyborgs which forces the redrawing of our ontological boundaries in acknowledgment.

Haraway's first contention, then, is that Nature is a socially constructed category, posing as an absolute with the power to dictate permissible social, moral, political, and technoscientific norms and practices. The illusion of naturally given norms appears in many contexts, giving rise to Haraway's characterization of Nature as an imploded, densely packed location. This imploded location is where attitudes and practices regarding gender, religion, science and technology, politics and family, race and identity come together, to be explained under the same rubric of natural givens and norms. Haraway's first goal is to dispel the illusion of self-evident necessity surrounding natural discourse wherever it appears. "Queering what counts as nature is my categorical imperative ... not for the easy *frisson* of transgression, but for the hope of livable worlds."[57] Whatever nature is, it is not a simple given, and Haraway's plea is that we recognize our responsibility in its construction, and our complicity in its destruction. Haraway's second goal, equally important, is to resist reinscribing the same logic through an imposed "nature of no nature," in which all that is nonhuman, dispossessed of previously presumed natural teleology and thus bereft of independent moral status or agency, passively receives the assigned teleology of human technoscience. Instead, she seeks to articulate a position in which the importance of human agency and the

---

[55] Donna J. Haraway, "The Promises of Monsters: A Regenerative Politics for Inappropriate/D Others," in Lawrence Grossberg, Cary Nelson, and Paula Treichler (eds), *Cultural Studies* (New York, 1992), p. 297.

[56] Donna J. Haraway, "Situated Knowledges: The Science Question in Feminism and the Privilege of Partial Perspective," *Simians, Cyborgs and Women: The Reinvention of Nature* (New York, 1991), p. 199.

[57] Donna J. Haraway, "When Man is on the Menu," in Jonathan Crary and Sanford Kwinter (eds), *Incorporations* (New York, 1992), p. 43.

constructed nature of ontological categories is evident—and which simultaneously recognizes that human agents are not the only agents present within the realm of technoscience.

## The Death of God/dess

Haraway writes in the manifesto that not only is God dead, but so is the goddess.[58] This declaration clearly sets the cyborg in opposition, not just to the culturally dominant and influential Christian narrative, but the religious articulations of female affinity to nature, as described above, in the figure of the goddess, as well. This double rejection of religious narrative makes theological engagement with the cyborg a somewhat fraught enterprise.

And yet, as Joseph Schneider observes, "the stories [Haraway] tells of herself almost always note the importance of her early life as a 'good Catholic girl.'"[59] Despite her renunciation of Catholic belief as an adult, Haraway openly acknowledges the importance of "Catholic sacramentalism" in shaping her analytic vision, even while describing herself as atheist and even "anti-Catholic."[60] True to her own vision of permeable boundaries, Haraway does not seek to keep her personal biography separate from her academic work, but frequently references her own social location and history; it is not surprising, therefore, that her posthuman figures share her suspicion of, while simultaneously drawing from, the narrative symbolism of Christianity.

Haraway characterizes the context of her writing as the "Second Millennium," a chronotope defined by its heritage of "disreputable history of Christian realism and its practices of figuration."[61] This characterization of the cyborg's chronotope as "the Second (Christian) Millennium" indicates Haraway's assessment of the importance of the Christian narrative as a major factor in setting cultural norms and expectations in the contemporary United States. One point to be emphasized, already seen in Haraway's rejection of technoscience as a "culture of no culture" which manipulates a "nature of no nature," is Haraway's refusal to allow the easy separation of science and technology from its surrounding culture, including, of course, pervasive Christian influences on U.S. culture.

A second point, and Haraway's main concern, is that Christian symbolism within technoscientific discourse infuses it with an apocalyptic dimension; a

---

[58] Haraway, "A Cyborg Manifesto," p. 162.
[59] Schneider, *Donna Haraway*, p. 6.
[60] Ibid.
[61] Donna J. Haraway, "Modest_Witness@Second_Millenium," *Modest_Witness@ Second_Millennium.Femaleman©_Meets_Oncomouse™: Feminism and Technoscience* (New York, 1997), p. 43. For the importance of Lynn Randolph's painting, "The Laboratory/ The Passion of OncoMouse" (1994), see Donna J. Haraway, "Living Images: Conversations with Lynn Randolph," www.lynnrandolph.com/essays.haraway-2.html.

Figure 1.2  Lynn Randolph, in the collection of Donna Haraway, "The Laboratory/The Passion of the OncoMouse," oil on masonite, 10" x 7" (1994). Reproduced with permission

symbolic way of communicating a sense of the gravity, immediacy, and universality of technoscience's import for our lives. Haraway writes, "In the United States, at least, technoscience is a millenniarian discourse about beginnings and ends, first and last things, suffering and progress, figure and fulfillment."[62] One does not have to be explicitly Christian to be fluent in this apocalyptic technoscientific discourse, for it manifests itself in secular guise as well, as "disaster-and-salvation stories maintained by people who have inherited the practices of Christian realism, not all of whom are Christian, to say the least."[63]

Haraway herself critically engages in this religious and apocalyptic rhetoric in her description of the cyborg as "outside of salvation history." In rejection of the paradigmatic teleological narrative of original wholeness, subsequent estrangement and sin, and ultimate salvation and restoration, Haraway claims the cyborg "does not expect its father to save it through a restoration of the garden," and "would not recognize the Garden of Eden; it is not made of mud and cannot dream of returning to dust."[64] Cyborg hybridity challenges not just notions of ontological boundaries and natural givens, but also the religious structures, narratives, symbols, and beliefs which frequently and authoritatively articulate and undergird those notions. Linking Christianity firmly with the narrative of natural, organic, originary union, Haraway identifies God the Father as part, even source, of the problem the cyborg is meant to address, with its ontological hybridity and unnatural origins. However, Haraway's use of Christian figures and narrative is more complex and ambivalent than simple wholesale rejection.

These themes are readily evident in Haraway's descriptions of Lynn Randolph's painting, "The Laboratory/The Passion of the OncoMouse." Haraway describes her interdisciplinary collaboration with Randolph in an interview, as "never a conscious decision ... the relationship developed into an interchange between the two of us where we never deliberately collaborated but, in fact, we were constantly collaborating." This unintentional collaboration resulted in the incorporation of many of Randolph's images into Haraway's *Modest_Witness*, for which, Haraway says, "I think of her visual contributions to the book as arguments, not just illustrations." In particular, "The Laboratory/The Passion of the OncoMouse" was painted in response to Haraway's text, but, Haraway says, "after I saw it I did more writing."[65] Of the painting, Haraway writes:

> In Randolph's rendering, the white, female, breast-endowed, trans-specific cyborg creature is crowned with thorns: She is a female Christ figure, and her story is that of the Passion: She is a figure in the sacred-secular drama of

---

[62] Donna J. Haraway, *Modest_Witness@Second_Millennium.Femaleman©_Meets_Oncomouse™: Feminism and Technoscience* (New York, 1997), p. 10.

[63] Ibid., p. 43.

[64] Haraway, "A Cyborg Manifesto," p. 151.

[65] Donna J. Haraway, *How Like a Leaf: An Interview with Thyza Nichols Goodeve* (New York, 1998).

technoscientific salvation history, encapsulating all of the disavowed links to Christian narrative that pervade U.S. scientific discourse. The laboratory animal is sacrificed; her suffering promises to relieve our own; she is a scapegoat and a surrogate. She bears our diseases, literally. Circled by peering eyes of many colors, she is the object of transnational technoscientific surveillance and scrutiny the center of a multi-hued optical drama. The bare-breasted hybrid mammal seems also to look at the viewer from inside a natural history diorama in a museum of natural-technical truth. Perhaps we also leer at her through a keyhole to a pornographic peep show; Her eyes lock with ours in a troubling and highly ambivalent gaze that, to me, suggests compassion, anger, reflection, pain, and curiosity; Her Passion transpires in a box that mimes the observation chambers of the laboratory, rooted in the dramas of the birth of modern science. OncoMouse is a figure both in secularized Christian salvation history and in the linked narratives of the Scientific Revolution and the New World Order—with their promises of progress, cures, profit, and if not eternal life, then at least life itself.[66]

As a secular Christ figure, OncoMouse "suffers, physically, repeatedly, and profoundly, that I and my sisters may live."[67] While Haraway is undeniably critical of the cultural and religious logic that requires vicarious suffering to achieve salvation and renders OncoMouse a victim of technoscientific sacrifice, this is not Haraway's final comment on Lynn Randolph's painting. In *When Species Meet*, Haraway returns to the image, writing, "It is tempting to see my sister OncoMouse as a sacrifice, and certainly, the barely secular Christian theater of the suffering servant in science and the everyday lab idiom of sacrificing experimental animals invite that thinking ... But something the biologist Barbara Smuts calls copresence with animals is what keeps me from resting easily with the idiom of sacrifice."[68] While human usage of nonhuman animals in experimental laboratory contexts is undeniably unequal, Haraway resists the rhetoric of victimhood, with its implication of passivity, submission to the inevitable, and most importantly, identification of animal as sacrificial object to humanity's sacrificing subject.

Haraway's resistance to interpreting this murine Christ figure as victim suggests that her interpretation of Jesus as Christ is similarly complex—not uncritical, but not dismissive either. Seeking a figure for humanity outside the narrative of humanism, Haraway offers Jesus as a "trickster figure," one who has often been interpreted as the kind of problematic universal representative of the Human, but whose narrative, when taken in its full detail, "makes of man a most promising mockery," which can and must be "read ironically by post-Christians

---

[66] Haraway, "Living Images: Conversations with Lynn Randolph."
[67] Haraway, *Modest_Witness@Second_Millennium.Femaleman©_Meets_Oncomouse™*, p. 79.
[68] Donna J. Haraway, *When Species Meet*, ed. Cary Wolfe, Posthumanities (Minneapolis, MN, 2008), p. 76.

and other post-humanists."[69] To "redeem" the figure of Jesus as a cyborg figure, as Haraway does, signals even more definitively that despite the evident atheism, anti-Catholicism and cynicism in Haraway's critical appraisal of Christianity, her relationship to the Christian narrative is one marked more by irony and ironic subversion than straightforward rejection and opposition. Haraway thus "reiterates the importance of Christian figural realism in the history and present of technoscience even as she seeks to confound and rework, to remould these stories for today and tomorrow."[70] In this, Haraway is entirely consistent, as the same can be said with regard to her positioning with regard to technoscientific discourse; indeed, this is the intent of the cyborg as an ironic figure altogether.

Just as her use of "figuration" is inherited from her religious upbringing, she bluntly acknowledges the way in which the Catholic notion of sacramentality is integral to her cyborg vision. Describing her "sacramental consciousness" as an "indelible mark of having grown up as an Irish Catholic in the United States," she comments, "understanding that the sign is the thing in itself, the implosion of the sign and substance—that is part of being blessed and cursed with a sacramental consciousness. The literalness of metaphor, the materiality of trope, the tropic quality of materiality, the implosion of semioticity and materiality, always simply seemed the case about the world, as opposed to a particularly fancy theoretical insight— or mistake."[71] Haraway's materialism is therefore a deliberately sacramental materialism, and this sacramentality stems as much from her religious heritage, despite her repudiation of it, as it does from purely philosophical conviction.

This sacramentality, however, does not translate into an embrace of the material as the sacred natural; Haraway's rejection of God the Father does not take the form of veneration of the goddess. This is not because Haraway rejects the celebration of the material within goddess talk, for Haraway's sacramental view of the material world aligns her with and not against this particular aspect of goddess worship. Lynn Randolph's now iconic "Cyborg," painted in response to her reading of Haraway's manifesto, presents an image of a woman embraced by a figure of totemic power—while literally plugged in to a keyboard. Randolph's shamanic cyborg image captures the both/and of Haraway's embrace of materiality: not just the natural, but the technological.

Rather, Haraway's rejection of the goddess comes from her conviction that "there is nothing about being 'female' that naturally binds women."[72] As a self-conscious alternative construction to the masculine Father God, the goddess becomes a feminist mirror image of the same logic of gender identity, a universally

---

[69] Donna J. Haraway, "Ecce Homo, Ain't (Ar'n't) I a Woman, and Inappropriate/D Others: The Human in a Post-Humanist Landscape," in Judith Butler and Joan W. Scott (eds), *Feminists Theorize the Political* (New York, 1992), p. 90.

[70] Schneider, *Donna Haraway*, p. 20.

[71] Donna J. Haraway, "Cyborgs, Dogs and Companion Species" (video lecture), www.youtube.com/view_play_list?p=C017E496EEE63132.

[72] Haraway, "A Cyborg Manifesto," p. 155.

*The Cyborg Manifesto* 35

Figure 1.3　Lynn Randolph, "Cyborg," oil on canvas, 36" x 28" (1989). Reproduced with permission

representative figure, the divinized Woman. Cyborg feminists, however, Haraway insists, "argue that 'we' do not want any more natural matrix of unity and that no construction is whole," and understand that "we do not need a totality in order to work well."[73] This is the context for Haraway's plea for a feminist "heteroglossia," yet another powerful biblical image borrowed and recast in the cyborg context.[74]

Haraway's now famous concluding line, "Though both are bound in the spiral dance, I would rather be a cyborg than a goddess," makes clear that Haraway prefers the cyborg, even while acknowledging that these feminist identities are bound together, hinting that no construction, not even the preferred cyborg, is sufficient alone.[75] Haraway rejects the goddess as universal identity; in this sense, the goddess is dead. And yet her last statement opens the possibility for the resurrection of the goddess as one identity among others, alongside the cyborg.

## Cyborgs for Earthly Survival

The issues problematized thus far can be characterized as theoretical, as challenges to concepts and categories which no longer usefully describe our lived experiences in the technologized social reality we have constructed. Yet these are not, in the end, Haraway's ultimate concerns. For Haraway, the theoretical is of interest insofar as it describes and enables the practical—that is, the political and the ethical. Haraway writes, "Cyborgs are not about the Machine and the Human, as if such Things and Subjects universally existed. Instead, cyborgs are about specific historical machines and people in interaction."[76] Her interest in cyborgs is driven, not out of a desire to conceptually define what is human (and not), but to encourage the creation of alternative social practices—"for *responsibility* in [boundary] construction."[77]

This plea for responsibility is based in Haraway's sense of urgency of the need for recognizing that our collective human social reality is one in which we make choices for some ways of living together and against others. Haraway speaks of being "interpellated" by technoscience:

> I belong to the "culture" whose members answer to the "hey, you!" issuing from technoscience's authoritative practices and discourses. My people answer that "hey, you!" in many ways: we squirm, organize, revel, decry, preach, teach, deny, equivocate, analyze, resist, collaborate, contribute, denounce, expand, placate, withhold. The only thing my people cannot do in response to the meanings and practices that claim us body and soul is remain neutral. We must cast our lot with some ways of life on this planet, and not with other ways.[78]

---

[73] Ibid., pp. 157–73.
[74] Ibid., p. 181.
[75] Ibid.
[76] Haraway, "Femaleman©_Meets_Oncomouse™," p. 51.
[77] Haraway, "A Cyborg Manifesto," p. 150.
[78] Haraway, "Femaleman©_Meets_Oncomouse™," pp. 49–51.

What Haraway means by interpellation is not the simple fact of being implicated in the practices and discourse of technoscience by virtue of one's location. Interpellation goes beyond a resigned recognition of individual complicity and participation in larger systems; interpellation requires an acknowledgment of the possibility and necessity of active response.

The cyborg, then, is at heart an ethical and political figure. As Haraway puts it: our cyborg ontology gives us our politics.[79] But what might this mean? As "cyborg ontology" is hybrid, first, it means that a cyborg politics begins with refusing the option of identity politics based on essentialist and universalized group identities. That much is clear; but this leaves the question of cyborg political identity an open one. Haraway asks, "Which identities are available to ground such a potent political myth called 'us,' and what could motivate enlistment in this collectivity?"[80] Cyborg identity, then, is offered as a flexible alternative to the rigidity of universal identities, though Malini J. Schueller detects the possibility of a covert disregard for particularity in Haraway's use of figures like the cyborg and the vampire: "But where and how, within the specific matrices of racial and gendered/sexual oppression, can vampirism be a choice? I suggest that like the postmodern figure of the cyborg, the vampire, recuperated metaphorically for illegitimacy and racial crossing, can function to metaphorize the specificities of race and sex out of existence and once again make room for universalizing analogy."[81] Schueller's suspicions notwithstanding, it is clear that Haraway's intent is not to promise a new, truly universal narrative to replace the old failed ones, but to articulate an alternative to the dead end of "endless splitting and searches for a new essential identity."[82] Thus, Haraway prescribes a different course of political action: coalition, or, affinity rather than identity.

Michelle Bastian argues that this political cyborg characteristic, so central to Haraway's vision, has dropped out of sight over the decades of ensuing intellectual discourse.[83] The cyborg figure presented by Haraway is not, therefore, the "technoborg" we are most familiar with, but rather "the coalition cyborg, who remembers her beginnings in U.S. third-world feminism just as much as those in

---

[79] Haraway, "A Cyborg Manifesto," p. 150.

[80] Ibid., p. 155.

[81] Malini J. Schueller, "Analogy and (White) Feminist Theory: Thinking Race and the Color of the Cyborg Body," *Signs: Journal of Women in Culture and Society* 31/1 (2005).

[82] Haraway, "A Cyborg Manifesto," p. 155.

[83] Michelle Bastian, "Haraway's Lost Cyborg and the Possibilities of Transversalism," *Signs: Journal of Women in Culture & Society* 31/4 (2006). Bastian cites Bartsch, DiPalma, and Sells, who point out that, while the cyborg was conceived primarily to act as a political metaphor, "academic work that treats a political coalition in cyborg terms ... barely exists." Ingrid Bartsch, Carolyn DiPalma, and Laura Sells, "Witnessing the Postmodern Jeremiad: (Mis)Understanding Donna Haraway's Method of Inquiry," *Configurations* 9/1 (2001): p. 142.

modern technoscience."[84] Haraway herself comments that there are readers "who would take the 'Cyborg Manifesto' for its technological analysis" but are inclined to "drop the feminism."[85] This prompts Bastian to describe Haraway's cyborg as the "lost" cyborg.

The disappearance of the coalition cyborg from the discourse leaves only the militaristic technoborg, with its temptations to theoretical discourse about Man and Machine, and political solutions that tend more toward annihilation than coalition. Perhaps for this reason, Haraway now "resituates her friend the cyborg as more relevant to the recent past," as a "dated and less effective resource for potent cultural criticism and political work in the new millennium."[86] But while Haraway has moved on, Bastian has taken up the project of recovering the feminist and political "lost cyborg." The permanently partial identity and heterogeneous subjectivity of the cyborg, she argues, implies that "political groups can be released from both the pressures of unity and the frightening prospect of a homogeneous enemy, focusing instead on developing the skills to become more able to handle unstable, pragmatic coalitions that focus more on attaining specific goals than on proving the group's common identity or innocence."[87] Bastian connects Haraway's cyborg to the work of Nira Yuval-Davis and Cynthia Cockburn on the political practice of transversalism, which concretizes the notions of cyborg subjectivity and offers specific recommendations for political strategies not based on group identity.[88]

Yet Haraway's notion of ontological, and therefore political and ethical, kinship goes beyond the ethical mandate for crossing the boundaries of human identity categories; cyborg kinship is kinship of the human with the nonhuman, and therefore democratization of technoscience includes not just all interpellated human beings, but the interpellated nonhuman actors of technoscience as well. In her words, "mice and molecules ... cooperate too."[89]

It was a nameless rat, implanted with a Rose osmotic pump, who served as Clynes and Kline's example of a functioning cyborg in 1960. "Rose," as Andy Clark nicknames "the whole rat-pump system," illuminated a line of possible scientific inquiry with multiple future implications for human bodies and human

---

[84] Haraway, *The Haraway Reader*, p. 325.

[85] N. Gane and D. Haraway, "When We Have Never Been Human, What Is to Be Done? Interview with Donna Haraway," *Theory Culture & Society* 23/7–8 (2006): p. 136, quoted in Schneider, *Donna Haraway*, pp. 57–8.

[86] Bastian, "Haraway's Lost Cyborg and the Possibilities of Transversalism."

[87] Ibid., pp. 1035–6.

[88] Haraway, "Femaleman©_Meets_Oncomouse™," pp. 96, Bastian, "Haraway's Lost Cyborg and the Possibilities of Transversalism," 1039–42. The naming of this practice indicates the authors' desire for an alternative to universalism/relativism, and thus, is an intriguing, non-coincidental political parallel to the epistemological theorizing of Calvin Schrag and J. Wentzel van Huyssteen, who use the same image to avoid the same dichotomy within the context of epistemology and interdisciplinary academic work.

[89] Clark, *Natural-Born Cyborgs*, p. 15.

lives.[90] Like OncoMouse, Rose's significance lies in her kinship with the humans who constructed her cyborg body, observed the effects, and extrapolated from the data. The chimpanzee Ham (whose name is an acronym for the Holloman Aeromedical Research Laboratory), the first literal "man-in-space cyborg," demonstrates how the primate bodies of our close genetic kin stand in for human bodies and illuminate possibilities for those human bodies to follow in their wake—in this case, both spatially and technologically.[91]

Here we return to the way in which the negotiation of constructed ontological boundaries affects real world practices. Mice and other laboratory animals are both "us" and "not us." The logic of animal experimentation depends crucially but implicitly upon a recognition of kinship between the human and the nonhuman; without such kinship, there is nothing to learn from Rose, from OncoMouse and her dial-a-mouse variations, or from monitoring the physical effects of Ham's excursion into space. At the same time, however, a denial of kinship often functions as the rationalization for the morality and necessity of nonhuman animal experimentation. They are us insofar as we can learn from them and their bodies; they are not us, so we can do what's necessary to their bodies in order to learn from them. Without categorically denying the permissibility of this technoscientific practice, Haraway seeks to articulate an alternative which recognizes not only the interpellation of those human actors often excluded but the nonhumans whose bodies are (re) constructed, patented, and experimented upon; this alternative means recognizing that there is no "transcendent excellence of the Human over the Animal, which can then be killed without the charge of murder being brought," but recognition of the contingent, historical, material relationships between the human and nonhuman that prevents "inequality from becoming commonsensical or obviously okay."[92]

Even as human interventions on murine bodies make them unnatural enough to be classified as patentable objects of human ingenuity rather than as examples of a natural kind, the kinship between human and nonhuman genetically modified, cyborg animals becomes more crucial and more evident. Now that human bodies, too, are increasingly modified into "self-regulating man-machine systems," we are even more obviously akin to Rose the "rat-pump system," the genetically modified OncoMouse and her dial-a-mouse cohort, and Ham the wired-up space chimp, in our own technologically manipulable physical systems, than we might previously have thought. This is what "cyborg anthropology," and therefore cyborg politics, is about:

> Cyborg anthropology attempts to refigure provocatively the border relations among specific humans, other organisms, and machines. The interface between specifically located people, other organisms, and machines turns out to be an excellent field site for ethnographic inquiry into what counts as self-acting and as collective empowerment. I call that field site the culture and practice

---

[90] Haraway, "Cyborgs, Dogs and Companion Species."
[91] Haraway, *When Species Meet*, p. 77.
[92] Haraway, "Femaleman©_Meets_Oncomouse™," p. 52.

of technoscience ... The relocated [murine] gaze forces me to pay attention to kinship. Who are my kin ... Who are my familiars, my siblings, and what kind of liveable world are we trying to build?[93]

Haraway's posthuman discourse is organized around the central figure of the cyborg, a simultaneously epistemological, ontological, political, and moral position deliberately taken up outside the categorical boundaries of nature and culture, science and politics, man and woman, human and nonhuman. This posthuman figure is a harbinger of the dissolution of those boundaries, a reality both threatening and hopeful. Haraway's hope lies in the possibility of the transgressive power and potential agency of the cyborg and its posthuman kin; the threat lies in the possibility of the continuing exploitation of those who find themselves already out-of-bounds with respect to the powerful discourses defining identity within technoscience.

---

[93] Ibid.

# Chapter 2
# The Transhumanist Manifesto

Simon Young's 2006 *Designer Evolution: A Transhumanist Manifesto* provides a counterpoint to Haraway's "A Cyborg Manifesto" with a very different posthuman vision. Written as an enthusiastic call to action, Young's rhetoric, like Haraway's, deliberately echoes Marx: "People of the world, unite. You have nothing to lose but your biological chains!"[1] Though Young's manifesto is a popular, rather than scholarly work, as a call to action it serves as a bookend to the sense of ethical urgency also evident in Haraway's writing.

It is not, however, a text that can single-handedly represent the transhumanist movement as a whole; there is no such text, as the diverse historical roots and divergent current manifestations render any single account less than comprehensively representative. In this chapter, therefore, I will draw upon Young, and several other representative and foundational thinkers of specific facets of the transhumanist movement: James Hughes, Nick Bostrom, David Pearce, Max More, and others, whose works aim at exploring the philosophical implications of, explaining, defending, and/or popularizing their preferred versions of transhumanism. In addition, much of the discourse that has contributed to the formation of transhumanism as a movement has taken place in the vibrant online communities that characterize transhumanism, including email networks, personal blogs, and official websites.

## Humanity, Plus

As noted in the Introduction, a certain amount of terminological confusion complicates discussions of the posthuman. The World Transhumanist Association (WTA) carefully distinguishes the terms "transhuman" and "posthuman" in its collaboratively authored document, the "Transhumanist FAQ."[2] The posthuman is defined as "possible future beings whose basic capacities so radically exceed those of present humans as to be no longer unambiguously human by our current

---

[1] Simon Young, *Designer Evolution: A Transhumanist Manifesto* (Amherst, NY, 2006), p. 31.

[2] The World Transhumanist Association is now known as Humanity+. References to the World Transhumanist Association (WTA) are retained in this chapter for material published or promoted under that name; references to Humanity+ refer to material distributed after the name change. URLs cited for WTA are automatically redirected to the corresponding material under Humanity+.

standards."[3] This rather open-ended definition acknowledges the plurality inherent in the concept of the posthuman, an umbrella term which encompasses many possible forms, including completely synthetic artificial intelligences, enhanced uploads, or the result of making many smaller but cumulatively profound augmentations to a biological human. These biological augmentations "would probably require either the redesign of the human organism using advanced nanotechnology or its radical enhancement using some combination of technologies such as genetic engineering, psychopharmacology, anti-aging therapies, neural interfaces, advanced information management tools, memory enhancing drugs, wearable computers, and cognitive techniques."[4] In contrast, the term transhuman "refers to an intermediary form between the human and the posthuman"; and "transhumanist" simply means someone who advocates transhumanism.[5] Interestingly, though some thinkers (such as N. Katherine Hayles and Andy Clark, for example) make the claim that we are already posthuman, transhumanists resist this extension of the notion: "Some authors write as though simply by changing our self-conception, we have become or could become posthuman. This is a confusion or corruption of the original meaning of the term. The changes required to make us posthuman are too profound to be achievable by merely altering some aspect of psychological theory or the way we think about ourselves. Radical technological modifications to our brains and bodies are needed."[6]

So what is transhumanism? Simon Young defines it in his manifesto as "the belief in overcoming human limitations through reason, science, and technology."[7] Similarly, though somewhat more cautiously, the "Transhumanist FAQ" offers this basic definition: "The intellectual and cultural movement that affirms the possibility and desirability of fundamentally improving the human condition through applied reason, especially by developing and making widely available technologies to eliminate aging and to greatly enhance human intellectual, physical, and psychological capacities."[8] Transhumanism is therefore a highly specific term, unlike the term posthuman, which carries with it a conglomeration of multiple possible and contested meanings. Nonetheless, the two terms are semantically connected, in that a transhumanist is someone who advocates the desirability of becoming (some form of) posthuman. Though transhumanism is not by any means a monolithic movement, all transhumanists share in common the goals and means encapsulated in the definitions above.

The phrase "better than well," which functioned as the slogan for the World Transhumanist Association, is descriptive of the basic conviction that characterizes

---

[3] N. Bostrom, "The Transhumanist FAQ: A General Introduction," The World Transhumanist Association, http://humanityplus.org/learn/transhumanist-faq/.

[4] Ibid.

[5] Ibid.

[6] Ibid.

[7] Young, *Designer Evolution*, p. 15.

[8] Bostrom, "The Transhumanist FAQ."

the transhumanist movement.⁹ To aim for a state of being that is "better than well" indicates transhumanism's rejection of the assumption that a dividing line between health and illness defines the limits of human experience and technological capability. The goal is not to be well, that is, to achieve the optimal level of health possible within the limits of a naturally given human embodiment, but to become better than well, by using technologies to redefine or remove the naturally given limits of human embodiment that have historically shaped definitions of health and wellbeing. This is, in bioethical terms, human enhancement, defined in terms of transcending biological limitations. Transhumanist goals of enhancement explicitly include the pursuit of longevity and the elimination of aging, disease, pain, and suffering.

This desire to be better than well is characterized by transhumanist apologists as an original and innate desire of humanity, that is, an expression of our essential humanness. This line of argument reaches toward both the technological and religious impulses evident within what we might call "human nature" for its force, as there is both a pragmatic and a spiritual dimension to the quest for transcendence of biological limits. James Hughes contends that transhumanism, as "the idea that humans can use reason to transcend the limitations of the human condition," has "ancient roots" and includes the "transcendent religious traditions" as evidence of the universality of human the desire to transcend sickness, aging, and death.¹⁰ Bostrom, too, cites religious practices such as prehistoric humans' burial rites and the quest for immortality narrated in the *Epic of Gilgamesh* as traces of this quintessentially human quest to "expand the boundaries of their existence."¹¹ As such, to be human means to be transhuman, in the sense that it is basic to humanity to desire becoming posthuman.

This is intriguing, given the typical resistance of transhumanists to characterizations of the movement as quasi-religious. As a movement, Bostrom locates transhumanism's roots in Enlightenment "rational humanism."¹² Humanism is seen as a crucial philosophical turning point, the beginning of a merger of the religious impulse toward transcendence and an appreciation of technological human agency.¹³ Bostrom summarizes, "this [humanist] heritage from the Renaissance combines with the influences of Isaac Newton, Thomas Hobbes, John Locke, Immanuel Kant, Marquis de Condorcet, and others to form the basis

---

⁹ The slogan "better than well" is less prominent after the redesign of the organization's website, but can still be seen here: http://humanityplus.org/get-involved.

¹⁰ James Hughes, *Citizen Cyborg: Why Democratic Societies Must Respond to the Redesigned Human of the Future* (Cambridge, MA, 2004), p. 156.

¹¹ Bostrom, "The Transhumanist FAQ."

¹² Ibid.

¹³ Hughes quotes, for example, Pico della Mirandola's 1486 *Oration on the Dignity of Man*, in which God says to humankind, "to you is granted the power, contained in your intellect and judgment, to be reborn into the higher forms, the divine." Hughes, *Citizen Cyborg*, p. 157.

for rational humanism, which emphasizes science and critical reasoning—rather than revelation and divine authority—as ways of learning about the world and the destiny and nature of man and of providing a grounding for morality."[14] Thus, transhumanism as a current movement and worldview is indeed an expression of the innate human quest for transcendence—but, crucially, through the means of human agency in the form of technological innovation, and not through religious expectation of salvation through divine agency.

The first direct intellectual precursors to the transhumanist movement appeared in the 1920s and 1930s, with J.B.S. Haldane's 1923 essay, "Daedalus: Science and the Future," J.D. Bernal's "The World, the Flesh and the Devil," and Herman J. Muller's *Out of the Night: A Biologist's View of the Future*.[15] These works proposed extrauterine gestation, genetic enhancement, bionic implants, and the possibility of a superior future form of humanity. Hughes credits Julian Huxley with the original coinage of the term "transhumanism," from his 1927 book on humanism, entitled *Religion Without Revelation*: "The human species can, if it wishes, transcend itself—not just sporadically, an individual here in one way, an individual there in another way, but in its entirety, as humanity. We need a name for this new belief. Perhaps *transhumanism* will serve: man remaining man, but transcending himself, by realizing new possibilities of and for his human nature."[16] In Huxley's coinage, once again, it becomes apparent that the "trans" of transhumanism refers not simply to the aspect of change but to the possibility of the transcendent.

The notion that humanity might transcend or technologically transform its own nature collectively, rather than sporadically and individually, in these intellectual and historical precursors to transhumanism brings with it the specter of eugenics. As Nikolas Rose notes, the "murderous form that eugenics took in Germany" forms the inevitable backdrop to contemporary evaluations of biotechnology.[17] Simon Young writes, "One can fully understand the sentiment behind the view that any kind of connection between biology and behavior should remain forever taboo, on the grounds that eugenicists made the same connection some eighty years ago, and the terrible end result was the ideology we might call 'Hitlerism.'"[18]

The transhumanist rebuttal to what is often a rhetorical, rather than substantive, association of transhumanism and eugenics—a sort of bioethical equivalent to the Internet's "Godwin's Law"—is to emphasize the movement's grounding in Enlightenment humanism and the importance of the individual person in its philosophy. Young writes, "this 120-year-old term [eugenics] describes

---

[14] Bostrom, "The Transhumanist FAQ."
[15] Hughes, *Citizen Cyborg*, pp. 157–8.
[16] Ibid., p. 158.
[17] Nikolas Rose, *The Politics of Life Itself: Biomedicine, Power, and Subjectivity in the Twenty-First Century* (Princeton, NJ, 2007), pp. 59–60. Rose provides a brief but thorough analysis of eugenics and its relevance to contemporary biopolitics (pp. 54–64).
[18] Young, *Designer Evolution*, p. 166.

the systematic attempt *by the state* to improve the constitution of a population through enforced sterilization and selective breeding. In short, eugenics means state control of reproduction." In contrast, Young says, transhumanism advocates "*voluntary consumer* access to Superbiology, enabling individuals to enhance their bodies and minds as they see fit, in their *own* interests ... we do not live under totalitarian regimes, but in democracies, in which individuals are free to do as they please."[19] Bostrom, too, identifies the problem of eugenics as totalitarian utopianism which imposes a centralized vision of a new and better world.[20] The negation of the individual seen historically in the totalitarian state's application of eugenics is contrasted with the positive valuation of the individual person within transhumanism. Here, it becomes crucial to define transhumanism as "humanity plus," emphasizing that technological proposals for human enhancement do not, from the transhumanist point of view, threaten the human at all; the autonomy, dignity, rationality, and self-determination of the individual human person are not simply preserved, but indeed increased, in transhumanist visions of the posthuman.

A related debate, both within the movement and among outside critics, is transhumanism's degree of similarity to and dependence upon Nietzschean philosophy. Critics of transhumanism, both religious and secular, often characterize transhumanism's vision of the posthuman as the technological pursuit of Nietzsche's *Übermensch*.[21] Stefan Sorgner argues that there are certain fundamental similarities between Nietzsche's concept of "overhumans" and transhumanism's posthuman; specifically, he names the rejection of a traditional Christian worldview and a corresponding embrace of critical thinking and scientific inquiry, the notion of individual enhancement, and a dialectical tension between evolutionary progress and ontological discontinuity with the posthuman/overhuman.[22] In response, Max More affirms not simply parallels with

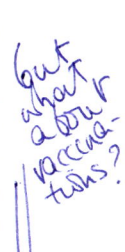

---

[19] Ibid., p. 65. Young's penchant for idiosyncratic terminology uses "Superbiology" as an equivalent for human enhancement.

[20] Nick Bostrom, "A History of Transhumanist Thought," *Journal of Evolution and Technology* 14/1 (2005): p. 7.

[21] For example, Jürgen Habermas, *Die Zukunft der Menschlichen Natur: Auf Dem Weg zu einer liberalen Eugenik?* (Frankfurt am Main, 2001). For a theological interpretation of transhumanism as Nietzschean nihilism, see Brent Waters, *From Human to Posthuman: Christian Theology and Technology in a Postmodern World* (Burlington, VT, 2006). For a contrasting theological interpretation, see Elaine Graham, "'Nietzsche Gets a Modem': Transhumanism and the Technological Sublime," *Literature & Theology* 16/1 (2002), Elaine Graham, *Representations of the Post/Human: Monsters, Aliens and Others in Popular Culture* (New Brunswick, NJ, 2002).

[22] Stefan L. Sorgner, "Nietzsche, the Overhuman and the Transhuman," *Journal of Evolution and Technology* 20/1 (2009): pp. 32–9. Sorgner's original article generated several responses, both positive and negative, on both the proper interpretation of Nietzsche as a philosopher and Nietzsche's relation and importance to transhumanism: William S. Bainbridge, "Burglarizing Nietzsche's Tomb," *Journal of Evolution and Technology* 21/1 (2010), Russell Blackford, "Editorial: Nietzsche and European Posthumanisms," *Journal*

Nietzschean philosophy, but direct influence, writing, "such an influence does indeed exist. I know that because his ideas influenced my own thinking."[23] Nick Bostrom, however, firmly rejects anything beyond a "surface-level similarity" with the Nietzschean vision: "What Nietzsche had in mind was not technological transformation but a kind of personal soaring growth and cultural refinement in exceptional individuals ... transhumanism—with its Enlightenment roots, its emphasis on individual liberties, and its humanistic concern for the welfare of all humans (and other sentient beings)—probably has as much or more in common with Nietzsche's contemporary the English liberal thinker and utilitarian John Stuart Mill."[24] Likewise, Ray Kurzweil writes that transhumanism represents an embrace of a slippery slope that leads "not down into Nietzsche's abyss," but "up toward greater promise."[25]

This ongoing internal and external debate on the proper interpretation of transhumanism as Nietzschean or a version of liberal humanism is a debate of some consequence, as well as an indication of the complexity and diversity of the movement. Is transhumanism best understood as a modernist movement, a conscious philosophical extension of Enlightenment rational humanism, or as a radically postmodern movement, drawing upon Nietzschean philosophy? Or is it simply not possible to characterize transhumanism as a holistic movement at all? This internal debate within transhumanism about how best to understand and characterize its own philosophical heritage highlights the difficulty and necessity of making interpretive choices as interdisciplinary dialogue partners with transhumanism.

Negotiating this difficulty requires scrupulous specificity in interdisciplinary dialogue with transhumanist ideas, as no one presentation of transhumanism or single thinker can be presumed to be representative of the whole. To that end, a brief description of the major "currents" of transhumanism (extropianism, democratic transhumanism, singularitarianism, and the hedonistic imperative) follows.[26] At the same time, however, I will begin building the argument that there

---

*of Evolution and Technology* 21/1 (2010), Michael Hauskeller, "Nietzsche, the Overhuman and the Posthuman: A Reply to Stefan Sorgner," *Journal of Evolution and Technology* 21/1 (2010), Bill Hibbard, "Nietzsche's Overhuman Is an Ideal Whereas Posthumans Will Be Real," *Journal of Early Christian Studies* 21/1 (2010), David Roden, "Deconstruction and Excision in Philosophical Posthumanism," *Journal of Evolution and Technology* 21/1 (2010). For a counter-response from Sorgner, see Stefan L. Sorgner, "Beyond Humanism: Reflections on Trans- and Posthumanism," *Journal of Evolution and Technology* 21/2 (2010).

[23]   Max More, "The Overhuman in the Transhuman," *Journal of Evolution and Technology* 21/1 (2010).

[24]   Bostrom, "A History of Transhumanist Thought," p. 4.

[25]   Ray Kurzweil, *The Singularity Is Near: When Humans Transcend Biology* (New York, 2005), p. 374.

[26]   Bostrom, "The Transhumanist FAQ." The FAQ also includes the following three categories: theoretical transhumanism, salon transhumanism, and transhumanism in arts and culture. However, these categories are not parallel to the first four, and I leave them out in the interest of clarity.

are significant philosophical overlaps between these distinctive currents, in the way in which transhumanism consistently advocates for a notion of "humanity, plus." In this two-pronged approach, which attempts to both honor the genuine diversity within the movement while identifying substantive similarities between various versions of transhumanism, I follow the lead of transhumanists like James Hughes and Nick Bostrom in their attempts to identify common values and beliefs among those who identify as transhumanists.[27] These attempts ultimately paint a picture of the transhumanist movement as an extension of Enlightenment humanism, with its emphases on individual will, freedom, rationality, and optimistic faith in human agency.

*Extropianism*

The name "extropianism" is derived from the term "extropy," coined as a metaphorical opposite to entropy, and referring to "the extent of a system's intelligence, information, order, vitality, and capacity for improvement."[28] Max More and Tom Morrow published the first issue of *Extropy Magazine* in 1988, and in 1992 founded the Extropy Institute, which hosted an active email listserv which provided the initial introduction to transhumanist ideas for many.[29] More describes extropianism as "the most developed form of transhumanism," and articulates a full-fledged philosophy of living that fulfills and replaces the meaning-giving function of religion. The purpose of life is its own expansion; More writes, "We behold a life of unlimited growth and possibility with excitement and joy. We seek to void all limits to life, intelligence, freedom, knowledge, and happiness. Science, technology and reason must be harnessed to our extropic values to abolish the greatest evil: death ... [this] is essential

---

[27] The two founding documents of the World Transhumanist Association (the *Transhumanist Declaration* and the *Transhumanist FAQ*), for example, are collaborative compositions which attempt to identify common themes and beliefs across the spectrum of transhumanism (see Bostrom, "A History of Transhumanist Thought," pp. 15–16). James Hughes cites more recent empirical research into commonly held values among transhumanists in James Hughes, "The Compatibility of Religious and Transhumanist Views of Metaphysics, Suffering, Virtue and Transcendence in an Enhanced Future," *The Global Spiral* 2 (2007), www.metanexus.net/magazine/tabid/68/id/9930/Default.aspx.

[28] Bostrom, "The Transhumanist FAQ."

[29] In 2006, The Extropy Institute closed its doors, announcing that its mission, "to bring great minds together to incubate ideas about emerging technologies, life extension and the future," and its specific goals, "(1) develop an elegant, focused philosophy for transhumanism—the philosophy of Extropy; (2) encourage discussions and debates on improving the human condition; and (3) develop a culture for activists, energized and devoted to bringing these ideas to the public," were "essentially completed." The website now functions as the "Library of Transhumanism, Extropy and the Future." Natasha Vita-More, "Next Steps," The Extropy Institute, www.extropy.org/future.htm.

to any philosophy of optimism and transcendence relevant to the individual."[30] This expansive vision is further enumerated in the "Extropian Principles," also authored by More: perpetual progress, self-transformation, practical optimism or "proaction," intelligent technology, open society (information and democracy), self-direction, and rational thinking.[31]

James Hughes characterizes extropianism as "libertarian transhumanism." The extropian principle of "open society" is a recent substitution for the original "spontaneous order," a belief Hughes describes as "distilled from the work of Friedrich Hayek and Ayn Rand, that an anarchistic market creates free and dynamic order, while the state and its life-stealing authoritarianism is entropic."[32] Bostrom interprets this movement away from the original libertarian principle as an indication that More has since distanced himself from this aspect of early extropianism.[33] Hughes argues, however, that the majority of extropians remain staunch libertarians, citing a 2002 online survey in which 56 percent of extropians identified as "libertarian" or "anarchist" in political outlook.[34]

As one of the earliest and strongest historical contributing streams to the current transhumanist movement, extropianism's libertarian vision of transhumanism remains an influential and perhaps majority voice within the movement. Simon Young's manifesto, for example, fits within this stream of the transhumanist movement in its blunt advocacy of free market solutions to issues of accessibility to current, emerging, and potential technologies, and its opposition to the notion of government regulation of technological research and development.[35] However, it is difficult to gauge from the outside the relative strengths and representations of the various factions within the transhumanist movement, and James Hughes's "democratic transhumanism" or "technoprogressivism," to which we now turn, constitutes a deliberate internal challenge and political alternative to extropian libertarianism.

*Democratic Transhumanism/Technoprogressivism*

Democratic transhumanism advocates both the right to use technology to transcend the limitations of the human body, and the extension of democratic concerns beyond formal legal equality and liberty into economic and cultural liberty and equality, in order to protect values such as equality, solidarity, and democratic

---

[30] Max More, "Transhumanism: A Futurist Philosophy," www.maxmore.com/transhum.htm.

[31] Max More, "Principles of Extropy Version 3.11," Extropy Institute, www.extropy.org/principles.htm.

[32] Bostrom, "A History of Transhumanist Thought," p. 15, Hughes, *Citizen Cyborg*, pp. 164–6.

[33] Bostrom, "A History of Transhumanist Thought," p. 15.

[34] Hughes, *Citizen Cyborg*, pp. 168–9.

[35] Young, *Designer Evolution*.

participation in a transhuman and ultimately posthuman context.[36] James Hughes, co-founder along with Nick Bostrom of the Institute for Ethics and Emerging Technologies (IEET), is at the forefront of defining and creating this distinctive current of transhumanism. Deliberately positioning democratic transhumanism as an alternative to extropianism's libertarian political ideology, Hughes argues that democratic transhumanism successfully addresses both "the legitimate concerns of the bioLuddites for equity, solidarity and public safety, and libertarian concerns with our right to control our bodies and minds."[37] Hughes seeks, in other words, to split the difference between those who seek unregulated technological progress (extropians), and those who fear it ("bioLuddites," or less pejoratively, "bioconservatives"), by creating a middle ground that allows for the freedom to pursue enhancement technologies with the provision of a certain judicious amount of regulation and universal provision.

Hughes outlines an "eleven-point program" for democratic transhumanists, arguing the need for multiple strategic political alliances, including a directive to "solidarize with sexual, cultural, and racial minorities, especially with morphological minorities such as the disabled and transgendered."[38] Hughes sees democratic transhumanism as an umbrella under which disparate groups and movements may establish common cause, listing advocates of reproductive rights, disability rights, universal basic income, drug decriminalization, and transgender rights as examples.[39] Though he admits that "currently all the self-described 'democratic transhumanists' in the world could hold a convention in

---

[36] Bostrom, "The Transhumanist FAQ."

[37] Hughes, *Citizen Cyborg*, p. 187.

[38] James Hughes, "Democratic Transhumanism 2.0," www.changesurfer.com/Acad/DemocraticTranshumanism.htm. The full 11-point list is as follows: (1) Build the transhumanist movement, (2) Guarantee morphological freedom and bodily autonomy, (3) Defend scientific research from Luddite bans, while embracing legitimate safety and efficacy regulations, (4) Protect scientific access to knowledge from overly aggressive intellectual property law, (5) Expand federal funding for research into transhuman technologies, (6) Create national health plans which include transhuman tech, (7) Expand federal support to education, (8) Provide job retraining and an income to the structurally unemployed, (9) Solidarize with sexual, cultural, and racial minorities, especially with morphological minorities such as the disabled and transgendered, (10) Support rights for Great Apes, dolphins and whales, (11) Strengthen democratic world government.

[39] Hughes, *Citizen Cyborg*, pp. 207–8. Here, Hughes approaches the coalition-building possibilities of Haraway's political cyborg, and is indeed the only transhumanist who seems aware of the posthuman discourse stemming from Haraway's "Cyborg Manifesto." As yet, however, as Hughes himself notes, "there has been little cross-pollination between the left-wing academic cyborgologists and the transhumanists," Hughes, *Citizen Cyborg*, p. 208. The underlying disjuncture between transhumanist anthropology and cyborg anthropology provide a reason for the lack of cross-pollination between these two posthuman discourses, an argument I will pursue in Chapter 3, in a more detailed analysis of the underlying anthropologies in these divergent posthuman visions.

a large classroom," Hughes argues that "there is a latent majority constituency for social justice, technological progress and health and longevity for all."[40] Significantly, this broad and inclusive vision also includes dialogue with religious faiths is a necessary and important element in crafting an inclusive and democratic transhumanism and posthuman future. This makes democratic transhumanism the most obviously sympathetic and potentially constructive dialogue partner for Christian theologians interested in transhumanist visions of the posthuman—though often, it is versions of extropianism or singularitarianism that remain the primary dialogue partners in Christian theological engagements.

*Hedonistic Transhumanism*

A third transhumanist current is "paradise-engineering," a transhumanist program outlined by David Pearce, the co-founder (along with Nick Bostrom) of the WTA.[41] The combination of the transhumanist view of the unnecessary character of biological finitude and its negative consequences, and classical utilitarian philosophy yields what Pearce labels "the hedonistic imperative." Pearce takes the typical transhumanist view of bodily pain, suffering, and infirmity to its logical and philosophical conclusion in arguing for the elimination of all forms of pain, for all people, and eventually, all organisms. This long-term goal Pearce calls "the abolitionist project."[42]

Pearce lists the technologies he considers most useful for achieving the goals of the abolitionist project in "ascending order of sociological plausibility": wireheading, utopian designer drugs, and genetic engineering leading to reproductive revolution. "Wireheading" is Pearce's term for "intracranial self-stimulation," that is, stimulation of the brain's pleasure centers through implanted electrodes. Though not against it, Pearce is doubtful of the plausibility of the wirehead scenario attaining widespread social acceptability. Wireheading is not, in Pearce's analysis, an evolutionarily stable solution, but worse, the uniform and constant state of bliss attained by wireheading conflicts with Pearce's long-term abolitionist goals, as "direct neurostimulation of the reward centres destroys informational sensitivity to environmental stimuli."[43] Further, he argues, there simply "isn't a moral urgency to maximizing superhappiness in the same way as there is to abolishing suffering."[44] A better goal, in Pearce's estimation, is to aim for both "superhappiness" and "superintelligence" by creating "an informational economy of mind based entirely on [adaptive] gradients of cerebral bliss." As long as the signaling function of pain is preserved in the hedonistic state, the subjective quality of pain can be replaced, in Pearce's phrase, by "gradients of

---

[40] Hughes, *Citizen Cyborg*, p. 216.
[41] Bostrom, "The Transhumanist FAQ."
[42] David Pearce, "The Abolitionist Project," The Hedonistic Imperative, www.hedweb.com/abolitionist-project/index.html.
[43] Ibid.
[44] Ibid.

bliss." Pearce's reluctance to stop short of achieving a state of gradients of bliss for all organisms, then, seems to be his main motivation for rejecting wireheading as the obvious technological means of obeying the hedonistic imperative.

The second technological means for eradicating suffering is also short-term: designer mood drugs. This is short-term, in Pearce's estimation, not because of its interference with the long-term goals of the abolitionist project, nor because of indefeasible social unacceptability, but because the effects achieved require a constant dependence on drugs.[45] This minor inconvenience is tolerable, but given the possibility of genetically engineering our genome to a predisposition of happiness as a constant state, will probably eventually become unnecessary. Pearce points to the rare condition of hyperthymia as an indication of the genetic possibility of the future, anticipating the use of both germline and somatic gene therapy. He writes, "Hyperthymic people aren't manic or bipolar; but by contemporary standards, they are always exceedingly happy, albeit sometimes happier than others. Hyperthymic people respond 'appropriately' and adaptively to their environment. Indeed they are characteristically energetic, productive and creative. Even when they are blissful, they aren't 'blissed out.'"[46]

It is difficult to say how widespread this hedonistic philosophy is within transhumanism as a movement; however, Nick Bostrom's list of identifying core transhumanist values includes "caring about the well-being of all sentience," a defining tenet for Pearce's utilitarian transhumanism.[47] Further, James Hughes cites a WTA survey of its members in which 81 percent of respondents agreed that their "ethical code advocate[s] the well-being of all sentient beings, whether in artificial intellects, humans, posthumans, or non-human animals."[48] Thus, while it is doubtful that scenarios of "wireheading" or espousal of hedonism characterize transhumanists in a general sense, at least one major facet of Pearce's hedonistic transhumanism does seem to describe a core transhumanist value held by a majority of transhumanists.

*Singularitarianism*

Singularitarianism may be the best known public face of transhumanism, due to the high public profiles of figures such as Ray Kurzweil and Hans Moravec. The Singularity, a term coined by Vernor Vinge, is "a point in the future when the rate of technological development becomes so rapid that the progress-curve

---

[45] Ibid. Intriguingly, Gregory Stock's argument for "fyborgization" over a more literal and permanent future merger of flesh and technology is based on the opposite assessment—that temporary and short-term alliances with technology provides more degrees of freedom than permanent and "invisible" cyborg mergers: Gregory Stock, *Redesigning Humans: Choosing Our Genes, Changing Our Future* (New York, 2002).

[46] Pearce, "The Abolitionist Project."

[47] Hughes, "The Compatibility of Religious and Transhumanist Views of Metaphysics, Suffering, Virtue and Transcendence in an Enhanced Future."

[48] Ibid.

becomes nearly vertical," the most likely cause of which would be the creation of some form of rapidly self-enhancing greater-than-human intelligence.[49] Therefore, singularitarianism is described in the "Transhumanist FAQ" as a "focus on transhuman technologies that can potentially lead to the rise of smarter-than-human intelligence," examples of which would be brain–computer interfacing or the development of true Artificial Intelligence (AI).[50] Alternatively, singularitarianism might be thought of as a preference for the enhancement of human intelligence as a specific transhumanist goal, rather than as a focus on specific technologies, as which technologies or AI strategies seem most likely to produce the Singularity is a matter of continuing investigation and internal debate.

Like More's ongoing revision of the Extropian Principles, there is a distinct aversion to strictly defining the boundaries of singularitarianism, but at the same time, a desire to identify of a core set of beliefs and practices that can be called singularitarian. Independent scholar and AI researcher Eliezer S. Yudkowsky's online document "Singularitarian Principles," therefore, charts a singularitarianism in which the Singularity itself is broadly defined, and a movement which is inclusive of various interpretations.[51] Michael Anissimov, however, argues that singularitarianism, strictly speaking, refers only to the advocacy of the development of posthuman (greater than human) intelligence, despite the association of singularitarianism with belief in the exponential growth of technology generally, pursuit of radical life extension, belief in the possibility and desirability of mind uploading and belief in the feasibility of strong AI.[52] The definition of the Singularity offered by the Singularity Institute for Artificial Intelligence (SAIA), authored by Anissimov, therefore consciously privileges the "intelligence explosion" definition: "When humanity builds machines with greater-than-human intelligence, they will also be better than we are at creating still smarter machines. Those improved machines will be even *more* capable of improving themselves or their successors. This is a positive feedback loop that

---

[49] Bostrom, "The Transhumanist FAQ", Vernor Vinge, "The Coming Technological Singularity," *Whole Earth Review* Winter (1993), www.ugcs.caltech.edu/~phoenix/vinge/vinge-sing.html.

[50] Bostrom, "The Transhumanist FAQ."

[51] Eliezer Yudkowsky, "The Singularitarian Principles," http://yudkowsky.net/sing/principles.ext.html#desc. Yudkowsky provides four "definitional principles" and five "descriptive principles." The "definitional principles" include: singularity, activism, "ultratechnology," and globalism; the "descriptive principles" include: apotheosis, solidarity, intelligence, independence, and nonsuppression. A full explanation of each principle can be found online.

[52] Michael Anissimov, "The Word 'Singularity' Has Lost All Meaning," Accelerating Future, www.acceleratingfuture.com/michael/blog/?p=504.

could, before losing steam, produce a machine with vastly greater than human intelligence: *machine superintelligence*."[53]

Singularitarians often express a sense of urgency with regard to the task of ensuring that AI and the resulting Singularity are human-friendly. The Singularity Institute actively funds research into friendly AI and other technologies anticipated by singularitarians to play a key role in the advent of the Singularity.[54] Yudkowsky's singularitarian activism, however, goes beyond the necessity of creating safeguards against the possibility of global catastrophes triggered by out-of-control human technologies, and the common SF scenarios of vindictive AI as depicted in *Terminator* and *Battlestar Galactica*, for example.[55] Yudkowsky and others make a positive argument for pursuing research into enhancing human intelligence as a means of ameliorating the human condition by pointing out that social problems such as poverty, illness, and the like are more likely to be solved through the creation of greater intelligence than by pursuit of individual solutions to specific problems at our current level of human intelligence.[56]

*The Upload Scenario*

Uploading is not categorized as its own "current" of transhumanism in the "Transhumanist FAQ," though it is, as Anissimov's analysis suggests, often inaccurately associated specifically with singularitarianism. Rather, uploading, "the process of transferring an intellect from a biological brain to a computer," is treated as a particular type of potential, future technology. Ray Kurzweil describes uploading as a process of "scanning all of the salient details and then reinstantiating those details into a suitably powerful computational substrate. This process would capture a person's entire personality, memory, skills, and history."[57] This, of course, remains a speculative possibility that would require progress both in neuroscience, to develop an adequately detailed three-dimensional map of the brain as well as adequate computing capacity, in order to "run the upload and provide some way for the upload to interact with the external world or with a virtual reality."[58] However, extrapolating from the exponential rapidity of

---

[53] "The Singularity FAQ," The Singularity Institute for Artificial Intelligence (SAIA), http://singinst.org/singularityfaq#WhatIsTheSingularity.

[54] Ibid.

[55] Michael Anissimov, "Ideas for Mitigating Extinction Risk," Accelerating Future, www.acceleratingfuture.com/michael/blog/2008/09/ideas-for-mitigating-extinction-risk/. See also the follow-up posts entitled, "A Bare Minimum for Extinction Safeguards," and "The IEET."

[56] Eliezer Yudkowsky, "What Is the Singularity?," The Singularity Institute for Artificial Intelligence, www.singinst.org/overview/whatisthesingularity.

[57] Kurzweil, *The Singularity Is Near*, pp. 198–9.

[58] Bostrom, "The Transhumanist FAQ." This is also sometimes referred to as "downloading," "mind uploading," and "brain reconstruction."

technological advances in scanning and sensing tools and anticipating the advent of nanotechnology, Kurzweil predicts that the technology for "scanning from within the brain using nanobots" will be available by the late 2020s, the basic computational resources by the early 2030s, and that successful uploading will take place by the end of the 2030s.[59]

Kurzweil offers three potential future scenarios. First, Kurzweil claims, by the late 2020s we will be able to create nonbiological systems which match and exceed the complex intelligence of humans—that is, true artificial intelligence. The second scenario is uploading, the transfer of the patterns of human intelligence to a nonbiological substrate. The third scenario is the gradual augmentation of the biological human with nonbiological components, a process which begins with cyborgs but ends, Kurzweil predicts, with the complete replacement of the biological with the superior nonbiological, as the nonbiological portion of our intelligence will expand its powers exponentially.[60] While the first two scenarios have their proponents within transhumanism (singularitarians and uploaders), the third scenario, the gradual cyborgization of humanity leading to a fully nonbiological future, seems to reach beyond specific sub-groups within transhumanism and describe a future most transhumanists view as both plausible and desirable.[61] This gradual merger of biology and technology, however, proceeds with the same assumptions that undergird the singularitarian and upload scenarios: that nonbiological systems are capable of intelligence, are superior to biological intelligence, are compatible with biological intellects, and represent the future of humanity. Thus this last scenario, as Kurzweil himself comments, describes a future in which "we will have effectively uploaded ourselves, albeit gradually, never quite noticing the transfer."[62]

Distinctions are therefore sometimes made between hypothetical scenarios of destructive, non-destructive. In destructive uploading, the original biological brain is physically destroyed in the uploading process. As a hypothetical scenario, destructive uploading simplifies the philosophical issues surrounding personal identity and continuity that uploading presents. Non-destructive uploading presumably results in the simultaneous existence of the original brain and the upload, prompting several questions: "Tricky cases arise, however, if we imagine that several similar copies are made of your uploaded mind. Which one of them is you? Are they all you, or are none of them you? Who owns your property? Who is married to your spouse? Philosophical, legal, and ethical challenges abound."[63]

---

[59] Kurzweil, *The Singularity Is Near*, pp. 197–200.

[60] Ibid., p. 377.

[61] Ibid., p. 374. James Hughes, Gregory Stock, and Nick Bostrom all seem to subscribe to some version of scenario three; see Hughes, *Citizen Cyborg*, Andrés Lomeña, "Interview with Nick Bostrom and David Pearce," The Hedonistic Imperative, www.hedweb.com/transhumanism/index.html, Stock, *Redesigning Humans*.

[62] Kurzweil, *The Singularity Is Near*, p. 202.

[63] Bostrom, "The Transhumanist FAQ."

Canadian SF author Robert Sawyer's novel *Mindscan* offers a narrative treatment of precisely these questions, through the *novum* of following the protagonist, Jake, through the non-destructive upload process, and then following the bifurcated identities of the dual protagonists that result—both of whom self-identify as the personal continuation of the original.[64] Biological Jake wakes up following the scanning procedure, raging that it didn't work—for he is still trapped in his biological body; artificial Jake wakes up, pleased that the procedure has worked, though the quirks of the artificial body take some getting used to. All of Jake's family and friends reject the artificial Jake and refuse to recognize him as the real Jake, and biological Jake, stripped of his legal identity and consigned to a luxury resort on the moon, also understandably refuses to recognize artificial Jake as the real Jake. Yet the structure of the novel, narrated in the double first person in the two voices of Jake, presumes that both Jakes are real, privileging the psychological continuity produced by the scanning procedure over physical continuity and social recognition as affirmations of personal identity.

**Email to Mother Nature**

The basic transhumanist conviction that human technologies can and should be employed to transcend the natural, biological limitations of the human organism—specifically, morbidity, senescence, and mortality—implies a certain attitude with regard to the "natural" as a concept and ontological category. First, and most obviously, this conviction directly challenges the notion of the immutability, givenness, or sacredness of these biological limitations. Second, this conviction presupposes a dichotomous opposition of the "natural" and the "technological," precisely by framing human technologies as the solution to the problems of the natural. Nature, therefore, is transformed from the common, culturally valorized notion associated with the good, the wholesome, and the desirable, into a negative concept associated with arbitrary limitation, vulnerability, and suffering.

There is, therefore, a broad similarity in one respect between cyborg and transhumanist attitudes toward the concept of the natural, in that both posthuman discourses reject its necessity, inviolability, and sacredness. This similarity is most obvious in James Hughes, who, like Haraway, draws on the work of Mary Douglas on cultural taboo and boundary transgression to challenge the notions of immutable nature: "Today the 'abominations' enraging the bioLuddites are lives that blur the ancient cognitive categories that separate animals and humans, humans and machines, the living and the dead, the real and the artificial, men and women, the young and the old."[65] The increased vigilance and patrol of those defunct boundaries, by conservative bioethicists and others, functions as

---

[64] Robert Sawyer, *Mindscan* (New York, 2005).
[65] Hughes, *Citizen Cyborg*, p. 77.

evidence for Hughes of what he calls "human racism": a reactionary exclusion of the nonhuman other.[66] Hughes, however, is unique among transhumanists in even briefly drawing on this philosophical discourse of ontological boundaries and notions of nature. For most transhumanists, the self-evident desirability of a posthuman state in which arbitrary biological limitations have been transcended is the focal point of discussion; the implications of ontological hybridity are beside the point.

For most transhumanists, discussions of nature occur either in the context of natural versus cultural (technological, self-directed, transhumanist) evolution, or in the context of environmental ethical objections to emerging technologies. In both contexts, the concept of nature functions as the opposite of technology. The "Transhumanist FAQ" asserts, for example, that "tampering with nature" is precisely what transhumanism is about, and that "there is no moral reason why we shouldn't intervene in nature and improve it if we can, whether by eradicating diseases, improving agricultural yields to feed a growing world population, putting communication satellites into orbit to provide homes with news and entertainment, or inserting contact lenses in our eyes so we can see better. Changing nature for the better is a noble and glorious thing for humans to do."[67] Though the document also acknowledges that one might alternatively view technology as part of nature, the dominant framework adopted in this official statement treats nature as a categorical given which human technologies may and indeed should improve.

This attitude then leads to rhetoric of "designer evolution," or the supersession of the biological evolution of humanity by its self-directed technological evolution. Kurzweil argues that the "the transformation underlying the Singularity is not just another in a long line of steps in biological evolution" but that transhumanism is "upending biological evolution altogether."[68] Nor is singularitarianism the only form of transhumanism to adopt this rhetoric. Simon Young opens his manifesto with a prologue entitled, "E-mail to Nature," which details the unsatisfactory aspects of the human condition that biological evolution has produced, and suggests several possible improvements: "the current model [*Homo sapiens*] is limited by numerous design faults. Terminal breakdowns occur frequently in all parts ... could not a program of automatic self-repair be included in an upgraded model?" Young's prologue is inspired by Max More's "A Letter to Mother Nature," which enumerates seven proposed amendments to the human constitution: ending senescence and mortality; expanding the physical senses; improving the brain and creating an external, networked "metabrain"; correcting and removing genetic defects and maximizing morphological freedom; taking control of emotional responses and motivations; integrating the biological and nonbiological.[69] While More does not provide an imagined response from Mother Nature, Young's email

---

[66] Ibid., pp. 78–9.
[67] Bostrom, "The Transhumanist FAQ."
[68] Kurzweil, *The Singularity Is Near*, p. 374.
[69] Max More, "A Letter to Mother Nature," www.maxmore.com/mother.htm.

exchange does. Nature's "most disappointing" reply justifies the human condition on the grounds that "it is quite beyond our power to rectify the problems you mention, as our manufacturing equipment is entirely automated." Young therefore responds, "We, the human species, therefore formally advise you of our intention to take over the business of Evolution, in order to improve the design of *Homo sapiens*, in our own interests of ever-increasing survivability and well-being."[70]

While More and Young both rather begrudgingly acknowledge that Nature is owed some amount of gratitude for a process of evolution which has resulted in humanity's current state of aptitude and intelligence, overall, humanity's natural condition is depicted as overwhelmingly negative. This attitude toward nature is also evident in transhumanist considerations of environmental activism. Transhumanist techno-optimism puts the movement at odds with those who consider nature and natural kinds to have an inherent value which must be preserved—making political enemies on both the extreme right and left of the U.S. political spectrum. Simon Young writes rather scornfully of an "eco-fundamentalism," an "extreme ideology" espousing "belief in the primacy of nature over humans."[71] This form of environmentalism differs, in Young's estimation, from "the perfectly sensible ... recognition of the interdependence of humankind and nature, and the consequent need to protect the ecological balance upon which our survival depends," and he characterizes this veneration of Nature as a religious "cryptopantheism."[72]

James Hughes, like Young, sees an affinity between religious faith and this sort of "deep ecology," and he too categorizes it alongside "religious right bioconservatives" rather than "left-wing."[73] Deep ecology activists view Nature as inherently valuable, are non-anthropocentric, and view environmentalism as a moral obligation rather than a pragmatic action. Left-wing bioconservatives, in contrast, object to technologies because they assume that "all technologies will therefore serve the interests of corporations, men and the rich," which presumably exclude care for sustainable environmental practices.[74]

Constructively, Hughes seeks to make an alternative case that transhumanism is not in necessary opposition to environmentalist concerns, arguing that "a combination of judicious regulation and ecologically-oriented technologies can prevent and remediate ecological damage."[75] Like the efforts to reclaim the ecologically damaged Earth of Kim S. Robinson's near-future *Science in the Capital* series, the assumption is not that ecologies must be preserved unchanged or that nature be somehow re-pristinated, but that the pragmatic goal of creating sustainable ecosystems for humans

---

[70] Young, *Designer Evolution: A Transhumanist Manifesto*, pp. 27–9.
[71] Ibid., p. 54.
[72] Ibid.
[73] "Overview of Biopolitics," Institute of Ethics and Emerging Technologies, http://ieet.org/index.php/IEET/biopolitics.
[74] Hughes, *Citizen Cyborg*, p. 126.
[75] IEET, "Overview of Biopolitics."

and other organisms requires human agency and technological intervention.[76] Again, Hughes comes closer than any other transhumanist thinker to an articulation of the relationship of human technology and nature reminiscent of the cyborg; yet, whether this is simply a more ecologically sensitive view of nature as resource or a view of humans as embedded within nature precisely as technological creatures, is difficult to say—and this is the crucial distinction.

**Playing God**

Most transhumanists identify as secular atheists, an unsurprising observation given transhumanism's roots in the Enlightenment tradition, in which faith functions as the irrational term in the dichotomy of faith and reason. The WTA's 2006 survey of members yielded a majority view of secular atheism (62 percent); James Hughes writes, "Since transhumanists see themselves as a part of the Enlightenment humanist tradition, and since most are in fact atheist, many feel that one cannot be a theist transhumanist."[77] Religious faith of any variety is often therefore viewed as an impediment to an appreciation of transhumanist goals, stemming from an irrational, faith-based distrust of human reason and scientific progress.[78]

Religious objections to enhancement technologies as attempts to "play God" play into transhumanist assumptions of the irrationality of religious belief, and are therefore met with ridicule. Quoting Christian commentator David Bresnahan, Hughes characterizes the Christian Right's condemnation of transhumanism as "violating the divine prohibition against hubris," for "God is the author, the creator, the engineer of humanity. We are His creation, but when we abandon God and then try to take on His role we risk destruction."[79] As most transhumanists do not believe that a divine, supernatural "God" exists, most see little point in engaging this sort of religious critique. Simon Young's response is typical: "the quest to cure disease, enhance abilities, and extend life cannot seriously be called playing—more like *replacing* a God who is clearly either absent without leave or completely uninterested in reducing human suffering."[80] Further, if it is in fact possible for human beings to "play God," then there is no clear distinction between human and divine capabilities; if technology *per se* is "playing God," then no form of tool-use can be acceptable—a

---

[76] Kim S. Robinson, *Forty Signs of Rain* (New York, 2004), Kim S. Robinson, *Fifty Degrees Below* (New York, 2005), Kim S. Robinson, *Sixty Days and Counting* (New York, 2007).

[77] James Hughes, "The Compatibility of Religious and Transhumanist Views of Metaphysics, Suffering, Virtue and Transcendence in an Enhanced Future," *The Global Spiral* 8/2 (2007), www.metanexus.net/magazine/tabid/68/id/9930/Default.aspx.

[78] See, for example, William S. Bainbridge, "The Transhuman Heresy," *The Journal of Evolution and Technology* 14/2 (2005): pp. 91–100.

[79] Bresnahan, David, quoted in Hughes, *Citizen Cyborg*, p. 110.

[80] Young, *Designer Evolution*, p. 49.

position vulnerable to an easy *reductio ad absurdum*, in which we "challenge the 'will of God' every time we put on our spectacles."[81]

Many transhumanists view the utility of religious faith as a historical means of coping with mortality, by producing resignation to the natural evils of suffering and death—making suffering a cornerstone of virtue, and death the necessary prerequisite to an afterlife.[82] Hughes quotes, for example, John Kilner and C. Ben Mitchell: "Much of what the Transhumanists long for is already available to Christians: eternal life and freedom from pain, suffering, and the burden of a frail body. As usual, however, the Transhumanists—like all of us in our failed attempts to save ourselves—trust in their own power rather than God's provision for a truly human future with him."[83] At its core, transhumanism is a refusal to resign oneself to this biological inevitability. Young writes, "Theists claim that suffering is an intrinsic part of the human condition. But transhumanists do not *believe* in the human condition—rather in its *transcendence*, through technology."[84] Or, one might say, transhumanists do believe in the human condition, and believe that it is pointlessly negative; this is the primary motivation for becoming posthuman.

Heidi Campbell notes, therefore, that "there is a common longing for transformation" in transhumanism and religious faith; however, she notes, "this longing for eternity represents two different futures, one where the posthuman directs the creative process and another where God directs the outcomes."[85] While transhumanism's Enlightenment philosophical heritage indeed presents an immediate obstacle to interdisciplinary dialogue with Christian theology and other forms of religious discourse, Campbell's observation highlights the more important disjuncture. Transhumanists emphasize the necessity and efficacy of human agency to transcend the limitations of the human condition, and decry religious belief specifically for undermining humanity's confidence in its own ability to act, through advocating reliance on notions of salvation through divine acts. Here, once again, transhumanism shows itself to be an extension of philosophical humanism.

One way to characterize transhumanism's relation to religious belief, then, is to consider that transhumanism has supplanted the need for religious belief: "While not a religion, transhumanism might serve a few of the same functions that people have traditionally sought in religion. It offers a sense of direction and purpose and suggests a vision that humans can achieve something greater than our present condition ... Some of the prospects that used to be the exclusive thunder of the religious institutions, such as very long lifespan, unfading bliss, and godlike intelligence, are being discussed by transhumanists as hypothetical future

---

[81] Ibid.
[82] Ibid., pp. 50–3.
[83] Hughes, *Citizen Cyborg*, p. 112.
[84] Young, *Designer Evolution*, p. 52.
[85] Heidi Campbell, "On Posthumans, Transhumanism and Cyborgs: Towards a Transhumanist-Christian Conversation," *Modern Believing* 47/2 (2006): p. 70.

engineering achievements."[86] However, a minority position within transhumanism makes the case for the compatibility of transhumanism and some forms of religious belief. Citing the 2006 WTA membership survey, Hughes notes that nearly a quarter of the respondents identified as religious, including the major world religious traditions: Buddhism, Hinduism, Christianity, Judaism, and Islam. Hughes cites the recent formation of two faith-centered transhumanist groups as further evidence that religious faith and transhumanism are not necessarily inherently incompatible.[87] The publication of a special issue of the *Journal of Evolution and Technology* on the topic of transhumanism and religion also indicates a desire within the movement to initiate more constructive conversations with adherents of religious faiths.[88]

Hughes argues that "elements of transhumanism are compatible with interpretations of all the world's faiths, and that these compatibilities are being and will be built upon to create new, syncretic 'trans-spiritualities' in which enhancement technologies are selectively incorporated by groups in all the religious traditions."[89] It is difficult to disagree with this statement, given the amount of hedging built into it, but clearly, significant questions remain. Which elements of transhumanism are being considered here, and which not, and which matter? Which interpretations of the world's religious faiths are compatible, and who is doing the interpreting? This is not theological nitpicking, for it is clear that, despite Hughes' belief in the possible convergence of various religious views and transhumanist goals, one corner of the religious world is not included in his optimism: the so-called "Christian Right."[90]

---

[86] Bostrom, "The Transhumanist FAQ."

[87] Hughes, "The Compatibility of Religious and Transhumanist Views of Metaphysics, Suffering, Virtue and Transcendence in an Enhanced Future."

[88] See Heidi Campbell and Mark Walker, "Religion and Transhumanism: Introducing a Conversation," *Journal of Evolution and Technology* 14/2 (2005): pp. i–xv. Other articles in this issue include Bainbridge, "The Transhuman Heresy," Patrick D. Hopkins, "Transcending the Animal: How Transhumanism and Religion Are and Are Not Alike," *Journal of Evolution and Technology* 14/2 (2005), Oliver Krueger, "Gnosis in Cyberspace? Body, Mind and Progress in Posthumanism," *Journal of Evolution and Technology* 14/2 (2005), Michael LaTorra, "Trans-Spirit: Religion, Spirituality and Transhumanism," *Journal of Evolution and Technology* 14/2 (2005), Stephen Garner, "Transhumanism and Christian Social Concern," *Journal of Evolution and Technology* 14/2 (2005), Todd Daly, "Life-Extension in Transhumanist and Christian Perspectives: Consonance and Conflict," *Journal of Evolution and Technology* 14/2 (2005), John Hedley Brooke, "Visions of Perfectibility," *Journal of Evolution and Technology* 14/2 (2005).

[89] Hughes, "The Compatibility of Religious and Transhumanist Views of Metaphysics, Suffering, Virtue and Transcendence in an Enhanced Future."

[90] Or, to put the issue in another context, these questions sketch out another inscription of the distinction between religion and science dialogue, and theology and science dialogue. Are "mainstream" religious beliefs and practices the better, more relevant conversation partners for the transhumanist movement, or academic theologies? In any case, it should

Finally, though Hughes views religious forms of transhumanism as a possibility, Young expresses the far more common attitude within the movement regarding the future of religious belief: "Once science declares death to be no longer necessary, the notion of an afterlife will wither away, and with it, the delusion of a deity."[91] This expectation explains the ire with which transhumanists receive the somewhat common critique of transhumanism as a pseudo-religious movement, a worldview which has transmuted Christian eschatological expectation into a secular, DIY-techno-salvation story.[92] Despite the insistence of transhumanists upon their adherence to their own very strict standards of human rationality which exclude religious belief, many characterizations of transhumanism in mainstream media draw this facile comparison, resulting in a caricatured "rapture of the geeks" image which haunts the transhumanist movement.[93] The parallels between the pursuit of longevity and immortality, amelioration of pain and suffering, even uploaded consciousnesses and disembodied souls are, indeed, easy to make. To conclude that transhumanism is therefore a pseudo-religion masked in the guise of scientific rationality, however, refuses to take transhumanism on its own terms and thus is at best an unhelpful criticism, precluding further dialogue between transhumanists and their critics on more substantive matters.

## Biopolitics and BioLuddites

Though the "Transhumanist Declaration" of the WTA disavows any affiliation with particular political parties, platforms, or politicians, it is clear that the transhumanist movement is in a general sense deeply political, in that it seeks to influence public opinion and the formation of public policies regarding research agendas and funding.[94] Specifically, many transhumanists, for example, believe strongly that the technologies of the near future signal as much threat to humanity as

---

be noted that these are different conversations, each with its own scope, assumptions, and possible outcomes.

[91] Young, *Designer Evolution: A Transhumanist Manifesto*, p. 53.

[92] For various expressions of this critique, see, for instance, Dale Carrico, "Superlative Summary," http://amormundi.blogspot.com/2007/10/superlative-summary.html, Michael W. DeLashmutt, "A Better Life through Information Technology? The Techno-Theological Eschatology of Posthuman Speculative Science," *Zygon* 41/2 (2006), Robert M. Geraci, "Apocalyptic A.I: Religion and the Promise of Artificial Intelligence," *Journal of the American Academy of Religion* 76/1 (2008), Graham, *Representations of the Post/Human*.

[93] Michael Anissimov, "Response to Cory Doctorow on the Singularity," Accelerating Future, www.acceleratingfuture.com/michael/blog/2007/06/response-to-cory-doctorow-on-the-singularity/.

[94] "The Transhumanist Declaration," World Transhumanist Association, http://transhumanism.org/index.php/WTA/declaration/. The Declaration, like the "Transhumanist FAQ," is a collaborative document and one of the founding documents of the World Transhumanist Association, now known as Humanity+.

they do promise, and therefore share a sense of urgency about preventative action. This kind of concern is inevitably political insofar as it involves the dimension of technology regulation and policy-making. And of course, the extropians' explicitly libertarian heritage predisposes this current of transhumanism to espouse policies against the regulation of technologies, preferring to allow the free market to regulate itself without government interference. At the same time, Hughes argues that the "Transhumanist FAQ" includes "an explicit embrace of political engagement, the need to defend and extend liberal democracy, and the inclusion of social democratic policy alternatives as legitimate points of discussion," in short, that the World Transhumanist Association (now Humanity+) has always embraced some version of democratic transhumanism.[95] This diversity within the movement, allowing a scope of political perspectives that includes opposite views on the central issue of technology regulation, makes it impossible to label any single set of political beliefs as "transhumanist politics."

The IEET's comprehensive "Overview of Biopolitics" provides an analysis of the divergences between extropians and technoprogressives on the issues of existential and ecological risk, accessibility to enhancement technologies and various concerns about the social impact of specific technologies.[96] There are, however, broad areas of agreement that unify transhumanism, even across the fault lines of democratic versus libertarian transhumanism. One such area is the advocacy of "personhood-based cyborg citizenship," a political application of the philosophical humanist roots shared by both extropians and technoprogressives.[97] James Hughes argues that the real insight of Western democracy is that "citizenship is for *persons*, not humans. Persons don't have to be human, and not all humans are persons. To create a transhuman democracy we will have to establish a new definition of citizenship, a 'cyborg citizenship,' based on personhood rather than humanness."[98] This redefined category of personhood can then be extended to include others, such as uplifted animals, uploads, and artificial intelligences, who would be definitionally excluded from the category of "human," a biological and specifically embodied category. This, for Hughes, is a victory against "human racism," a point of view which assumes that only humans can be persons, and accordingly discriminates against nonhuman persons. "Transhumanists, like their democratic humanist forebears," writes Hughes, "want to create a global society in which all persons, on the basis of their capacity for thought and feeling, can participate as equal citizens, control their own affairs and achieve their fullest potential, regardless of the characteristics of their bodies."[99] Among the specific goals that Humanity+ explicitly endorses is The Great Ape Project, a campaign for extending the status and rights of personhood to the great apes, as an immediate

---

[95] Hughes, *Citizen Cyborg*, p. 179.
[96] IEET, "Overview of Biopolitics."
[97] Ibid.
[98] Hughes, *Citizen Cyborg*, p. 79.
[99] Ibid., p. 82.

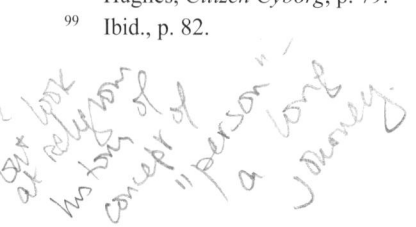

means of paving the way toward a more inclusive notion of personhood and legal status.[100]

There are also political points of view which transhumanists are univocal in opposing. Political advocates of banning or restricting research and development into or availability of enhancement technologies are referred to as "bioLuddites." Resistance to transhumanism can make for strange bedfellows: the "Christian Right," feminists and political liberal progressives find themselves stuck with the same pejorative label, though for various and mostly non-overlapping reasons.[101]

In recent years, Leon Kass, a George W. Bush appointee to the President's Council on Bioethics in 2001, has earned the label "arch-bioLuddite" for his opposition to technologies of human enhancement.[102] Kass, Francis Fukuyama, and Jürgen Habermas have each advanced versions of what Young calls "humanist" arguments against human enhancement, that is, arguments "that focus on the 'inviolacy' of human beings in their present biological state, any attempt to alter the human constitution is regarded as 'inhumane,' 'dehumanizing,' or an affront to 'human dignity.'"[103] Fukuyama's monograph, *Our Posthuman Future: Consequences of the Biotechnology Revolution*, for example, labels transhumanism "the world's most dangerous idea" and argues against enhancement technologies and the pursuit of the posthuman on the basis that the consequences will undermine the concept of human dignity, the sole effective basis for human rights worldwide.[104]

These humanist objections to transhumanist aspirations and current human enhancement technologies, however, are most effectively refuted by transhumanist characterization of the movement as an extension of humanism, rather than the erosion of it. The transhumanist impatience with bioLuddite, or the slightly more tactful "bioconservative," opposition to proposals of human enhancement, to characterizations of enhancement as the new eugenics and to anti-human constructions of the posthuman in SF "narratives of apprehension," is the result of frustration with critics' lack of comprehension that these technological proposals do not, from the transhumanist point of view, threaten the human at all. The autonomy, dignity, rationality, and self-determination of the liberal humanist

---

[100] "Humanity+ Goals," Humanity+, http://humanityplus.org/projects/goals/, Paola Cavalieri and Peter Singer, "The Great Ape Project—and Beyond," in Paola Cavalieri and Peter Singer (eds), *The Great Ape Project* (New York, 1993). The detailed list of categorical goals and specific strategies and actions for achieving them, last accessed November 8, 2010, has subsequently been revised to a simplified mission statement.

[101] "Overview of Biopolitics."

[102] Hughes, *Citizen Cyborg*, p. 62.

[103] Young, *Designer Evolution: A Transhumanist Manifesto*, p. 58. See Francis Fukuyama, *Our Posthuman Future: Consequences of the Biotechnology Revolution* (New York, 2002), Habermas, *Die Zukunft der Menschlichen Natur*, Leon Kass, "The Wisdom of Repugnance," *New Republic* 216/22 (1997), Leon Kass, *Life, Liberty and the Defense of Dignity: The Challenge for Bioethics* (San Francisco, CA, 2002).

[104] Fukuyama, *Our Posthuman Future*.

subject remain theoretically preserved, indeed increased, in transhumanist visions of the posthuman.

In contrast, the objections of left-wing so-called "bioLuddites" focus less on ontological concepts of human nature and human dignity, and more on concerns regarding equality of access to new technologies, unjust and oppressive social effects of new technologies on certain groups of people, and the need to regulate technologies to restrict damaging environmental impact. To these objections, transhumanists are much less univocal. Here, the internal political diversity of transhumanism, specifically the difference between technoprogressive/democratic transhumanism and extropian/libertarian transhumanism, intersects with the concerns of left-wing critics to produce vastly different responses. Extropians answer the first of these objections with a confidence that with time, access to technologies will become widely distributed through the free market. Young writes, "Yes, initially some people more than others will be able to afford bioenhancement beyond the level of 'normal' good health. It's called living in the free world … Only the most ideological of extremists could seriously wish to deprive everyone of the benefits of bioenhancement on the grounds that the rich will be the first to benefit."[105] The "Transhumanist FAQ" similarly concludes, "Initially, however, the greatest advantages will go to those who have the resources, the skills, and the willingness to learn to use new tools. One can speculate that some technologies may cause social inequalities to widen … Trying to ban technological innovation on these grounds, however, would be misguided."[106] Likewise, the free market is assumed to be an adequate mechanism for managing environmental impact and other existential risks represented by future technologies. Others, however, such as Hughes and other technoprogressive, democratic transhumanists, see a necessary role for government regulation as a means of assuring prudential risk management, amelioration of environmental impacts, and equality of distribution and access to enhancement technologies for all. Hughes writes, "on questions of regulating technology, the democratic transhumanists side with most of the rest of the world against the libertarian and Luddite extremes: appropriately regulate technology and avoid bans."[107]

Despite their disagreement regarding the necessity and extent of government regulation of research and development, access and distribution, and assessment and management of potential existential risks of enhancement technologies, both extropians and technoprogressives, however, argue strongly against blanket bans on research or particular technologies on both principled and pragmatic grounds. This, then, is what unites transhumanists of various types within the political context. The "bioLuddite" impulse to heavily restrict or outright ban the pursuit of enhancement technologies, for whatever reason (religious, secular, right-wing, or

---

[105] Young, *Designer Evolution*, p. 63.
[106] Bostrom, "The Transhumanist FAQ."
[107] Hughes, *Citizen Cyborg*, p. 216.

left-wing) prompts a univocal transhumanist response. Technology is the solution to humanity's problems, not the source of them.

The divergence between these two posthuman discourses of transhumanism and the cyborg is clearly evident, despite surface similarities. Both discourses suppose that the boundaries which previously defined and safeguarded human identity are porous and flexible in ways that require reformulation of the notions of human nature and identity; both acknowledge the role of technoscience in questioning and redrawing those boundaries; both advocate some mixture of anticipation and caution with regard to the consequences of the technologies on the horizon. Both discourses evince a suspicion, at times even hostility, to organized religion and religious belief, and to the discourses of natural kinds and natural law. That said, it is clear that the specific ways in which the posthuman takes shape in these visions makes an enormous differences for precisely how the human is redefined in response to the posthuman challenge. The next chapters will therefore take up the question of anthropology: what anthropologies are at work in these posthuman visions? How do these anthropologies intersect with theological anthropology? What theological insights might be gained by engaging in these posthuman conversations, and what might be offered?

# Chapter 3
# Post-Anthropologies

The first and second chapters have briefly sketched the major points of two distinct posthuman discourses. Though the term "posthuman" is utilized in both, it signifies vastly different constructions, and the conversations themselves are all but hermetically sealed off from one another, differing not only in the scholars and resources engaged but in philosophical stance, moral assumptions, and political goals. This chapter will offer a more detailed consideration and contrast of the differing anthropologies embedded within these two posthuman visions, the cyborg and the upload, summarized in Table 3.1.

Both Haraway and the transhumanists scorn a rejection of the posthuman on the basis of repugnance, implausibility, or impossibility. Accepting the possibility of the posthuman means moving beyond the knee-jerk reactions of disgust or denial and into considering the desirability and implications of the advent of the posthuman. On this point, though perhaps nothing else, Haraway and the transhumanists agree: neither views human nature as static or unchangeable. Beyond this basic agreement, however, the divergence of their posthuman anthropologies is dramatic.

The differences can be traced to a fundamental divergence in transhumanism's embrace of their Enlightenment anthropological roots, and the firm rejection of this Enlightenment anthropology by Haraway. As Cary Wolfe comments, transhumanism "derives directly from ideals of human perfectibility, rationality and agency inherited from Renaissance humanism and the Enlightenment," and therefore "has little in common with Haraway's playful, ironic, and ambivalent sensibility in 'A Cyborg Manifesto,' which is suspicious—to put it mildly—of the capacity of reason to steer, much less optimize, what it hath wrought."[1]

N. Katherine Hayles's 1999 *How We Became Posthuman* is a useful entry point into the exploration of the divergence of these posthuman anthropologies, as Hayles critically analyzes transhumanism, or in her term, the "cybernetic posthuman," and finds both continuities and discontinuities within the cybernetic posthuman with what she calls "the liberal humanist subject."[2] These continuities

---

[1] Cary Wolfe, *What Is Posthumanism?* (Minneapolis, MN, 2010), p. xiii.

[2] N.K. Hayles, *How We Became Posthuman: Virtual Bodies in Cybernetics, Literature, and Informatics* (Chicago, IL, 1999). In the interest of accuracy to Hayles's 1999 text, in the summary that follows I will use her term "cybernetic posthuman" (p. 5). It is clear from subsequent work, however, that this term references a transhumanist posthuman (see N.K. Hayles, "Wrestling with Transhumanism," *The Global Spiral* 9/3 (June 2008), http://metanexus.net/magazine/tabid/68/id/10543/Default.aspx).

Table 3.1    Key differences between the cyborg and upload

| Cyborg | Transhumanism |
| --- | --- |
| "heterogeneous, collective" self | extension of liberal humanist self |
| social, relational | individualistic |
| material embodiment | virtual, simulated embodiment |
| hybrid | assimilative |
| immanence | transcendence |
| technological ambivalence | techno-optimism |
| kinship with machines | pursuit of AI |
| kinship with nonhuman animals | uplift of nonhuman animals |

and discontinuities are evidence of two intermingled posthuman constructions, one of which is indeed constructed as Enlightenment "humanity plus," and one of which ironically subverts this construction. Hayles's alertness to this ambivalence within posthuman discourse is to her credit, though I contend here that at this point we would do better to treat these constructions as distinct discourses rather than a single discourse containing continuities and discontinuities, as Hayles does. Wolfe, in fact, criticizes Hayles for using the term posthuman in a way that firmly associates it with "a kind of triumphant disembodiment," even while she herself insists that "the posthuman need not be recuperated back into liberal humanism."[3]

Hayles structures her analysis of the cybernetic posthuman as "three interrelated stories," the first of which is the story of "*how information lost its body*, that is, how it came to be conceptualized as an entity separate from the material forms in which it is thought to be embedded." This leads to the second story, "how *the cyborg was created technical artifact and cultural icon* in the years following World War II, for when information loses its body, equating humans and computers is especially easy, for the materiality of the thinking mind appears incidental to its essential nature." The third story, "deeply implicated with the first two," is "the unfolding story of how a historically specific construction called *the human is giving way to a different construction called the posthuman.*"[4] The cybernetic posthuman, in Hayles's definition, privileges informational pattern over material instantiation, views consciousness as an epiphenomenon and the body as a sort of "original prosthesis," and configures human being so that it may be seamlessly articulated with intelligent machines.[5]

---

[3] Wolfe, *What Is Posthumanism?*, p. xv.
[4] Hayles, *How We Became Posthuman*, p. 2. Italics original.
[5] Ibid., p. 3.

Hayles is careful to emphasize that "the human" being supplanted by "the posthuman" is a historically specific construction, the "liberal humanist subject."[6] It is this specific historical construction of the human that is presumed by the cyberneticists she analyzes, even as their own work produces a posthuman result which (at least potentially) undermines that construction. Hayles writes of Norbert Wiener's pioneering work in cybernetics: "The revolutionary implications of this [cybernetic] paradigm notwithstanding, Wiener did not intend to dismantle the liberal humanist subject. He was less interested in seeing humans as machines than he was in fashioning human and machine alike in the image of an autonomous, self-directed individual ... For Wiener, cybernetics was a means to extend liberal humanism, not subvert it."[7]

In one sense, Hayles argues that this cybernetic posthuman implies "the deconstruction of the liberal humanist subject," through the unbounded flow of information between the subject and the environment.[8] The essence of liberal humanist subject is autonomy; yet the posthuman subject, a "material-informational entity," is enmeshed with its environment in ways that are negotiable and unfixed. Hayles writes, "We have only to recall how Robocop's memory flashes that interfere with his programmed directives to understand how the distributed cognition of the posthuman complicates individual agency. If 'human essence is freedom from the wills of others,' the posthuman is 'post' not because it is necessarily unfree but because there is no *a priori* way to identify a self-will that can be distinguished from an other-will."[9] Hayles therefore perceives the flexible and porous boundaries of the posthuman self as a challenge to the fixity and stability of the autonomous, self-directing liberal humanist subject.

Yet at the same time, the perceived bodilessness of the information processes that define the cybernetic posthuman deconstructs the liberal humanist subject quite differently than the deconstructions of feminist or postcolonial critiques. "Because information had lost its body," Hayles writes, "this [cybernetic] construction implied that embodiment is not essential to human being. Embodiment has been systematically downplayed or erased in the cybernetic construction of the posthuman in ways that have not occurred in other critiques of the liberal humanist subject, especially in feminist and postcolonial theories."[10] Hayles argues that erasure of embodiment is a feature of the liberal humanist subject continued, indeed strengthened, in the cybernetic posthuman: "Although in many ways the posthuman deconstructs the liberal humanist subject, it thus shares

---

[6] Ibid., p. 5. Moreover, it is clear that this specific construction of "the human" is one which Hayles herself does not endorse; she writes, "I am not trying to recuperate the liberal subject ... I do not mourn the passing of a concept so deeply entwined with projects of domination and oppression" (p. 2).

[7] Ibid., p. 7.

[8] Ibid., p. 2.

[9] Ibid., p. 4.

[10] Ibid.

with its predecessor an emphasis on cognition rather than embodiment ... To the extent that the posthuman constructs embodiment as the instantiation of thought/information, it continues the liberal tradition rather than disrupts it."[11]

Hayles's perception of the continuity between the liberal humanist subject and the transhumanist self is verified in the transhumanists' own characterization of their movement as a direct philosophical heir to Enlightenment philosophy and Renaissance humanism. As a response to "narratives of apprehension," in which the encroachment of technology represents the invasion of autonomy and the erasure of the individual self, and the lingering specter of the eugenics movement, the transhumanist insistence on the posthuman as "humanity plus" fulfills an apologetic function, seeking to reassure that enhancement technologies augment and do not diminish the human. This humanist emphasis within transhumanist anthropology is also evident in transhumanist arguments on the nature of personhood as the foundation for legal rights and moral status of the individual, as seen in James Hughes's arguments for "cyborg citizenship" and the support of The Great Ape Project by Humanity+ and the Institute for Ethics and Emerging Technologies.

In contrast to transhumanism's continuity with the liberal humanist subject, Haraway's appropriation of the cyborg as a feminist icon is a self-consciously ironic move. Haraway is well aware of Clynes and Kline's original vision of the cyborg as the self-sufficient space explorer liberated from bodily needs, or, in her summation, "the awful apocalyptic *telos* of the 'West's' escalating dominations of abstract individuation, an ultimate self untied at last from all dependency, a man in space."[12] Haraway's objective is one of subversion of this dominant narrative of the self; her vision is that the cyborg, despite its advent as the definitive "man in space," may be unfaithful to its origins, and constructed differently: "The cyborg is a kind of disassembled and reassembled, postmodern collective and personal self. This is the self feminists must code."[13]

The posthuman challenge to the stability and fixity of the boundaries of the liberal humanist subject perceived by Hayles is exactly the disassembled, reassembled, collective, and personal self that Haraway celebrates as the cyborg.[14] Not coincidentally, it is these characteristics that Hayles identifies as the challenges the posthuman represents to the specific historical construction of the human she tags as "the liberal humanist subject." The transgression of natural boundaries, and the fluidity of the boundary between self and other, means that this subversive posthuman self is not defined as a single, autonomous "thinking mind," but is embedded within constant, if constantly shifting, social and physical relationships.

---

[11] Ibid., p. 5.

[12] Donna J. Haraway, "A Cyborg Manifesto: Science, Technology and Socialist-Feminism in the Late Twentieth Century," in *Simians, Cyborgs and Women: The Reinvention of Nature* (New York, 1991), p. 151.

[13] Ibid., p. 163.

[14] Ibid., pp. 164ff.

## Heart and Soul

This continued erasure of embodiment is a fundamental aspect of the construction of the cybernetic posthuman that Hayles analyzes, and is the result of what she names as the lethal grafting of the posthuman on to a liberal humanist view of the self. Michael Hauskeller makes this connection very clear:

> Transhumanists continue the logocentric tradition of Western philosophy. By and large they believe that what makes us human, and what is most valuable about our humanity, is the particularity of our *minds*. We are thinking beings, conscious of ourselves and the world, rational agents that use our environment including our own bodies to pursue our own freely chosen ends. And because our essence consists in our thinking, it is at least conceivable that we may one day be able to transfer ("upload") our very being to a computer (or another biological brain) and thus achieve some kind of personal immortality. Generally, the organic body is held to be replaceable.[15]

The envisioned cybernetic melding of humans and machines depend upon the conception of human identity as mind, further interpreted as a pattern of information, which may flow freely between biological and mechanical substrates. The biological human body, therefore, as non-essential, can be partially or wholly replaced, or theoretically discarded altogether by the transfer of informational pattern into virtual reality, without the disruption of human identity as informational pattern. The body is, in Hayles's phrase, the "original prosthesis."[16]

Hayles's analysis of the cybernetic posthuman thus leads directly to the contested issue of embodiment, a locus that offers what is perhaps the starkest contrast between Haraway and the transhumanists, and which is foundational for the other loci of disagreement explored in this chapter (gender, epistemology, and kinship with nonhuman animals).

*All Heart? Transhumanists on Embodiment*

Transhumanism contains both materialistic and dualistic anthropological elements. This is in part explicable by the diversity of the movement.[17] It might

---

[15] Michael Hauskeller, "Nietzsche, the Overhuman and the Posthuman: A Reply to Stefan Sorgner," *Journal of Evolution and Technology* 21/1 (2010).

[16] Hayles, *How We Became Posthuman*, p. 5.

[17] Stephen Garner, "Transhumanism and the *Imago Dei*: Narratives of Apprehension and Hope" (PhD Dissertation, The University of Auckland, 2006). Garner regards this as a sufficient explanation, identifying a materialistic anthropology at work in transhumanist AI, and a dualistic anthropology at work in transhumanist focus on virtual reality. However, for reasons explored in my analysis of Garner's theological response to transhumanism, I contend that Garner attributes a stronger materialism to Humanity+ than is warranted.

be suspected at this point that the construction of a general "transhumanist anthropology" is a lost cause, if diversity of opinion on such a basic anthropological issue exists within the movement. Yet Hayles's analysis of transhumanism's continuity with the "liberal humanist subject" of the Enlightenment, a continuity foregrounded in transhumanist self-descriptions, indicates that there is indeed a common ground to be found, even if individual transhumanist thinkers or distinct branches of the movement parse out the details in differing or competing ways. Following Hayles, I argue that transhumanist anthropology is indeed dualistic, and that claims to a materialist anthropology within transhumanism are qualified by a basic dualism which derives from the Enlightenment roots of transhumanist anthropology. This is true not only in the primary example of transhumanist uploaders, but evident within the anthropologies of transhumanists committed to improvement of the human body rather than the uploading of the mind, as well.

The dualistic elements implicit within transhumanism contrast sharply with the materialism that shapes Haraway's cyborg vision. Unlike the transhumanists, for whom the essence of the (post)human remains located in the autonomous, free, rational mind, Haraway defines the posthuman ontology of the cyborg in terms of its bodily hybridity. Haraway's rejection of anthropological dualism flows consistently from her feminist suspicion of dualisms and universalisms in general.

As the ultimate goal is to provide an understanding of these posthuman discourses for the purpose of interdisciplinary engagement with theological anthropology, I also briefly reference notions of the soul. Both transhumanists and Haraway reject notions of the soul in their construction of the posthuman. For transhumanists, rejection of the soul is a manifestation of their philosophical inheritance of the Enlightenment schism of faith and reason, the result of a larger general rejection of religious faith. For Haraway, the soul is yet another inscription of disembodied essence into anthropology, and is rejected on the same basis as her rejection of other forms of disembodiment. Intriguingly, however, Haraway hints at a materialistic sacramentality embedded within her philosophy, opening the door to the possibility of understanding cyborg anthropology as more than reductively materialistic.

*Uploads, Sims, and Virtual Embodiment* Hayles begins *How We Became Posthuman* with the straightforward declaration, "This book began with a roboticist's dream that struck me as a nightmare."[18] The roboticist in question is Hans Moravec, whose dream of uploading human consciousness into a computer struck Hayles not simply as implausible but conceptually flawed; for, she asks, "how could anyone think that consciousness in an entirely different medium would remain unchanged, as if it had no connection with embodiment?"[19]

---

[18] Hayles, *How We Became Posthuman*, p. 1.
[19] Ibid.

Moravec and other uploaders within the transhumanist movement are particularly vulnerable to charges of anthropological dualism that privileges mind over body, or in Hayles's words, informational pattern over material instantiation. Ray Kurzweil explicitly embraces a dualistic anthropology: "Though I have been called a materialist, I regard myself as a 'patternist' ... Since the material stuff of which we are made turns over quickly, it is the transcendent power of our patterns that persists ... The pattern is far more important than the material stuff that constitutes it."[20] Simon Young not only frankly acknowledges this dualism but overtly celebrates it: "Those who speak of the 'Cartesian dichotomy of mind and body' are sorely mistaken. *Cartesian dualism is not the cause of our problems, but the beginning of the solution* ... Descartes is not the villain but the hero of the piece. Cartesian duality marks the beginning of human evolution from *Homo sapiens* to *Homo cyberneticus*—man the steersman of his own destiny."[21]

Yet not everyone is so willing to bite the Cartesian bullet; Nick Bostrom's discomfort with the label of dualism shows up in his comments in an interview with the magazine *Cronopis*: "I think that uploading could, under the right circumstance, preserve both consciousness and personal identity. But I would not call myself a dualist. I think my mind currently is running on a kind of protein computer, and if exactly the same computational processes were implemented on a silicone computer I believe I wouldn't notice any difference."[22] Bostrom's answer describes precisely the anthropological quandary of the uploaders: how to combine a materialistic commitment within transhumanist anthropology with a view of human consciousness and identity that is theoretically, if not yet practicably, separable from its material instantiation.

It seems clear, however, that in uploading, a philosophy of personal identity is at work which not only distinguishes between mental and physical continuity, but privileges mental continuity as the sole required factor for continuity of personal identity. As the "Transhumanist FAQ" puts it, "A widely accepted position is that you survive so long as certain information patterns are conserved, such as your memories, values, attitudes, and emotional dispositions, and so long as there is causal continuity so that earlier stages of yourself help determine later stages of yourself." Thus, physical continuity completely drops out: "For the continuation of personhood, on this view, it matters little whether you are implemented on a silicon chip inside a computer or in that gray, cheesy lump inside your skull, assuming both implementations are conscious."[23]

---

[20] Ray Kurzweil, *The Singularity Is Near: When Humans Transcend Biology* (New York, 2005), p. 388.

[21] Simon Young, *Designer Evolution: A Transhumanist Manifesto* (Amherst, NY, 2006), p. 34.

[22] Andrés Lomeña, "Interview with Nick Bostrom and David Pearce," The Hedonistic Imperative, www.hedweb.com/transhumanism/index.html.

[23] N. Bostrom, "The Transhumanist FAQ: A General Introduction," The World Transhumanist Association, http://humanityplus.org/learn/transhumanist-faq/.

Precisely what "conscious" means in this context (or any) is, of course, a vexed question. Kurzweil addresses the issue "for the purpose of illustrating this vexing and paradoxical (and, therefore, profound) nature of consciousness: how one set of assumptions (that is, a copy of my mind file either shares or does not share my consciousness) leads ultimately to the opposite view, and vice versa."[24] Defining consciousness as "first-person 'subjective' experience," inaccessible to all entities other than the self, he predicts, on the basis of this inaccessibility, that human beings will eventually come to attribute consciousness to nonbiological entities on the same basis that we attribute it to other human beings.[25] The question of whether or not an upload would be conscious is therefore answered with a presumptive "yes."

Whether or not this presumptive consciousness is continuous with the consciousness of the biological original, and whether or not this matters for continuity of identity, is unclear. Kurzweil contends that "both the data capture and the reinstantiation of a dynamic entity constitute the upload scenario," and describes the difference between the scanned informational pattern and an instantiated upload as the difference "between a computer program that resides on a computer disk (a static picture) and a program that is actively running on a suitable computer (a dynamic, interacting entity.)"[26] Here, consciousness seems to be an emergent phenomenon dependent upon a physical substrate, not an inherent property of the uploadable informational pattern; the consciousness of a successful upload, then, would be generated by its new physical substrate, just as the consciousness of the original biological person was previously generated by the biological body. If, however, consciousness is ontologically dependent on the original material substrate of the brain, this would imply that an upload's consciousness would be a different consciousness, discontinuous with the first-person subjective experience of the original substrate.

When Bostrom says "I believe *I* wouldn't notice the difference," then, this is actually fudging between the first- and third-person perspectives on consciousness; perhaps others wouldn't be able to tell the difference between biological Bostrom and upload Bostrom, but Bostrom himself would. Kurzweil seems to acknowledge this in his consideration of non-destructive upload scenarios: "Although the copy shares my pattern, it would be hard to say that the copy is me because I would—or could—still be here. You could even scan and copy me while I was sleeping. If you come to me in the morning and say, 'Good news, Ray, we've successfully reinstantiated you into a more durable substrate, so we won't be needing your old body and brain anymore,' I may beg to differ."[27] This is precisely the dilemma traced out in narrative form by Robert Sawyer in the novel *Mindscan*. Yet, uploaders retain the belief that an upload is

---

[24] Kurzweil, *The Singularity Is Near*, p. 389.
[25] Ibid., p. 385.
[26] Ibid., p. 201.
[27] Ibid., p. 384.

indeed a continuation of personal identity, despite this issue of a disjuncture of first-person consciousness. It seems, then, that continuity of personal identity from the biological original to the upload depends upon the mental continuity represented by the informational pattern, and not continuity of consciousness; like physical continuity, consciousness is non-essential for the continuation of personal identity.

As physical continuity as a criterion for personal identity drops out of the upload scenario, a common critique is that this necessarily implies disembodiment. Bostrom, however, offers this rebuttal to critics: "an upload's experience could in principle be identical to that of a biological human. An upload could have a virtual (simulated) body giving the same sensations and the same possibilities for interaction as a non-simulated body. With advanced virtual reality, uploads could enjoy food and drink, and upload sex could be as gloriously messy as one could wish. And uploads wouldn't have to be confined to virtual reality: they could interact with people on the outside and even rent robot bodies in order to work in or explore physical reality."[28] Ray Kurzweil's vision echoes this; though "a reinstantiated mind will need a body, since so much of our thinking is directed toward physical needs and desires," eventually, "the human body version 2.0 will include virtual bodies in completely realistic virtual environments, nanotechnology-based physical bodies, and more."[29] Yet this counter to the disembodiment critique simply presumes that there would be no difference between a simulated and a non-simulated bodily experience.[30]

Nick Bostrom's simulation argument offers the most detailed defense of this position. Bostrom proposes that one of the three following propositions is true: 1) the human race is very likely to become extinct before reaching a posthuman stage; 2) any posthuman civilization is extremely unlikely to run a significant number of simulations of it evolutionary history (or variations thereof); 3) we are almost certainly living in a computer simulation.[31] While Bostrom argues that "in the dark forest of our current ignorance, it makes sense to apportion one's credence roughly evenly" between the three propositions, he also notes that the third possibility is the most interesting, indicating, among other things, a possible disjunction between the physics of the simulated universe we could empirically observe and the physics of the universe of the computer running the

---

[28] Bostrom, "The Transhumanist FAQ."

[29] Kurzweil, *The Singularity Is Near*, p. 199.

[30] Ibid., p. 203. In the concluding italicized dialogue section, Kurzweil writes, "The word 'virtual' is somewhat unfortunate. It implies 'not real' but the reality will be that a virtual body is just as real as a physical body in all the ways that matter … there's no discernible difference."

[31] See Nick Bostrom, "Are We Living in a Computer Simulation?" *Philosophical Quarterly* 53/211 (2003), Brian Weatherson, "Are You a Sim?" *Philosophical Quarterly* 53/212 (2003), Nick Bostrom, "The Simulation Argument: Reply to Weatherson," *Philosophical Quarterly* 55/218 (2005).

simulation. Though the simulated universe is significantly "real," as far as its simulated inhabitants are concerned, it does not exist at the most fundamental level of reality.

Thus, the perceived materiality of simulated bodies is informational pattern, not material reality, but sims can't tell the difference. Sim embodiment is therefore simultaneously "real" and virtual. Thus, the simulation argument presumes that material embodiment and virtual embodiment are indistinguishable from one another, and this presumption is carried over from the simulation argument as a general presumption in other contexts, such as the upload scenario, in which Bostrom denies being a "neurotic body-loather" precisely on the grounds that virtual embodiment is indistinguishable from material embodiment. This not only passes over the issue of the physical discontinuity at the heart of the upload scenario, but also, by presuming that bodily experiences are replicable without a material body, defines "embodiment" at the start as a subjective *mental* experience, rather than a material reality.[32]

Kurzweil's "patternism," with its central assumption that a person is "principally a pattern that persists in time," which is "far more important than the material stuff that constitutes it," is a dualistic anthropology, separating the essential person from the physical substrate as the first conceptual step in arguing that the substrate can be replaced. As Noreen Herzfeld points out, however, at the same time there is an underlying reductive materialist assumption at work, crucial to the upload scenario, in which scanning the physical organ of the brain is equivalent to mapping the mind.[33] This stands in unresolved tension with the identification of human identity as an immaterial informational pattern. This tension has been noted by Ted Peters, who makes a distinction between the

---

[32] In his reply to Phil Weatherson's response to the original argument, Bostrom even suggests that "we should distrust our senses in regard to ... how we are physically implemented," contending that we exist in a "special circumstance" analogous to a hall of carnival mirrors (Bostrom, "The Simulation Argument: Reply to Weatherson," p. 94). Bostrom argues that, knowing we exist in a hall of mirrors, we shouldn't conclude we possess three hands even if the mirror shows us that we do. Inexplicably, however, this passes over that it is *one's direct bodily experience* which contradicts the mirror's testimony of three hands; it is not that, but rather our additional knowledge that the mirrors are untrustworthy, that is key for Bostrom. The example changes if one removes the mediating technology and posits that one has direct bodily experience of possessing three hands; not only is the example more relevant to Bostrom's point, but the "special circumstances" in which one should distrust such sensory input are circumscribed more narrowly, weakening Bostrom's argument. It also seems to contradict transhumanism's general commitment to scientific empiricism, which, of course, relies on sensory and technologically mediated sensory perception of the material world, implying a general epistemic trust, rather than distrust, of observations.

[33] Noreen Herzfeld, "Cybernetic Immortality Versus Christian Resurrection," in Ted Peters, Robert J. Russell, and Michael Welker (eds), *Resurrection: Theological and Scientific Assessments* (Grand Rapids, MI, 2002), p. 194.

reductionist impulse present in much of neuroscience, and the dualism present in transhumanist upload scenarios: "The tendency in the science is toward reductionism, toward reducing our minds and our souls to biological activity. The contrary tendency in transhumanist technology is to view the mind or soul as immaterial, as something that can become dis-embodied and re-embodied. The first tends toward a substance monism or materialism, the second toward a substance dualism."[34] It seems, then, that both materialistic and dualistic assumptions are equally necessary for the success of the upload scenario, enshrining an unresolved philosophical contradiction at its very heart.

*The Body as Property* As we have noted, however, transhumanism's visions of the posthuman include more possibilities than the upload scenario. The transhumanist definition of posthuman explicitly includes the possibility of a posthuman future which "could be the result of making many smaller but cumulatively profound augmentations to a biological human" alongside the possibilities of completely synthetic artificial intelligences or uploads.[35] It is therefore worth considering whether the anthropological dualism evident in uploading is also present in other currents of transhumanism and their visions of the posthuman, and to what extent. Do transhumanist proposals for enhancement of the human body also demonstrate dualistic anthropological assumptions?

One of transhumanism's central goals, one which unites transhumanists of all the various types, is the extension of the human lifespan. Unlike Kurzweil's upload scenario, Aubrey de Grey's research focuses on the enhancement of the biological body in pursuit of this goal. De Grey writes, "To design therapies [for aging], all you have to understand is aging damage itself: the molecular and cellular lesions that impair the structure and function of the body's tissues."[36] Rather than seeking the biological causes of aging, a complex matter, de Grey proposes that, at least as a first step, addressing the damaging effects of aging is sufficient to make progress toward the goal of "negligible senescence." There are seven types of molecular and cellular damage identified by de Grey, each of which he matches with a specific strategic fix.[37]

This focus on the specific interventions on the aging body might suggest an anthropology that conceptualizes one's specific embodiment as inherently valuable and perhaps even indispensable for personal identity. Yet de Grey's description of the human body is a "machine," a metaphor which harkens back

---

[34] Ted Peters, *Anticipating Omega: Science, Faith and Our Ultimate Future* (Göttingen, 2006), pp. 130–1.

[35] Bostrom, "The Transhumanist FAQ."

[36] Aubrey de Grey and Michael Rae, *Ending Aging: The Rejuvenation Breakthroughs That Could Reverse Human Aging in Our Lifetime* (New York, 2007), pp. 5–6.

[37] Ibid., p. 43.

to the mechanistic assumptions of the Enlightenment.[38] De Grey argues that combating aging is in principle no different from maintaining man-made machines such as cars: "when we want to keep a car on the road for an exceptionally long time ... we *fix damage as it happens* ... we all know that a car can be kept going more or less indefinitely with sufficient maintenance ... the analogy to humans (at the cell, tissue and organ level) is strikingly exact."[39] De Grey dismisses the option of "getting a new car," as uploaders advocate, but the metaphor of body as machine is, in the end, a variation of the Enlightenment view of the body as personal property. (The recurring and "strikingly exact" analogy of car maintenance suggests that we might also fruitfully inquire, who's driving?)

This attitude toward the human body at work in transhumanists who explicitly advocate bodily improvement is also articulated by James Hughes. Hughes enumerates the first of "the four motivations leading us to push the envelope of humanness" as achieving control over our bodies (meaning less pain, disease, and disability).[40] This rhetoric of "control over the body" is instructive, for it is certainly possible to articulate the goals of ameliorating pain, disease, and disability without the notion of control—notions of human "flourishing" come easily to mind, for example. Yet the question of whether or not "control" is the best way to articulate one's relationship with one's body is unaddressed; for Hughes, it is simply axiomatic that "in democratic societies we try to give each other as much control over our own bodies and minds as possible," and also that "soon, unlimited technological control over the human body and mind will be possible."[41]

As N. Katherine Hayles has noted, the origins of the "liberal humanist subject" are economic in nature: the human body is conceived of as "original property," an object in some sense owned by the self in a relation that precedes market relations and functions as the natural foundation for economic exchange.[42] This too is present in Hughes's description of the body; Hughes approvingly quotes Lori Andrews, asserting, "It is time to start acknowledging that people's body parts are their personal property," even if, as Hughes acknowledges, "this sounds to many like

---

[38] See Ann M. Pederson, "A Christian Theological Response to Aubrey De Grey's Prospects for the Biomedical Postponement of Aging, or What Does It Mean to Love Long and Prosper?" in James Haag, Michael L. Spezio, and Gregory R. Peterson (eds), *Routledge Companion to Religion and Science* (New York, 2011).

[39] de Grey and Rae, *Ending Aging*, pp. 44–5.

[40] James Hughes, *Citizen Cyborg: Why Democratic Societies Must Respond to the Redesigned Human of the Future* (Cambridge, MA, 2004), p. xvi. The remaining three motivations Hughes names are living longer; becoming smarter; and becoming happier, all of which are further expressions of greater control over the biological body.

[41] Ibid., p. 11.

[42] Hayles, *How We Became Posthuman*, p. 3. Here, Hayles is using C.B. Macpherson's analysis of "possessive individualism" as a baseline.

capitalism run amok."[43] As personal property, the body is an object of individual sovereignty: one may do with it as one wishes.

The freedom to enhance the body is thus articulated as the freedom to dispose of the body as one wills, in an argument clearly continuous with liberal humanist arguments for bodily autonomy, integrity, and freedom. In this sense, Hughes, more than any other prominent transhumanist thinker, is willing to take issues of embodiment and "morphological freedom" seriously. "Morphological freedom" refers to the right of an individual to configure the body in ways that may deviate from accepted social norms. This furnishes the connection Hughes sees between disability, reproductive and LGBTQ rights activism, and transhumanism; when the body is construed as original property, these discourses can be articulated as arguments to dispose of one's property according to one's wishes as a political right.[44] This leads to an envisioned future in which not only "the deaf hear, blind see and lame walk," but in which "people [may] reshape their bodies to fit their personal aesthetics, lifestyles and whims."[45]

The question for Hughes is not whether control should be the goal, nor even how much control over our bodies and minds we as a democratic society should be aiming for, but how to make sure that we do in fact achieve that technologically mediated, potentially unlimited, control of the body for each individual citizen. Thus despite Hughes's focus on deliberate improvement of the body, the body is viewed as a possession of the self, not part of or definitive of the self. It is something one controls; in Hayles's words, the "original prosthesis."[46] This anthropological framework prevents Hughes from seeing embodiment as formative or constitutive for human identity, preserving an inherent though implicit dualism of mind and body easily detectable in his rhetoric of bodily control.

It is, moreover, a small step from Hughes's enhancement of the body as one's original prosthesis to the uploaders' desire to replace or discard it; one has only to make the further quite typical transhumanist assumption that biological bodies are

---

[43] Lori B. Andrews, "My Body, My Property," *The Hastings Center Report* 28 (1986). Quoted in Hughes, *Citizen Cyborg*, p. 231. Among other failings, this approach to embodiment fails to offer any possibility of resistance to the organ trade. If someone wants to sell their own kidney, it is their body/property, and they may dispose of it as they choose.

[44] As Cary Wolfe observes, the liberal humanist underpinnings to much of disability studies and activism, in which recognition, access, privileges, rights, and participation are the explicit goals, is understandable for all sorts of historical, institutional, and strategic reasons; yet, as Wolfe argues, this is not the only way to construct disability studies or activism. Rather, Wolfe advocates "an ethics based not on ability, activity, agency, and empowerment but on a *compassion* that is rooted in our vulnerability" (Wolfe, *What Is Posthumanism?*, p. 141).

[45] Hughes, *Citizen Cyborg*, pp. 18–19. This vision, we might note in passing, N. Katherine Hayles describes as a "nightmare" culture of "posthumans who regard their bodies as fashion accessories rather than the ground of being," *How We Became Posthuman*, p. 5.

[46] Hayles, *How We Became Posthuman*, p. 3.

inferior to nonbiological bodies. Indeed, Hughes himself makes this assumption in his discussion of life extension: "Since anti-aging and life extension medicine will likely have added at least 50 years to life expectancy by the 2050s, the average child today can expect to live well into the 2100s, when the convergence of cognitive science, nanomedicine and artificial intelligence will allow consciousness to be backed up and sustained in forms far more durable than the human body."[47] Hughes seems to follow Kurzweil's third scenario, in which improvement of the biological body is a pragmatic and proximate goal, which will function as the precursor to inevitable post-biological existence.

*All Heart: Cyborgs and Hybrid Bodies*

In strong contrast to the acknowledged or unacknowledged, explicit or implicit, anthropological dualism of transhumanism is Haraway's thoroughgoing commitment to materialism in the figure of the cyborg. Arguing from the same cybernetic insights regarding the flow of information between mechanical and electronic systems and biological organisms, Haraway moves not to the conclusion that human persons are bodiless patterns of information, but that information is variously embodied. Thus the significance of emerging technologies is not how they allow the mind to extend or instantiate itself in novel ways, but the way in which technologies extend and reconfigure the body. "Communications technologies and biotechnologies are the crucial tools for recrafting our *bodies*," she writes, emphasizing that the cyborg's significance lies in its power to reshape the body, not reinscribe the mind.[48]

For Haraway, materialism is the counter not only to the Enlightenment dualism which defined the human as disembodied rationality, but also to the biological essentialism of some second-wave feminists, exemplified in discourses such as that of natural childbirth and goddess-talk, which opposed the (female) natural to the (male) technological. She therefore introduced the cyborg to feminist discourse to counter the second-wave tendency to "see deepened dualisms of mind and body, animal and machine, idealism and materialism in the social practices, symbolic formulations, and physical artifacts associated with 'high technology' and scientific culture."[49] The cyborg is not a flight from the body nor does it mark the disappearance of embodiment; rather, the cyborg stands as evidence of the multiple possibilities of embodiment that cross the boundaries of identity politics.

Haraway never loses sight, therefore, of the importance of embodiment in her development of the cyborg as metaphor: "These ontologically confusing *bodies*, and the practices that produce specific embodiment, are what we have to

---

[47] Hughes, *Citizen Cyborg*, pp. 29–30.
[48] Haraway, "A Cyborg Manifesto," p. 164.
[49] Ibid., p. 154.

address, not the false problem of *dis*embodiment."[50] Indeed, without a continuing emphasis on the importance of embodied experience, the cyborg loses its salience as an image. Haraway's positive vision of the posthuman is one which validates embodied existence through its celebration of hybridity. Hybridity is the result of an incorporative transgression of boundaries: organism *and* machine, human *and* animal. The embodied hybridity of the cyborg is its metaphorical appeal.

This is a materialism that takes seriously not simply the fact of human embodiment generally, but the specificity of the differences between human bodies and the impact those differences make in defining what it means to be (post)human. Haraway's starting point is the observation that women are embodied not just differently from men but differently from each other as well; these differences split apart the identity of Woman, fracturing feminism as a movement. Homogeneous identity categories presuming that differences in female embodiments were negligible or non-existent proved oppressive, and were consequently contested by women whose different bodies marked them as other within the movement. This lesson, that the body matters, not simply in its generic reality but in its specificity, is exactly what is theorized by Haraway in the construction of the cyborg. The cyborg's hybrid embodiment is not a generic universality, but a specificity, and a multiplicity.

The contrast between this emphasis on specific, multiple, hybrid cyborg embodiments as *de facto* realities which must be acknowledged and the discourse of morphological freedom offered within transhumanist technoprogressivism is illustrative. For Haraway, it is the differences which already exist unacknowledged that must be addressed, the multiplicities and hybridities of gender, ethnicity, race—all the permutations of "natural" categories which existing cyborg bodies immediately challenge. Often, even more often than not, these cyborg embodiments are experienced as negative, carrying social and personal penalties for their deviation from the categorical and natural norms: Haraway writes, "We are excruciatingly conscious of what it means to have a historically constituted body."[51] In contrast, Hughes's morphological freedom emphasizes what ought to be available to persons in the future, a discourse of legal rights of the individual over the body, and anticipates an optimistic future in which personal whims rather than social and historical realities define bodily experience for the individual self.

*Posthumans Without a Soul*

Despite the tendency toward dualism embedded within transhumanism as a result of its conscious continuation of Enlightenment anthropology, leading to a disembodied notion of rationality as the essence of human nature, there is a consistent and strong rejection of a notion of disembodied spiritual essence.

---

[50] Donna J. Haraway, "Fetus: The Virtual Speculum in the New World Order," in *Modest_Witness@Second_Millennium.Femaleman©_Meets_Oncomouse™: Feminism and Technoscience* (New York, 1997), p. 186.

[51] Haraway, "A Cyborg Manifesto," p. 157.

The concept of a soul is viewed as paradigmatically superstitious, an obsolete and non-empirical belief which rational appraisal in the light of current scientific knowledge reveals to be untrue.

Thus, despite James Hughes's arguments for the compatibility of many religious and transhumanist views, and the emerging efforts at articulating a variety of syncretistic transhumanist religions, supernatural notions, including that of a soul, tend not to be among the religious beliefs deemed compatible with transhumanism.[52] Patrick Hopkins, for instance, identifies a desire for transcendence as a common characteristic of religions and transhumanism, but notes, "in religious terms, [transcendence] tends to imply some kind of 'higher' ontological order, usually some sort of supernatural domain ... Does true transcendence require supernaturalism, or is supernaturalism a superfluous concept for what is essentially a phenomenal condition?"[53] Thus while some strands of transhumanism certainly incorporate a dualism in which the essential self is separable from the inessential body as informational pattern, supernatural articulations of this idea remain unacceptable. The problem, it seems, is not the dualism, but the unscientific soul-talk it comes packaged in.

In contrast to the straightforward, categorical rejection of souls or possible spiritual realities of most transhumanists, Haraway's position on spirituality and the posthuman is much more complex. Emphatically uninterested in disembodied essences such as souls, as we have seen, Haraway nonetheless readily acknowledges that she incorporates a kind of "Catholic sacramentality" into her work, a perspective in which the material becomes the sacred. Haraway's resistance to the separation of the material and the semiotic can be seen as the philosophical result of a sacramentalism that accepts the material instantiation of the symbolic and sacred. Examples of Haraway's incorporation of both a general sense of sacramentalism and specific use of Christian figures abound: her characterization of the current technoscientific moment as "The Second Christian Millennium," her references to the OncoMouse as a suffering Christ figure, her allusions to the creation narrative of Genesis within the "A Cyborg Manifesto," and even eucharistic overtones in Haraway's final "parting bite" in her recent *When Species Meet*.[54]

Pastoral theologian Elaine Graham's engagement with Haraway on this point encourages what she characterizes as a "heretical" reading of her work. As Graham correctly observes, Haraway rejects both God and goddess as "totalizing narratives

---

[52] James Hughes, "The Compatibility of Religious and Transhumanist Views of Metaphysics, Suffering, Virtue and Transcendence in an Enhanced Future," *The Global Spiral* 8/2 (2007), www.metanexus.net/magazine/tabid/68/id/9930/Default.aspx.

[53] Patrick D. Hopkins, "Transcending the Animal: How Transhumanism and Religion Are and Are Not Alike," *Journal of Evolution and Technology* 14/2 (2005): p. 18.

[54] Donna J. Haraway, *When Species Meet*, ed. Cary Wolfe, Posthumanities (Minneapolis, MN, 2008), pp. 285–301.

of ultimate resolution and closure."[55] However, Graham attributes this rejection of religious narrative wholly to Haraway's socialist-feminist secularism, leading her to characterize Haraway's rejection of the goddess as part of a larger rejection of spiritual other-worldliness. Reading of Haraway as not simply materialistic, but anti-spiritual, leads Graham to suspect "an unresolved dualism of transcendence and immanence, sacred and secular."[56] Thus Graham sees the oft-quoted concluding statement to Haraway's manifesto, "I would rather be a cyborg than a goddess," as a rigid dichotomy which, she observes, is "strangely incongruous" in an essay which celebrates the end of dualisms.

Though others have also read Haraway in this way, the strange incongruity ought to suggest that this is, in fact, a misreading.[57] Indeed, as we have noted, the full syntax of Haraway's final statement includes the acknowledgment, "Though both are bound in the spiral dance …"[58] This acknowledgment that goddess and cyborg are inextricably bound together, overlapping—even perichoretic, to recontextualize a theological term!—options, rather than mutually exclusive options, indicates clearly that Haraway is not in fact setting up a new dualism along material/spiritual lines. Graham's lengthy defense of the importance of the notion of divine immanence of much of thealogy, as represented by Carol P. Christ and others, is therefore somewhat misdirected.[59] Haraway's rejection of the goddess is a rejection of essentialism, not a rejection of an inaccurately attributed anti-materialistic spirituality.

Unlike Graham, therefore, I am more inclined to interpret the ubiquitous religious symbols and allusions in Haraway's prose, her consistent references to her childhood spiritual formation within the Roman-Catholic tradition, and her frank acknowledgment of a deliberate sacramentalism in her work, as indicative of a latent spirituality within Haraway's cyborg writing. In other words, seeing sacramentality in the cyborg is not a heretical appropriation, but rather a faithful interpretation, of Haraway's own sense of sacramental materiality. This, clearly, opens the door to explicit theological engagement, without the need for lengthy apologetics and explanations.

---

[55] Elaine Graham, *Representations of the Post/Human: Monsters, Aliens and Others in Popular Culture* (New Brunswick, NJ, 2002), p. 211.

[56] Ibid., p. 216.

[57] For instance, Katharyn Privett, "Sacred Cyborgs and 21st Century Goddesses," *Reconstruction* 7/4 (2007).

[58] For a lengthier defense of Haraway on this point, see Anna Mercedes and Jennifer Thweatt-Bates, "Bound in the Spiral Dance: Spirituality and Technology in the Third Wave," in Chris Klassen (ed.), *Feminist Spirituality: The Next Generation* (Lanham, MD, 2009).

[59] Graham, *Representations of the Post/Human*, pp. 212–14. Here, Ruth Mantin's question, "can goddesses travel with nomads and cyborgs?" seems more to the point. See Ruth Mantin, "Can Goddesses Travel with Nomads and Cyborgs? Feminist Thealogies in a Postmodern Context," *Feminist Theology* 26 (2001).

At the same time, Haraway's rejection of essentialism in both its patriarchal and feminist articulations, in both secular and religious forms, means that we must read the cyborg as rejecting the notion of soul, as an inner, disembodied essential self—while maintaining a sense of spirituality consistent with Haraway's sacramental vision of material reality. As we will see in Chapter 4, contemporary Christian theological anthropologies, which move away from the classical anthropological dualism of body and soul, provide multiple possibilities for transversal connections with this kind of sacramental materialism.

The first major site at which transhumanist anthropology and cyborg anthropology diverge, therefore, is the issue of embodiment. While transhumanism admittedly incorporates materialistic claims, particularly in specifically technological contexts, the underlying dualism of Enlightenment anthropology, defining the human self as essentially a mind which can be mapped as an informational pattern and conceiving of the human body as an individual's property and an object of control, remains the larger philosophical framework within which occasional reductive materialistic claims are made. In contrast, Haraway's cyborg discourse repudiates the Enlightenment's "liberal humanist subject," and instead affirms a consistent materialism which makes the body constitutive for human identity, even while avoiding the claims of biological essentialism. Finally, and perhaps counterintuitively, it is the materialism of the Haraway cyborg, rather than the dualism of transhumanist anthropology, which makes space for the introduction of a spiritual dimension into the posthuman, in the form of a materialistic sacramentality.

**The FemaleMan**

Gender is, of course, high on the list of Haraway's conceptual priorities in her introduction of the cyborg as a feminist icon, and the topic of gender, linked as it is to embodiment, is one which marks an obvious divergence of Haraway's posthuman anthropology and that of the transhumanist movement. One cannot help noticing the gendered nature of the two discourses: not only does the gender of the participants divide neatly along ideological lines, but the gendering of the discourses themselves—Haraway's cyborg often takes the feminine pronoun, while Simon Young's 2008 "transhumanist manifesto" talks of the posthuman destiny of "man"—highlights the way in which gender is actively present in posthuman discourse, even when formally absent or systematically ignored.

Transhumanism's philosophical continuity with Enlightenment rational humanism results in an approach to gender issues that seeks to minimize the importance of bodily differences, emphasizing aspects of personhood which are independent of particular embodiments, while at the same time placing gender within the umbrella of a broad right to morphological freedom. Haraway, in contrast, seeks an approach to gender which recognizes the significance of different embodiments, incorporating into her cyborg approach the critical perspectives of feminist, womanist, postcolonial, and queer theories. Thus, just as "posthuman" is used in both discourses to signal very different visions, "postgender" in transhumanist discourse leads to a technologically mediated gender-less future, while Haraway's invocation of "postgender" invites a continuing renegotiation of the reality of gender rather than transcendence or negation of it.

*Psychological Androgyny and Artificial Wombs*

James Hughes stands as the exception to transhumanism's general indifference to the topic of gender, acknowledging and even lamenting transhumanism's largely homogeneous white male demographic, and building into his technoprogressivism a deliberate plea for coalition building that explicitly names Haraway and the "cyberfeminists."[60] In an ironic turn of phrase, Hughes sees feminists, cyberfeminists, gays, lesbians, and bisexuals as "natural allies" of democratic transhumanism in a shared quest for morphological freedom, as "the right to control one's own body means being able to share it with other consenting adults," as well as including enhanced reproductive rights and access to reproductive and contraceptive technologies.[61] While acknowledging that "as yet there has been little cross-pollination between the left-wing academic cyborgologists and the transhumanists," Hughes asserts that "mutual recognition and ties are growing," and indeed, this seems to be one aspect of the biopolitical and philosophical gap the IEET is intended to fill.[62]

In an Institute for Ethics and Emerging Technologies white paper, Hughes and co-author George Dvorsky offer a detailed proposal of transhumanist postgenderism, in which the biologically rooted injustices of gender can potentially be transcended by advances in neurotechnology, biotechnology, and reproductive technologies.[63] Importantly, Hughes and Dvorsky contend that "efforts to ameliorate patriarchy and the disabilities of binary gender through social, educational, political and economic reform can only achieve so much as long as the material basis, biological gendering of the body, brain, and reproduction, remain fixed."[64] In other words, these social, educational, political, and economic reform efforts must necessarily be complemented by technological interventions on the human body itself, for "only the blurring and erosion of biological sex, of the gendering of the brain, and of binary social roles by emerging technologies will enable individuals to access all human potentials and experiences regardless of their born sex or assumed gender."[65] The problem of gender injustice, according to Hughes and Dvorsky, resides primarily not in the social, but in the biological realm—not merely in human relationships, but within human bodies. The solution must therefore be not simply social, but

---

[60] Hughes, *Citizen Cyborg*, p. 72.
[61] Ibid., pp. 207–8.
[62] Ibid., p. 208.
[63] James Hughes and George Dvorsky, "Postgenderism: Beyond the Gender Binary," *IEET Monograph Series* (2008), http://ieet.org/archive/IEET-03-PostGender.pdf.
[64] Ibid.
[65] Ibid.

biological. This is the role of technology: to reshape the human body in ways that prevent the unjust and oppressive consequences of biological binary gender.

Hughes and Dvorsky therefore position their postgender proposal as one which "transcends essentialism and social constructivism by asserting that freedom from gender will require both social reform and technology."[66] It is clear that their construction of postgenderism repudiates strong forms of social constructivism, by locating the source of gender injustice in the body itself, rather than in the social constructions of gender projected upon the body. But for this reason it is correspondingly less clear how their postgenderism transcends essentialism, as it grounds gender so strongly in biology. The key to this claim of a *via media* between gender essentialism and constructivism is the basic transhumanist attitude toward the function of technology to transcend biological givens, in this case, biological sex and gender. Though both biological essentialists and Hughes and Dvorsky's postgenderism identify gender as a biological given, essentialists construct a necessary ontology from the biological given—a further move which Hughes and Dvorsky reject, instead viewing biological gender as a bodily reality which can, and should, be modified and even transcended through technology. Gender is a bodily reality which does not define the human person, as essentialists would contend; rather, gender is a bodily reality which negatively limits the full potential of the human person.

This view of gender as a bodily reality which constrains or limits, but does not define, the person, can only make sense when connected with the implicit dualism of transhumanist anthropology discussed above. The body, even when it makes a (negative) difference in the formation of personhood as Hughes and Dvorsky argue that gender currently does, is not ontologically definitive, because the body remains an inessential, upgradeable, and replaceable prosthesis. Technology can, and Hughes and Dvorsky argue, should, intervene and dispel the illusion of the ontological necessity and givenness of gender, in effect creating a space between person and gender (body) in which deliberate selection of traits can occur.[67] Here, as with other discussions of morphological freedom and enhancement, it is once again language of control over the body that frames the discussion of gender.

The goal of this transhumanist postgenderism, then, is enhanced control over the body by multiplying possibilities of gender and sexual expression, and making the selection of these traits a matter of deliberate individual choice. Hughes and Dvorsky claim that "bodies and personalities in our postgender future will no longer be constrained and circumscribed by gendered traits, but enriched by

---

[66] Ibid.

[67] Here, the question of whether the binary gendering of our current biological and social reality has influenced the character of our technologies is unaddressed, despite the existence of a rich feminist and philosophical discourse on the gendering of technoscience. Hughes and Dvorsky presume that the technological interventions they envision are themselves gender neutral. Given their attention to the "gendered brain" and "gendered occupational stratification" as problematic, this is a telling oversight.

their use in the palette of diverse self-expression."[68] On the surface, this stated goal contradicts my contention that transhumanist postgenderism envisions a gender-less future, in its apparent celebration of the possibilities of an unbounded proliferation of diverse gender trait self-expression.

Implicit in this description of the postgender future, however, is the assumption that the free choice of gender traits is performed in a context where persons have already been freed from the biological imperative of non-chosen gender traits; Hughes and Dvorsky even refer to this as "psychological androgyny."[69] The proliferation of possible gender configurations, then, is a second moment dependent upon first achieving a biologically nongendered, neutral (neuter?) state from which choice can be made, as an expression of the person's conscious control over the biological body. Thus despite their overt rejection of universal androgyny as a postgender goal, psychological androgyny is the necessary prerequisite to the diverse self-expression Hughes and Dvorsky describe as the postgender future. In the transhumanist postgender future, *bodies* may indeed be multiply gendered, but *persons* will not be; gender, as a bodily attribute, is non-essential, non-binding, non-permanent, and non-defining.

Even more problematic is the implicit evaluation in this postgender vision of some gender traits as valuable and others as undesirable. Which gender traits belong to the category of positive possibilities of self-expression, and which gender traits belong to the category of those which constrain and circumscribe? The lack of direct discussion gives the impression that the postgender future will leave this determination completely open to individual choice, and yet there are indications that there are some gendered realities which are considered to be wholly negative. Though Hughes and Dvorsky do name some "masculine" traits as negative, overall it is "feminine" traits are more often viewed negatively; for instance, "gendered brains" result in statistically shorter life expectancies and higher aggression in males, but it is women who are "impaired in the workforce," not only by the biological demands of pregnancy and childbirth, but by gendered occupational stratification resulting from "the different abilities and aspirations coded in the gendered brain."[70]

This is seen with particular clarity in the way that the anticipated successful development of artificial wombs is presumed to benefit women in particular through gifting them greater control of the body through technology. At first, Hughes anticipates, only women prone to at-risk pregnancies will likely use it, then childless women who prefer a machine to the emotional complications of a human surrogate. Eventually, however, Hughes claims, "artificial wombs will be attractive for all women, as an alternative to the burdens and risks of pregnancy and delivery, and to allow a level of control, purity and optimization of the uterine

---

[68] Hughes and Dvorsky, "Postgenderism."
[69] Ibid. Hughes and Dvorsky write, "psychological androgyny will allow future persons to explore both masculine and feminine aspects of personality."
[70] Ibid.

environment impossible in a woman's body."[71] A recent IEET blog post by Nikki Olson and Hank Pellissier echoes this sentiment, calling pregnancy one of the "most risky and unpleasant things a woman can expect to endure" and characterizing the womb as "a dark and dangerous place, a hazardous environment." Olson and Pellissier, like Hughes, anticipate that humanity will "return to the egg," an evolutionarily superior option, via artificial wombs.[72]

There is, of course, an obvious misstep in claiming that anything "will be attractive for all women," a universalizing pronouncement which ignores the lesson feminists themselves have had to painfully learn, as Haraway's "A Cyborg Manifesto" describes. But more significant is the way in which the transhumanist goal of "control of the body" leads directly into a characterization of women's bodies as out-of-control, impure, and sub-optimal. In addition to being simply insulting, the possibility that pregnancy and birth might be experienced as revelatory and pleasurable is apparently unthinkable.[73] Further, Hughes, Olson, and Pellissier make clear that a primary benefit of artificial wombs is that they will allow women's bodies to function more like men's bodies, by eliminating the socially problematic, physically dangerous, and altogether unpleasant embodied state of pregnancy and childbirth—an *andro*gynous postgender future indeed. Here, it becomes extremely clear that the default masculinity of Enlightenment anthropology is operative in this postgender vision.

In this transhumanist postgender vision, Donna Haraway is cited "as a postgender theorist arguing for technological transgression to liberate both women and men from the gender binary" who proposes the cyborg as a means of achieving "the integration of women and machines into a new liberatory androgynous archetype."[74] Placing Haraway under the umbrella of transhumanism in this way ignores not only her explicit repudiation of the movement but also crucial aspects of her project that do not dovetail neatly with transhumanist postgenderism— specifically, her insistence on rejecting universals for women, her ambivalence

---

[71] Hughes, *Citizen Cyborg*, p. 87.

[72] Nikki Olson and Hank Pellissier, "Artificial Wombs Will Spawn New Freedoms," Institute for Ethics and Emerging Technologies, http://ieet.org/index.php/IEET/more/olson20110526.

[73] For an exploration of childbirth as an embodied cyborg reality where feminism, technology and spirituality converge, see Mercedes and Thweatt-Bates, "Bound in the Spiral Dance: Spirituality and Technology in the Third Wave." For an explicit comparison of Hughes' artificial womb discussion and Haraway's "monstrous regeneration," see J. Jeanine Thweatt-Bates, "Artificial Wombs and Cyborg Births: Postgenderism and Theology," in Ron Cole-Turner (ed.), *Transhumanism and Transcendence: Christian Hope in an Age of Technological Enhancement* (Washington, DC, 2011).

[74] Hughes and Dvorsky, "Postgenderism." Cf. Hughes, *Citizen Cyborg*, p. 207.

toward and ironic use of the cyborg, and her characterization of the cyborg as female rather than androgynous.[75]

While Hughes grasps the importance of the boundary-transgressing aspect of Haraway's cyborg, to describe Haraway as proposing the cyborg "as the liberatory mythos for all women" is to miss a central aspect of Haraway's critique of feminist essentialism.[76] There is no liberating mythos for all women, because there is no universal or categorical identity that includes all women.[77] This is a major mistake in the interpretation of Haraway as a feminist thinker, but indicative of a broader error as well, in that Hughes and Dvorsky show little appreciation of the diversity and historicity of the feminist movement in the attempt to classify Haraway and the "cyberfeminists" as part of the transhumanist movement. The single feminist actually cited by Hughes, Dvorsky, Olson, and Pellissier is Shulamith Firestone, and the blatant differences in feminist viewpoint between Firestone and Haraway are not acknowledged, nor is the fact that Firestone is not a "cyberfeminist" but rather a second-wave radical feminist.[78] Firestone locates the source of women's social oppression in the reproductive function of women's bodies; Haraway, in contrast—even while finding the extension metaphor of organic birthing into universal female identity problematic—views attention to and valuing of women's bodies as a solution, not the source of the problem.

In addition, this transhumanist (mis)interpretation overlooks Haraway's delicate balancing between the oppressive and liberating potentials of the cyborg, an aspect of the manifesto clearly evident in Haraway's negative descriptions of the cyborg and insistence on its historical specificity as the prerequisite to its ironic potential. Haraway's attitude regarding posthuman technologies is not, like the transhumanists', easily labeled "techno-optimism," but a much more guarded and conditional hope, dependent upon the ties of kinship that are recognized and fostered, or not. The cyborg is an ironic and subversive figure, but it can only remain ironic and subversive if its potential threat is voiced along with its potential promise.

Most importantly, Hughes and Dvorsky misinterpret Haraway's manifesto in claiming the androgyny of the cyborg. Haraway's cyborg is, in her words, "a girl who's trying not to become Woman."[79] Women are cyborgs, though not the only cyborgs, precisely *as women*—historically relegated to the wrong side of the ontological tracks, cyborg women refuse to stay neatly put in their appointed universal category of Woman, universal Man's Other. The boundary crossing of

---

[75] See, for instance, Haraway's remarks on transhumanism in N. Gane and D. Haraway, "When We Have Never Been Human, What Is to Be Done? Interview with Donna Haraway," *Theory Culture & Society* 23/7–8 (2006).

[76] Hughes, *Citizen Cyborg*, p. 207.

[77] Haraway, "A Cyborg Manifesto," p. 155. Cf. pp. 173, 181.

[78] See Shulamith Firestone, *The Dialectic of Sex: The Case for Feminist Revolution* (New York, 1970).

[79] Donna J. Haraway, "Cyborgs at Large: Interview with Donna Haraway," in A. Penley and C. Ross (eds), *Technoculture* (Minneapolis, MN, 1991), p. 20.

these cyborg women does not result in the surrender of particular gender or a transcendent androgyny; this would simply replicate the logic Haraway seeks to subvert. Indeed, this annihilates identity in the name of liberation, a secular analog of the Gospel of Thomas's promise to Mary Magdalene that, in heaven, she will be saved by being made a man. Instead, this boundary crossing requires recognition of the gendered self in defiance of ontological categories.

The source of this transhumanist misappropriation of Haraway is the presumption of an anthropological dualism and the corresponding transhumanist goal of enhanced control of the body. Transhumanist postgenderism is thus another expression of transhumanism's continuity with, in Hayles's phrase, the "liberal humanist subject" resulting in a split of the person from his (and here the masculine pronoun is intentional, and not falsely universal) body.

*Beyond Gender "As We Know It"*

It is exactly this divorce of body and identity that Haraway resolutely refuses to accept, instead maintaining a consistent materialism that takes seriously the feminist slogan, "our bodies, ourselves," even while redefining it through her invocation of the cyborg.[80] Haraway's strategy is to pay close attention to material reality, in order to point out that our gendered bodies and identities do not in reality fit the universal, totalizing theories of identity we have socially constructed. That is, gender essentialism is itself the social construct. Once this move is made, biologically gendered bodies can be constitutive for identity without taking on the baggage of a socially constructed essentialism projected back onto those bodies, in an exercise of social power. Biology is not destiny; biology is not Nature.

The cyborg therefore does not negate or transcend biological gender, but is not constrained by social gender; this is the result, not of transcendence or denial of material reality, but the embrace of it. Only when gender is constructed as global identity must it be rejected—but cyborgs are free to consider the "partial, fluid, sometimes" aspect of sex and sexual embodiment. Haraway's use of cyborg imagery is apt, not simply for its obvious utility in advocating a "refusal of anti-science metaphysics," but also because it signals that "the production of universal, totalizing theory us a major mistake that misses most of reality, probably always, but certainly now."[81] The material reality of gendered bodies is therefore the key in deconstructing the totalizing identity of Woman.

Postgender, therefore, in the sense of somehow getting beyond gender entirely, is not a concept represented in the cyborg. Haraway is explicit about this. In a 2006 interview, Haraway comments, "I have trouble with the way people go for a utopian post-gender world – 'Ah, that means it doesn't matter whether you're a man or a woman any more.' … We're in a post-gender world in some ways, and in others

---

[80] Haraway, "A Cyborg Manifesto," p. 181.
[81] Ibid.

we're in a ferociously gender-in-place world."[82] For Haraway, then, postgender clearly does not mean that it no longer matters whether one is a man or a woman anymore—that is, a denial of the material reality of gender. Positively, postgender is about the ultimate goal of "a world without gender as we know it," but that is not to say without gender at all.[83] The cyborg is "postgender" in this limited and very specific sense, in a context in which the word "gender" signifies the social construct of essential and universal Woman, that is, "gender as we know it."

Haraway's reading of Joanna Russ's *The Female Man* provides an illustration of the disruption of universal gender categories through boundary transgressions which lead to an open-ended plurality, but not transcendence, of gender. Haraway adopts Russ's Female Man as a useful figure "not because she is an unmarked feminist utopian solution to a supposed universal masculine domination rooted in a coherent and singular masculine subject," but because she is the opposite—"as much a disruption of the story of the universal Female as of the universal Man."[84] Russ's generic title figure literally takes on flesh in the narrative multiply, as four genetic clones from four differing personal histories in disjunctive space/time continuums, who come together in the 1970s United States and produce a collective narrative in which, indeed, they are simultaneously postgender and gender-in-place. Haraway's reading of *The Female Man* highlights the ways in which these four protagonists subvert each other's certainties. The point, for Haraway, is precisely the way Russ uses her protagonists to interrogate each other, showing up the limits not only of 1970s United States heteronormativity, but also the uncertain, historically constructed nature of the origin stories of the utopian all-female Whileaway (what *did* happen to all the men, anyhow?). Only by accepting that none of these narratives is whole, or wholly true, can one begin to put together something that describes what it means to be gendered in a material sense. Not even genetically identical J-named protagonists turn out to be identically gendered; none of the four can claim to tell the whole story about gender; significantly, all of the four must negotiate how to live out their own diverging gender identities, for none of them transcend gender into androgynous postgenderism.

The primary and most crucial divergence of Haraway and the transhumanists on gender and postgender is that Haraway sees gendered bodies as the means of deconstructing gender as a socially constructed, falsely universalized essentialism, while Hughes and Dvorsky reject biologically gendered bodies precisely because they accept an inverted gender essentialism, in which gender is a negative given to be subordinated to technological control. Put simply, for Haraway, gendered bodies are the solution; for Hughes and Dvorsky, gendered

---

[82] Gane and Haraway, "When We Have Never Been Human, What Is to Be Done?" pp. 137–8.

[83] Ibid.

[84] Donna J. Haraway, "Femaleman©_Meets_Oncomouse™. Mice into Wormholes: A Technoscience Fugue in Two Parts," in *Modest_Witness@Second_Millennium. Femaleman©_Meets_Oncomouse*™ (New York, 1997), p. 70.

bodies are the problem. As a result, though Hughes and Dvorsky describe a postgender future of "a palette of diverse self-expression," which sounds on the face of it somewhat similar to Haraway's "partial, fluid, sometimes" aspect of sex and sexual embodiment, the two postgender visions are not at all equivalent.

**Know Thyself**

The question of how we perceive the world, and come to know it and ourselves, is one embedded into the core of the posthuman discussion. Cary Wolfe writes, "when we talk about posthumanism, we are not just talking about a thematics of decentering of the human in relation to either evolutionary, ecological or technological coordinates … we are also talking about *how* thinking confronts that thematics, what thought has become in the face of those challenges."[85] For Wolfe, posthumanism leads directly into the consideration of epistemology, and its transformation by the "decentering of the human."

If, as I have argued, transhumanism has not "decentered" the human, but instead seeks to enlarge and expand it (humanity, plus), then the operative epistemology within transhumanism will not significantly depart from its Enlightenment and modernist inheritance. This is, in fact, precisely what we find in the scattered clues regarding epistemology within transhumanist discourse, as well as in transhumanism's description of itself as an extension of rational humanism. In contrast, the distinctions between self and other that the cyborg figure calls into question, in the cyborg's liminal existence on the boundaries, is the starting point that Wolfe calls the "decentering" of the human. Thus what we find, once again, is that these two posthuman discourses, transhumanist and cyborg, are not only distinct but in active tension with one another.

*Rational Humanists and Bayesian Reasoners*

Nick Bostrom describes transhumanism's philosophical roots as "rational humanism," a dual inheritance of Francis Bacon's scientific methodology and Renaissance humanism, "which emphasizes science and critical reasoning – rather than revelation and religious authority – as ways of learning about the natural world and the destiny and nature of man and of providing a grounding for morality."[86] But what precisely does this broadly sketched allegiance to Enlightenment humanist values and scientific method tell us about the working epistemology of transhumanism? As with so many other aspects of this diverse movement, the topic of epistemology becomes a contested one within transhumanism itself, and various epistemologies, ranging from uncritical scientism to more sophisticated proposals of "Bayesian reasoning," exist.

---

[85] Wolfe, *What Is Posthumanism?*, p. xvi.
[86] Bostrom, "The Transhumanist FAQ."

Simon Young, for example, defines knowledge in his manifesto as an "accurate representation of the world"; then, blithely skipping over the philosophical quagmires embedded in that definition, in the next sentence defines science as "the pursuit of knowledge."[87] Young goes on to advocate a "new scientism," or "a renewed respect" for the scientific method and its successes, as the middle ground between theistic absolutism and postmodern epistemological relativism. Young writes, "The New Scientism rejects both theistic absolutism and postmodern epistemological relativism for a renewed respect for the scientific method of observation, hypothesis, and experimentation as the knowledge base responsible for the miraculous technowonderland of the modern world. Science is not the source of our eventual downfall but the greatest hope for our transcendence."[88] Here, then, the transhumanist attitude toward scientific knowledge explicitly "represents *a renewal of modernity*—the belief in ongoing human progress through reason, science, and technology."[89]

Alongside the rather hyperbolic presentation of Young's "new scientism" are more nuanced considerations of scientific rationality, often centered on Bayesian reasoning. An active site for this is the community blog Less Wrong (sponsored by The Singularity Institute for Artificial Intelligence and the Future of Humanity Institute at Oxford University), the tagline of which reads, "refining the art of human rationality." In a "core sequence" of articles promoted on the site as recommended prerequisite reading for newcomers, Eliezer Yudkowsky's definition of rationality is "the art of obtaining beliefs that correspond to reality as closely as possible."[90] Improving the correspondence of one's mental map to the territory of reality, both for itself and for the achievement of pragmatic goals, is what it means to be rational. Specifically, this means "Bayesian-style belief-updating (with Occam priors) because ... this style of thinking gets us systematically closer to ... *accuracy,* the map that reflects the territory."[91]

Rather than getting sidetracked into wrangling over definitions, Yudkowsky's approach is to establish a communal consensus on the meaning of rationality as normative, and move on to the pragmatic consideration of how to become more rational: "What's left to discuss is not *what meaning* to attach to the syllables 'ra-tio-na-li-ty;' what's left to discuss is *what is a good way to think*."[92] Unpacking what is a "good way to think" includes not overthinking what, precisely, rationality is, beyond a quickly established communal consensus on a basic empiricism (beliefs that correspond to reality) and pragmatism (beliefs that achieve one's goals). Thus, underpinning these musings on rationality and how to improve it (in

---

[87] Young, *Designer Evolution*, p. 84.
[88] Ibid., p. 95.
[89] Ibid., p. 103.
[90] Eliezer Yudkowsky, "What Do We Mean by Rationality?" Less Wrong, http://lesswrong.com/lw/31/what_do_we_mean_by_rationality/.
[91] Ibid.
[92] Ibid.

both an immediate and technologically mediated future sense), is a presumptive representational, critical realist notion of rationality that remains fundamentally unchanged from transhumanism's original Enlightenment, rational humanist philosophical roots: rationality consists on constructing and constantly improving one's mental map of reality.

How closely our mental maps correspond to reality is taken to be a matter of probability, and the accuracy of our maps depends upon how good we are, as rational agents, at gauging the relative probabilities of our beliefs. Often, human reasoners are mistaken about the relative probabilities of their beliefs. But why is it that human reasoners are so bad at gauging the relative probabilities of the accuracy of our beliefs? Robin Hanson argues that this is the result of the human tendency to form beliefs for reasons other than truth-approximation: "If honest truth-seeking agents would not knowingly disagree, then how is it that humans do knowingly disagree, even when they are confident of their honesty? The obvious explanation is that humans do not seek only to believe the truth; they have other motivations influencing the choice of their beliefs, such as hope and self-respect (otherwise known as wishful-thinking and overconfidence)."[93] Bayes's Theorem, which provides a means of calculating the probabilities and therefore evaluating the accuracy of epistemic beliefs, is therefore invoked as a sort of epistemic therapy, in order to counteract the human tendency to weight evidence too strongly or too weakly, due to factors such as observational bias, self-deception, or emotional or idiosyncratic preferences.[94] Employing Bayes's Theorem as epistemic therapy in this way means acknowledging that our "mental maps" are only ongoing approximations of the territory. Thus, a core epistemic principle for transhumanism is that of epistemic fallibility, and a corresponding virtue is a conscious commitment to ongoing revision of beliefs in light of further evidence. Yudkowsky's "Twelve Virtues of Rationality" lists, among others, the virtues of "relinquishment, lightness, evenness," all of which describe attitudes necessary for achieving the right level of epistemic commitment in light of the fallible, probabilistic nature of human reasoning.[95]

This functions as the crucial distinction between reason and faith. Faith is seen as a determination to believe "no matter what," which resists the kind of probabilistic, tentative commitment that constitutes the central characteristic of the transhumanists' Bayesian rationality. Mikael Stenmark reflects, "It is this 'no-matter-what happens mentality' that bothers non-religious people … the strength

---

[93] Robin Hanson, "Enhancing Our Truth Orientation," in Julian Savulescu and Nick Bostrom (eds), *Human Enhancement* (London, 2009), p. 360.

[94] For an exploration of anthropic bias and observation selection effects considered from a Bayesian perspective, Nick Bostrom, *Anthropic Bias: Observation Selection Effects in Science and Philosophy*, ed. Robert Nozick, Studies in Philosophy (New York, 2002).

[95] Eliezer Yudkowsky, "Twelve Virtues of Epistemology," http://yudkowsky.net/rational/virtues.

with which the religious believer holds these beliefs seems unreasonable."[96] Stenmark calls this the "tentativeness" challenge to religious belief, a challenge which assumes that beliefs may be held with different degrees of acceptance: "we could say that a belief is *tentatively accepted* when one thinks there is a need to investigate it further, but one is willing to use it as a starting-point (a working hypothesis) for something one is doing. This further inquiry might be done in different ways. One is actively (or constantly) looking for defeaters (counter-evidence) of one view, or one is actively searching for justifiers (evidence) of it, or both."[97] This description of tentative acceptance of a belief, contrasted with full acceptance that presumes there is no need for further investigation, comes very close to the transhumanist explanation of precisely what it is about Bayesian reasoning that makes it definitively rational. All beliefs should be accepted tentatively, with degrees of acceptance ranging in correspondence to the probabilities given by the theorem; full acceptance, in Stenmark's sense, is therefore never rationally warranted. Since religious beliefs are typically accepted in a full rather than a tentative sense, they are, in the transhumanists' estimation, by definition irrational.[98]

To be rational, then, according to Yudkowsky, is to be Bayesian: "*Bayesian reasoner* is the technically precise codeword that we use to mean *rational mind*."[99] Despite this systematic acknowledgment of the probabilistic nature of human knowledge, and the employment of at least informal Bayesian reasoning as a means of correctly assessing the degree of probability of a belief's correspondence to reality, consideration of the human knower as an embodied, socially located epistemic agent is entirely lacking. The assumption seems to be that Bayes's Theorem is universally applicable and univocally articulated, regardless of the identity of the knower. Equating Bayesian reasoner with "rational *mind*" is not simply a casual elision of the embodied existence of the human person; it truly seems not to matter.

Further, Bayesian reasoning aside, Yudkowsky's stipulated working definition of rationality as the "map corresponding to territory" is a restatement of Simon Young's casual definition of knowledge as "accurate representation of the world."[100] A recent series of articles by James Hughes at the Institute for Ethics and Emerging Technologies, however, takes issue with the presumptive definitions of rationality at work in transhumanism, specifically those frequently encountered in the Less

---

[96] Mikael Stenmark, *Rationality in Science, Religion, and Everyday Life: A Critical Evaluation of Four Models of Rationality* (Notre Dame, IN, 1995), pp. 290–1.

[97] Ibid., p. 291.

[98] Stenmark's discussion goes on to discuss when full acceptance of a belief can be rational, and makes a further distinction between "full" and "dogmatic" acceptance. Ibid., pp. 293–9.

[99] Eliezer Yudkowsky, "An Intuitive Explanation of Bayesian Reasoning," Less Wrong, http://yudkowsky.net/rational/bayes.

[100] Young, *Designer Evolution*, Yudkowsky, "What Do We Mean by Rationality?"

Wrong posts and discussions. Hughes identifies "the unsustainable autonomy of reason" as the first of a list of inherited "contradictions of the Enlightenment" within transhumanism. Specifically taking to task Yudkowsky and extropian Max More, Hughes challenges transhumanists to move beyond the assumption that their inherited Enlightenment notion of rationality can be taken for granted as universal and self-evident.[101] However, in the article Hughes goes no further than suggesting that, for mainly apologetic reasons, transhumanists would do well to abandon their implicit foundationalism. Intriguingly, however, Hughes also lists as a separate item on his list of inherited "contradictions of the Enlightenment" the anthropological notion of the individual self. While Hughes does not explicitly connect this item to his epistemological concerns regarding the unsustainability of typical transhumanist notions of rationality, the intimate dependence of Enlightenment epistemology on its anthropology would suggest that in critically examining the Enlightenment notion of the individual self, he is also prepared to critically examine Enlightenment notions of the individual human knower.[102] Hopefully, this might include challenging the disembodied, abstract notions of rationality operative even in these transhumanist explorations of epistemology.

These disparate gleanings of transhumanist epistemology fall short of a systematic or fully representative description. They do, however, provide an indication that transhumanism, as a whole, remains firmly committed to strong Enlightenment notions of scientific objectivity, empiricism, and claims to universality, and as a whole, has not seriously examined the epistemological critiques of Enlightenment rationality. In particular, as Hughes points out, transhumanists must address the inherited split between reason and emotion, as well as postmodernist deconstructions of Enlightenment Reason, as represented, for example, by Derrida and Foucault.[103]

*Situated Knowledges*

Derrida and Foucault, of course, are looming background presences in Haraway's "Cyborg Manifesto." As a critique-of-a-critique of Enlightenment anthropology and epistemology, Haraway's cyborg in its hopeful, ironic, and subversive mode is well aware that Reason is a historical product of the Enlightenment's "modest witness," whose "subjectivity is his objectivity."[104] The assumption that the identity of the scientific observer, the so-called modest witness, disappears or is irrelevant

---

[101] James Hughes, "Problems of Transhumanism: The Unsustainable Autonomy of Reason," Institute for Ethics and Emerging Technologies, http://ieet.org/index.php/IEET/more/hughes20100108/.

[102] At the time of writing, this seventh and last installment of Hughes' planned series on "Problems of Transhumanism" has not yet been published on the IEET website.

[103] Hughes, "Problems of Transhumanism."

[104] Donna J. Haraway, "Modest_Witness@Second_Millenium," in *Modest_Witness@ Second_Millennium.Femaleman©_Meets_Oncomouse™: Feminism and Technoscience* (New York, 1997), pp. 23–4.

to the act of observation within the "culture of no culture" that is the laboratory is challenged by Haraway and other feminist philosophers of science. The objectivity produced by this faulty assumption is simply a particular subjectivity pretending to a universal objectivity.

Thus Haraway's "Situated Knowledges: The Science Question in Feminism and the Privilege of Partial Perspective," addresses an epistemological quandary very different from the transhumanists' preoccupation with the self-evident superiority of reason over faith or other forms of irrationality. In this essay, Haraway seeks to articulate an epistemology which remains true to her commitment to material reality, while acknowledging simultaneously that human knowledge is subjective and socially constructed. She begins with acknowledging the importance of the contested question of "what *we* might mean by the curious and inescapable term 'objectivity'" and describes feminist responses to the question of objectivity as having both "selectively and flexibly used and been trapped by two poles of a tempting dichotomy."[105] One pole is identified as strong social constructivism.[106] Unwilling to make a move that denies that "our appeals to real worlds are more than a desperate lurch away from cynicism and an act of faith like any other cult's," Haraway concludes, "the further I get with the description of the radical social constructionist programme and a particular version of postmodernism, coupled to the acid tools of critical discourse in the human sciences, the more nervous I get."[107] The second pole of the "tempting dichotomy" is the search for a feminist version of objectivity. This answers the feminist need to "insist on a better account of the world," which radical social constructivism cannot fulfill. Yet, Haraway writes, "Here, we, as feminists, find ourselves perversely conjoined with the discourse of many practicing scientists, who, when all is said and done, mostly believe they are describing and discovering things *by means of* all their constructing and arguing."[108] This is perverse, because, in Nancy Hartsock's term, the "abstract masculinity" that underlies the practice of science remains problematic, a "deadly fantasy that feminists and others have identified in some versions of objectivity doctrines in the service of hierarchical and positivist orderings of what can count as knowledge."[109]

The epistemological problem, then, is "how to have *simultaneously* an account of radical historical contingency for all knowledge claims and knowing subjects, a critical practice for recognizing our own 'semiotic technologies' for making meanings, *and* a no-nonsense commitment to faithful accounts of the 'real' world."[110] In an ironic move, Haraway adopts the metaphor of vision as

---

[105] Donna J. Haraway, "Situated Knowledges: The Science Question in Feminism and the Privilege of Partial Perspective," in *Simians, Cyborgs and Women: The Reinvention of Nature* (New York, 1991), p. 183.

[106] Ibid., p. 184.

[107] Ibid., p. 185.

[108] Ibid., p. 187.

[109] Ibid., pp. 186–8.

[110] Ibid., p. 187.

a therapeutic intervention, insisting on the "particularity and embodiment of all vision (though not necessarily organic embodiment and including technological mediation)."[111] This insistence on the importance of embodiment in Haraway's chosen epistemological metaphor signals the important role of the body in modifying the concept of objectivity itself: Haraway advocates an "embodied objectivity" which she names "situated knowledges."[112]

Such an objectivity is usable, though not innocent, by which Haraway means to say that no vantage point of vision may claim to be unmarked or universal. Embodied vision is always particular, but particularity is therefore the means to knowledge rather than an impediment to it: "So not so perversely, objectivity turns out to be about particular and specific embodiment, and definitely not about the false vision promising transcendence of all limits and responsibility. The moral is simple: only partial perspective promises objective vision."[113] Further, these partial perspectives are not complete in themselves. Haraway writes, "The knowing self is partial in all its guises, never finished, whole, simply there and original; it is always constructed and stitched together imperfectly, and *therefore* able to join with another, to see together without claiming to be another."[114]

In "Femaleman©_Meets_Oncomouse™," Haraway speaks of "the relocated gaze," choosing to deliberately position herself as sister to the laboratory mouse. As an example of the epistemological practice of embodied vision Haraway advocates in "Situated Knowledges," the relocated gaze of kinship is instructive. Refusing to speak on OncoMouse's behalf, a blatant anthropocentric power move, nonetheless Haraway seeks a way of "seeing together" through the mouse's vision. Thus, even while one's own location and specifically embodied vision must be acknowledged, precisely that acknowledgment enables the realization that other locations and other embodied visions are both possible and necessary. The relocated gaze, therefore, "forces [us] to pay attention to kinship."[115] As Baukje Prins observes, this epistemology of hybrid subject/object neatly aligns with the ontological hybridity of the cyborg: "the former 'subject' and 'object' of knowledge reappear as apparatuses of visual and bodily production. By giving them both the status of material-semiotic actors, Haraway blurs the epistemological boundary between subject and object."[116]

---

[111] Ibid., p. 189.

[112] Ibid., p. 188.

[113] Ibid., p. 190.

[114] Ibid., p. 193. Haraway addresses at length the issue of privileging some partial perspectives over others, arguing that while "there is good reason to believe vision is better from below the brilliant space platforms of the powerful," one must avoid both facile appropriation of the less powerful, and romanticizing that partial perspective into an "innocence" that leaves it unaccountable to other partial perspectives (p. 190).

[115] Haraway, "Femaleman©_Meets_Oncomouse™," p. 52.

[116] Baukje Prins, "The Ethics of Hybrid Subjects: Feminist Constructivism According to Donna Haraway," *Science, Technology, & Human Values* 20/3 (1995): p. 353.

Cary Wolfe's recent exploration of posthumanism as a mode of thought, rather than simply as a discussion of the decentering of the human in relation to technology, delves into the question of embodiment and epistemology through the work of Niklas Luhmann. In Luhmann's second-order systems theory, the distinction between self and other (system and environment), exists, but as a "temporally dynamic, recursive loop of systemic code and environmental complexity that is itself infected by the virus of paradoxical self-reference."[117] In a move similar to Haraway's cyborg irony and epistemological insistence on the necessity of partiality as a prerequisite for vision, this "paradoxical self-reference" is precisely what makes the world epistemologically accessible: "The very thing that separates us from the world *connects* us to the world, and self-referential, autopoietic closure, far from indicating a kind of solipsistic neo-Kantian idealism, actually is generative of openness to the environment."[118]

This means, as Wolfe observes, that not only can we no longer ignore the epistemological realities of embodiment and location, but further that we can no longer talk of "*the* body," or even "*a* body in the traditional sense," for the boundaries of what constitute body and environment are not stable, and these boundaries are produced in the paradoxical, self-referential interaction of system and environment. The payoff is that this enables the description of the human with greater specificity. "Far from surpassing or rejecting the human," he writes, "[this perspective] insists that we attend to the specificity of the human—its ways of being in the world, its ways of knowing, observing and describing—by (paradoxically, for humanism) acknowledging that it is a fundamentally prosthetic creature that has coevolved with various forms of technology and materiality, forms that are radically 'not-human' and yet nevertheless have made the human what it is."[119] This, of course, is to define the human as cyborg, in the boundary-crossing, hybrid mode that Haraway invokes.

The most significant and striking contrast between these posthuman epistemologies is their divergence on the importance of specific embodiments in human ways of knowing the world. For Haraway, a disembodied epistemology is by definition distorted; this is her central complaint about scientific assumptions of objectivity that attempt to erase the location and identity of the human knower. Specific embodiments, deliberate positioning, and communal accountability are her key prescriptions for correcting the distorted perspective of Enlightenment objectivity, prescriptions whose implications have been elaborated on in various ways by Wolfe. Transhumanism, however, retains the very notion of disembodied objectivity that Haraway's cyborg discourse rejects; the human knower in transhumanist discourse disappears, like the Enlightenment's "modest witness," even while engaging in the process of gathering and evaluating the evidence that informs his construction of a rational worldview.

---

[117] Wolfe, *What Is Posthumanism?*, p. xix.
[118] Ibid., p. xxi.
[119] Ibid., p. xxv.

## Am I My Sister's Keeper?

As Cary Wolfe observes, "'the animal question' is part of the larger question of posthumanism."[120] Transhumanist and cyborg discourses construct the relationship of the human and nonhuman quite differently, and nowhere is this seen more clearly than in specific discussions of ontological and ethical relationships of the (post)human to nonhuman animals. Transhumanist arguments for the abolition of nonhuman suffering and for the uplift of nonhuman animals rely upon, and indeed sharpen, the ontological boundary between human and nonhuman; in this way, transhumanism becomes an example of how, as Cary Wolfe complains, "the philosophical and theoretical frameworks used by humanism … reproduce the very kind of normative subjectivity—a specific concept of the human—that grounds discrimination against nonhuman animals and the disabled in the first place."[121] In contrast, Haraway's emphasis on cyborg kinship and specific embodiments allows for an articulation of relationship between human and nonhuman that can recognize agency on both sides of the ontological divide.

### *The Abolitionist Project and "Uplifting"*

There is, perhaps surprisingly, a strong impulse within transhumanism that advocates for (post)human ethical concern for the wellbeing of all sentient life. Nick Bostrom's identification of the "core values" of transhumanism include "caring about the well-being of all sentience," and the WTA 2005 survey includes an 81 percent positive response to the question, "Does your ethical code advocate the well-being of all sentient beings, whether in artificial intellects, humans, posthumans, or non-human animals?"[122]

David Pearce's hedonistic transhumanism, for example, identifies as an explicit goal the abolition of all pain and suffering, and this universal goal includes abolishing the pain and suffering of nonhuman animals. Pearce argues that to restrict the scope of the abolitionist project to the human species is to yield to a deeply rooted anthropocentric bias, one which he hopes the "superintelligent/ superempathetic descendants" of humanity will overcome, and view the abuse (and consumption) of nonhuman animals with as much moral horror as we view human child abuse today.[123] Pearce writes, "From a notional God's-eye perspective, I'd argue that morally we should care just as much about the abuse of functionally equivalent non-human animals as we do about members of our own species— about the abuse and killing of a pig as we do about the abuse or killing of a human

---

[120] Ibid., p. xxii.

[121] Ibid., p. xvii.

[122] Hughes, "The Compatibility of Religious and Transhumanist Views of Metaphysics, Suffering, Virtue and Transcendence in an Enhanced Future."

[123] David Pearce, "The Hedonistic Imperative," The Hedonistic Imperative, www.hedweb.com/hedab.htm.

toddler."[124] Pearce's advocacy goes beyond simply the abolition of human-caused suffering, to include the abolition of what might be called, in theological terms, "natural evils" as a cause of nonhuman animal suffering: "*If* we want to, we can use depot contraception, redesign the global ecosystem, and rewrite the vertebrate genome to get rid of suffering in the rest of the natural world too."[125]

In an ethic that strangely (and surely inadvertently) echoes traditional Christian arguments for the human stewardship of creation, Pearce see posthumanity as the caretakers of the nonhuman: "For non-human animals don't need liberating; they need *looking after*. We have a duty of care, just as we do to human babies and toddlers, to the old, and the mentally handicapped."[126] Pearce's view of the relationship of the (post)human and the nonhuman is therefore one of ethical concern, but not kinship; (post)humanity exists in a separate ontological category from that of nonhuman animals. While Pearce argues passionately for an "extended circle of compassion," and takes his commitment to the abolitionist project to include the suffering of nonhuman animals, the anthropocentrism he decries remains at work in his ordering of (post)human, nonhuman relationships. This is especially evident in his proposal to unilaterally reconstruct the global ecosystem and rewrite nonhuman animal genomes to achieve the posthuman goal of the abolitionist project.

James Hughes's argument for the philosophical, legal, and moral category of "person" rather than "human" is also in part driven by this same motivation to broaden ethical consideration to include these other categories of sentience, including nonhuman animals. Yet, Hughes's personhood argument makes rationality—moreover, a certain narrow and specific philosophical notion of rationality inherited from the Enlightenment—the standard of personhood. If one attains it (human or not), then one is a person. If not (human or not), one is not a person—and not entitled to the ethical consideration extended to sentient beings. This is consistent, and Hughes should not be criticized simply for being willing to bite the bullet of philosophical consistency. Yet, there is an implicit anthropocentricism at work within this democratic transhumanist plea for non-anthropocentrism, built into the working definition of personhood.

This logic leads to a second transhumanist position regarding the relationship and ethical responsibility of (post)humans and nonhuman animals, the case for "uplifting." Unlike Pearce, whose "duty of care" is comprehensively expressed in the abolition of pain and suffering, some transhumanists argue that a (post)human ethical responsibility for nonhuman animals includes the use of enhancement technologies with the goal of enabling nonhuman animals to achieve personhood status. George

---

[124] Ibid.
[125] Ibid.
[126] Ibid. Italics original.

Dvorsky argues that the moral question of uplifting is imminent, anticipating that various emerging technologies make the process of uplifting possible.[127]

Dvorsky argues that "through the application of Rawlsian moral frameworks, and in consideration of the acknowledgment of legally recognized nonhuman persons, it can be shown that the existence of uplift biotechnologies will represent a new primary good and will thus necessitate the inclusion of highly sapient nonhumans into what has traditionally been regarded as human society."[128] Dvorsky extends Rawls's concept of original position to include the possibility of nonhuman persons; as the veil of ignorance includes psychological and physical propensities, it also, Dvorsky concludes, includes knowledge of one's species. Dvorsky suggests that uplift biotechnologies mean that "for nonhuman animals these discrepancies in abilities qualify as a deficient primary good for the attainment of fair and equal opportunity," and thus that, "considering that the reference class should contain sapient nonhumans, it is fair and reasonable to assert that they would make contingencies for the uplift of nonhumans given the availability of the technologies that would allow for such endowments."[129]

The moral mandate for uplifting, of course, faces the same issues regarding consent that Pearce's proposal to abolish suffering through the rewriting of genomes and reconstruction of ecosystems does. Dvorsky, however, attempts to address this problem, likening the problem of informed consent for uplifting to the ethical quandary of genetic modifications and the consent of the unborn or young children; consent, or non-consent, must be deduced and inferred by proxy. Here, like Pearce, human beings are cast as caretakers of nonhuman animals; indeed, in Dvorsky's analogy, a paternalistic role. In order for this analogy to work, however, Dvorsky must assume that humans can adequately ascertain and represent the desires of nonhumans. Indeed, Dvorsky writes, "Assuming that a nonhuman would participate in the original position experiment as a free and rational decision-making agent, it's not unreasonable to conclude that they would, like humans, come to the same set of principles designed to protect the interests of the entire reference class."[130] Further, Dvorsky argues that persons in the original position would consider coming into the world as a non-uplifted animal as a "worst outcome" and would therefore ensure that uplift technologies would be fairly distributed and available. Consent can therefore be presumed.

In relying so heavily on Rawls, Dvorsky makes himself vulnerable to the criticisms of Rawls and his notion of the original position; these critiques include, most significantly, the disembodiment and specific notions of rationality

---

[127] George Dvorsky, "All Together Now: Developmental and Ethical Considerations for Biologically Uplifting Nonhuman Animals," *Journal of Evolution and Technology* 18/1 (2008): p. 130.
[128] Ibid., p. 131.
[129] Ibid., p. 137.
[130] Ibid., p. 138.

and personhood assumed in the concept of the original position.[131] Dvorsky's application of Rawls repeats his anthropocentrism; in extending Rawls' reference class to include nonhuman animals, Dvorsky assumes a nonhuman animal in the original position will "participate ... as a free and rational decision-making agent." As this is the basic criterion for personhood to begin with, conceiving of nonhuman animals as participants in Rawls's thought experiment means conceiving of them as already uplifted. The argument is both anthropocentric and circular.

Aware of the countering objection that uplifting is anthropocentric, Dvorsky protests that "the goal is not to transmutate [sic] animals into humans, but to improve their quality of life by endowing them with improved modes of functioning and increased health ... Moreover, uplift is primarily advocated by transhumanists who also make the case for *Homo sapiens* to move beyond human limitations – a rather non-anthropocentric position."[132] At issue in Dvorsky's statement is what the word "anthropocentrism" means; perhaps a better term might be "transanthropocentric," as Dvorsky expresses the transhumanist conviction that remaining merely human is deficient for all concerned, human and nonhuman alike. Yet, Dvorsky's rebuttal misses the key fact that relying on specific human notions of rationality and agency, incorporated into the transhumanist definition of personhood, is demonstrably anthropocentric in a highly specific sense, in that it originated within a historical context which not only categorically excluded nonhuman animals, but many human beings as well. The presumption of the universality and ahistoricity of the notions of rationality at work in transhumanist anthropology functions as a blinder to the anthropocentrism at work in the anthropological assumptions that undergird the notion of uplifting.

The implicit anthropocentrism in expressing our ethical responsibility to nonhuman animals through uplifting them to become more rational is consistent with a transhumanist anthropology which defines the (post)human person according to the criterion of rationality.[133] Moreover, the argument for uplifting implicitly maintains a sharp ontological distinction between the human and the nonhuman animal, a boundary defined primarily through the notion of rationality. Kinship between human and nonhuman is possible, but it must be technologically mediated and produced by humans through the uplift of the nonhuman to a human standard of rationality. From this perspective, uplifting nonhuman animals is to make them our kin by making them like us; and this action implies a discontinuity between the nonhuman animal's former self and uplifted self. This, Dvorsky recognizes, without acknowledging it as problematic: "there is the issue of identity and the potential destruction of a nonhuman animal's former self ... Indeed, the

---

[131] For a helpful summary of articulations of this critique, see Kevin M. Graham, "The Political Significance of Social Identity: A Critique of Rawl's Theory of Agency," *Social Theory & Practice* 26/2 (2000).

[132] Dvorsky, "All Together Now," p. 140.

[133] Garner, "Transhumanism and the *Imago Dei*," pp. 197–8.

uplifted animal will barely resemble its former self, and will for all intents-and-purposes be a new person."[134]

Yet making nonhuman animals over "in our own image," so to speak, fails to take into account the possibility that nonhuman animals possess their own agency, by which they express their intentions and desires through their own unique competencies.[135] It is this sense of the robust agency of nonhuman animals that forms the basis for Donna Haraway's sense of kinship with other animals, a position entirely consistent with her interpretation of the cyborg's breakdown of the ontological boundary between human and animal. This appreciation of nonhuman agency first expresses itself within her epistemology, in the essay "Situated Knowledges," heavily informs her "OncoMouse," and comes to fruition in her move away from technological and cyborg themes into her more recent scholarly focus on companion species.

*Human, Nonhuman, and Posthuman Kinship*

The groundwork for Haraway's expression of epistemological and political-ethical kinship with nonhuman animals is present in her "Cyborg Manifesto," as it places the cyborg not only at the ontological boundary between organism and machine, but at the boundary of human and animal as well. This conflation between chimera and cyborg is programmatic rather than sloppy, for it highlights Haraway's ultimate goal in dismantling disembodied notions of human uniqueness that place human beings in an ontological category which simultaneously denies both animal and machine kinship.

At the conclusion of "Situated Knowledges," Haraway describes the feminist "successor science" she would like to see practiced as envisioning the natural world as the "Coyote Trickster," an active participant in the process of the construction of human scientific knowledge, rather than as the inert object of scientific discovery, or Nature as the passive resource for human exploitation. In choosing the Coyote Trickster as her metaphor, Haraway highlights the agency of the nonhumans co-opted into human scientific practice, but also describes a collective agency to the natural world: "Acknowledging the agency of the world in knowledge makes room for some unsettling possibilities, including the world's independent sense of humour. Such a sense of humour is not comfortable for humanists and others committed to the world as resource ... Perhaps our hopes for accountability, for politics, for ecofeminism, turn on revisioning the world as coding trickster with whom we must learn to converse."[136]

---

[134] Dvorsky, "All Together Now," p. 140.

[135] Noreen Herzfeld observes the same move in the drive to develop working artificial intelligence. As most transhumanists are deeply interested in the development of AI, the symmetry is intriguing and certainly not coincidental.

[136] Haraway, "Situated Knowledges," pp. 199–201.

This appreciation of nonhuman agency present in Haraway's epistemology forms the basis for the explicitly ethical move of claiming kinship with the nonhuman agents implicated in human technoscience. In OncoMouse, Haraway's focus narrows to this individual nonhuman agent incorporated into human technoscientific practice, Haraway "relocates" her own gaze to deliberately position herself to see with "murine eyes"; she claims OncoMouse as a sibling, or more properly, a sister.[137] Recognizing this kinship, not just generally but within the specific context of the laboratories of technoscientific practice, means no longer seeing lab animals as "test systems, tools, means to brainier mammals' ends, and commodities," but understanding that "these sister mammals are both us and not-us; that is why we employ them."[138] It is neither clear nor uncomplicated exactly what the role of nonhuman animals in human technoscience should be, or how it should be determined. But it is clear that to allow the matter to slide into pragmatics or simply to disappear into the invisibility of ubiquitous technoscientific practice is ethically irresponsible.

Recognizing our own animality, and recognizing the agency of nonhuman animals, is yet another negotiation of the porous and unfixed boundary between the previously rigid categories of human and animal. The logic of Haraway's original "A Cyborg Manifesto" is consistently articulated with regard to both the organic/mechanical boundary and the human/animal boundary. In this sense, Haraway's current focus on companion species is an extension of her earlier work, despite her move away from the image of the cyborg and the term "posthuman." The point seems clear: we are responsible for the ways in which we construct our relationships with these nonhuman agents, in the laboratory, in the so-called wild, in our homes.

In the same vein, Cary Wolfe frames the recently emerged discipline of "animal studies" as part of posthumanism, arguing that what makes the field of animal studies significant are the challenges it poses to the "model of subjectivity and experience drawn from the liberal justice tradition and its central concept of rights, in which ethical standing and civic inclusion are predicated on rationality, autonomy and agency."[139] This opens up, Wolfe contends, "new lines of empathy, affinity, and respect between different forms of life, both human and nonhuman," which liberal humanism cannot account for philosophically or ethically.[140]

At this point, it becomes clear that even while expressing a sense of ethical obligation and concern for nonhuman animals, the anthropology of transhumanism maintains a sharp distinction between human (and *a fortiori*, posthuman) and nonhuman animals, consistent with an emphasis on (human) rationality as the

---

[137] Haraway, "Femaleman©_Meets_Oncomouse™," pp. 52, 79.

[138] Ibid., p. 82.

[139] Wolfe, *What Is Posthumanism?*, p. 127.

[140] Ibid., pp. 127–8. Wolfe connects animal studies and disability studies in this regard, as offering the same challenge to humanist notions of the human self, and elaborates on the connection between them in a fascinating exploration of the figure of Temple Grandin (Chapter 5, "Learning from Temple Grandin").

benchmark characteristic of personhood. While it is certainly laudable to insist that preconceived notions of who can be a person and who cannot are dangerous and often tinged with overtones of racist discourse, as both Haraway and Hughes argue, the means by which Hughes and other likeminded transhumanists propose to solve the problem is simply a reinscription of the same anthropological notions that historically produced the problem. In arguing the case for rational personhood or the uplifting of animals, the logic of Western patriarchy and colonialism is, albeit unknowingly, dominant. In contrast, Haraway's insistence on the cyborg's kinship with both machine and animal leads directly to her valuation of the agency and unique competencies of nonhuman animals. Haraway, unlike the transhumanists, considers nonhuman animals already to be "persons," if one must use that word to describe creatures with whom relationship is possible and indeed evident, rather than merely "potential persons" who have yet to achieve equivalent moral status and indeed must be transformed in order to do so. The ethical question, according to Haraway, is how to construct the boundaries and relationships with nonhuman animals in ways that respect them as agents; as the transhumanist proposition to uplift animals into human rationality bypasses, even negates, the agency nonhuman animals currently possess, it is at best a confused and anthropocentric expression of ethical obligation to nonhuman animals.

Despite surface similarities, in their rejection of rigid notions of human nature and acceptance of the relevance and potency of the role of current and emerging technologies in defining our sense of the human, the two branches of this bifurcated posthuman discourse operate with different, and indeed even opposing, anthropologies. Despite James Hughes's efforts to frame Haraway's cyborg discourse as a subset of transhumanist thought, the disparate anthropological visions at work in the two discourses make this a tough sell; Haraway, for one, isn't buying it, as her explanation for her repudiation of the term posthuman in her interview with Nicholas Gane makes clear:

> I've stopped using it [posthuman] … human/posthuman is much too easily appropriated by the blissed-out, "Let's all be posthumanists and find our next teleological evolutionary stage in some kind of transhumanist technoenhancement." … The reason I go to companion species is to get away from posthumanism. Companion species is my effort to be in alliance and in tension with posthumanist projects because I think species is in question.[141]

Not only do these two posthuman discourses offer different visions of the possible posthuman future, they contain different notions of the human. This is unsurprising; posthuman discourse, after all, is a way of interrogating what it means to be human. That these two discourses offer divergent answers to what it means to be human, and what we should value in the human, shapes the specific

---

[141] Gane and Haraway, "When We Have Never Been Human, What Is to Be Done?" pp. 139–40.

posthuman visions they each offer. Turning to theological anthropology, then, the task is to enter the conversation begun in these two differing posthuman discourses with theological notions of what it means to be human and what we should value in the human, in the hope of contributing constructively in the collective task of envisioning the posthuman.

# Chapter 4
# Theological Anthropologies

The Christian tradition offers a rich, historical diversity of interpretation of the question, "what does it mean to be human?" At the very center of Christian theological anthropology is the depiction of the creation of humankind in the image of God. And, as Noreen Herzfeld comments, "as a litmus test of humanity, the image of God not only contributes to defining what it is to be human but also to determining our relationship to the nonhuman."[1] Thus any theological dialogue with the posthuman must reference this central reference point for defining the human within the Christian tradition.

Despite, however, its importance and centrality, the biblical concept of the *imago dei* remains ambiguous, prompting a long history of theological interpretation of this primary and yet stubbornly mysterious aspect of human being. This chapter begins with a brief overview of the biblical texts referring to the *imago dei*, followed by a discussion of the three major categories of interpretations within the Christian tradition (substantive, functional, and relational). This overview sets the stage for the further consideration of the concepts of human uniqueness and sinfulness within the context of the posthuman in both its cyborg and transhumanist constructions.

An overview even as brief as the one that follows makes two points readily apparent. First, the multiplicity and variety of interpretations of the *imago dei* point to a plasticity that results from the ambiguity of the biblical text and the concept itself. Second, the contemporary theological and philosophical context shapes the interpretation of the doctrine at each historical point as much as scripture and the witness of past Christian tradition. Thus, this central theological notion of the *imago dei* exists within the Christian tradition "as a set of complex theological minitheories" rather than as a univocal concept.[2]

**Plastic Images of God**

The three scriptural references to the image of God in the Old Testament occur in Genesis within the material attributed to the Priestly source: Genesis 1:26–28, 5:3, and 9:6. Herzfeld makes two observations regarding Genesis 1:26–28: first, that the creation of human beings in God's image is connected to the phrase "male and

---

[1] Noreen Herzfeld, *In Our Image: Artificial Intelligence and the Human Spirit* (Minneapolis, MN, 2002), p. 15.

[2] J. Wentzel van Huyssteen, *Alone in the World? Human Uniqueness in Science and Theology*, The Gifford Lectures (Grand Rapids, MI, 2006), pp. 313–14.

female," and second, that the image is twice connected to the idea of dominion over the other animals.[3] Genesis 5:3 connects the creation of humankind in God's likeness to Adam's fathering of a son, Seth, in Adam's likeness; Herzfeld suggests that this indicates that the divine image is inherited by Seth, and that the image is transmitted from parent to child.[4] Genesis 9:6 connects the divine image with the ethical prohibition against murder, within the context of giving human beings permission to kill and eat the flesh of other animals. Herzfeld concludes from these passages: "(1) all human beings participate in the image of God, regardless of gender or generation, (2) only human beings are created in this image, thus they are distinguished from nonhuman animals, and (3) human life is to be valued because of God's image."[5] One might label these theological affirmations as the universality, ontological uniqueness and moral status of the image of God in humanity.

J. Wentzel van Huyssteen adds another Genesis passage to the three above, Genesis 3:22, in which Adam and Eve become like God, in possessing the knowledge of good and evil.[6] This suggestive addition to the canon of Genesis *imago dei* texts raises the possibility of what van Huyssteen calls an epistemological likeness, an albeit somewhat problematic one, as this passage also, of course, describes "the fall" of humankind into sin. Van Huyssteen suggests that nothing in the biblical narrative reconciles the contradiction between the created likeness and the epistemological likeness; while the text laments this development of human history, it is the human capacity for knowledge which marks humanity as unique, and uniquely capable of relationship and knowledge of God. Even more suggestive for our posthuman context, van Huyssteen describes this new dimension of the *imago dei* as one which questions the presumed boundary between human and divine: "the ultimate focus on this thin line between the divine and human worlds finally culminates in the breaking down of the necessary boundaries between these two worlds."[7] The implications of this added layer of epistemological and moral complexity to interpretations of the *imago dei* become very significant in theological discussions of the posthuman, as the Christian doctrine of sin intersects with the question of technology as a domain of human agency.

New Testament references to the image of God are equally sparse and no less ambiguous, but add an important new and specifically Christian dimension to the concept in the interpretation of Jesus the Christ as the paradigmatic and true image of God. In adding this Christological interpretation, humanity is linked to the divine image insofar as it resides in Christ, who is the true image of God. This not only establishes Christ as a mediating figure between humanity and divinity, but introduces a progressive, moral dimension to the image of God in that

---

[3] Herzfeld, *In Our Image*, pp. 11–12. For this brief overview of the biblical texts, I follow Herzfeld's summary.
[4] Ibid., p. 12.
[5] Ibid., p. 13.
[6] van Huyssteen, *Alone in the World?*, p. 123.
[7] Ibid.

becoming "Christ-like" means perfecting the image of God within ourselves to better conformity with the true image revealed in Jesus Christ.

Though these scriptural references to the image of God do provide some important theological content, Herzfeld is correct in noting at the conclusion of her synopsis of the Old Testament material that "none of these passages defines that image."[8] No more so do the various New Testament passages define the image, despite the important addition of a Christological layer of interpretation to the doctrine. It is therefore unsurprising that Christian interpretations of scriptural references to the image of God lead in several directions.

The typology of substantive, functional, and relational interpretations of the *imago dei* within the Christian theological tradition has proven influential. Substantively, the image of God is interpreted as something that human beings possess, as a trait or property of the human being, intrinsic and unique to our shared human nature. Functional interpretations explicitly draw on the historical, cultural, and literary contexts of the Genesis scriptures, as well as linguistic analysis, to make the case that the image of God should be connected to dominion and representation of God on earth. Relational interpretations locate the image of God, not within human nature or human individual soul, or in individual or corporate action, but in the relationships that constitute the human person.

*Substantive Interpretations*

Substantive interpretations of the *imago dei*, focusing on the human capacity for rationality, have historically been the dominant category of interpretation. This is due, as F. LeRon Shults points out, to the influence of Platonic and Aristotelian philosophical categories on the early formation and articulation of Christian doctrine, including theological anthropology.[9] Substance dualism and faculty psychology, as the dominant philosophical and cultural notions of anthropology, influenced the way in which notions of the image of God and human nature were articulated in the Christian tradition. The guiding questions became, therefore, how the substance of the soul and the substance of the body were related, such that they constituted one's personal identity, and, what were the faculties of the soul, and how did they relate to each other and to the body?

Substantive interpretations of the *imago dei*, whether classical or contemporary, coincide with anthropological constructions that privilege disembodied notions of intellect, rationality, mind, or soul as the essential aspect of human nature. Augustine of Hippo adopted a Neoplatonic anthropology in which the soul and body were distinguished as separate substances, and identified the self with the substance of the soul rather than the body.[10] Augustine identifies the soul as "a

---

[8] Herzfeld, *In Our Image*, p. 13.

[9] F. LeRon Shults, *Reforming Theological Anthropology: After the Philosophical Turn to Relationality* (Grand Rapids, MI, 2003), pp. 165–74.

[10] Ibid., pp. 167–8.

certain substance, sharing in reason and suited to the task of ruling the body."[11] Shults traces Augustine's influence through Boethius's definition of the human person as "an individual substance of a rational nature," which was subsequently taken up by and defended by Thomas Aquinas in the *Summa Theologica*. Adopting Aristotle's hylomorphism, Aquinas identifies the soul as the form of human being, and body as the matter, an anthropological construction less obviously dualistic than the Platonic dualism of identifying body and soul as distinct substances; however, as Robert Pasnau observes, "when it comes to explaining the human mind (intellect and will), Aquinas has special reason for ignoring the body, inasmuch as he believes that these capacities of the soul are entirely immaterial."[12] Unlike the nutritive and sensory faculties of the soul, which human beings share in common with all forms of life and which are linked to the body, the rational powers, described in terms of intellect and will, are the immaterial aspects of the soul, which both distinguish human beings as unique among God's creation and guarantee the promise of immortality.[13]

Nor have substantive interpretations disappeared in contemporary theological anthropologies. Herzfeld writes, "Among contemporary theologians, Reinhold Niebuhr follows Augustine quite closely, finding the divine image in a reason that encompasses rationality, free will and an ability to move beyond the self that Niebuhr defines as self-transcendence."[14] While it is self-transcendence that is the quality most quintessentially and uniquely human, Herzfeld notes that Niebuhr does not define the capacity for self-transcendence as a quality separate from reason, but rather as a consequence of reason; thus while the concept of reason is itself somewhat broad, it remains the substantive content of the divine image in humanity and the source of human uniqueness.

Criticisms of the substantive approach identify the inevitable anthropological dualism it entails as one of its major weaknesses; feminists, in particular, note both the problematic historical association of femaleness with the body and maleness with the mind, and that an anthropology which associates the divine only with the mental inevitably devalues the physical dimensions of human being.[15] Further, as theologians engage in interdisciplinary dialogue with the sciences on the locus of anthropology, the immateriality of the soul, mind, and reason implied by substantive notions of human nature become more and more difficult to articulate coherently. Shults observes, "one of the major factors in the rapid decline of the use of both substance dualism and faculty psychology as plausible explanatory models has been scientific research in the field of neurobiology ... In the light

---

[11] Ibid., p. 167. Shults quotes Augustine from *On the Greatness of the Soul*, 13.22.

[12] Robert Pasnau, "Introduction," *The Treatise on Human Nature: Summa Theologicae 1a, 75-89* (Indianapolis, IN, 2002).

[13] Ibid., pp. xvi–xvii.

[14] Herzfeld, *In Our Image*, p. 17.

[15] For a classic articulation of this feminist critique see Rosemary R. Ruether, *Sexism and God-Talk: Toward a Feminist Theology* (Boston, MA, 1983).

of contemporary neuroscience a hard dichotomy between soul and body and a classification of separate faculties of the soul are no longer tenable."[16]

*Functional Interpretations*

Functional interpretations of the image of God sidestep this issue, by returning to a holistic anthropology based on the biblical text, and defining the image in terms of human action rather than human nature. Functional interpretations were introduced though Old Testament scholars, as an exegetical corrective to theological interpretations that neglected important aspects of the historical and cultural context of the scriptural passages in Genesis. Johannes Hehn first proposed that the concept of the *imago dei* should be interpreted as a royal title or designation in 1915; Gerhard von Rad extended Hehn's approach into a functional interpretation that locates the image of God in humanity's representation of God on earth. Von Rad explicitly rejected substantive interpretations of the image of God which defined it as mental or spiritual aspects of human nature, arguing that the only thing made clear in the text is the function of humanity as "God's representative, summoned to maintain and enforce God's claim to dominion over the earth."[17]

Herzfeld notes that functional interpretation remains the favored category among Old Testament scholars, for three reasons: first, it emphasizes a holistic view of human beings, rather than the dualism presupposed by substantive interpretations; second, it interprets the enigmatic concept of the image through its textual connection with the concept of dominion; third, it takes into account the historical, cultural, and literary context of the Priestly writer. It also, as Herzfeld notes, provides a starting point for the recovery of a Christian theology of responsibility for the environment, a crucial current issue.[18]

Stephen Garner goes further, stating that the functional interpretation is the dominant view generally; moreover, he contends that the functional interpretation is particularly pertinent to discussions regarding the relationship of human beings and their technologies, and asks, "does the functional interpretation of the *imago dei* in a sense demand that human beings be technological?" It may be, Garner suggests, that "playing God" is in fact in line with a functional interpretation of the *imago dei* in the context of human technologies.[19]

---

[16] Shults, *Reforming Theological Anthropology*, p. 179. See also Warren S. Brown, Nancey Murphy, and H. Newton Malony, eds, *Whatever Happened to the Soul? Scientific and Theological Portraits of Human Nature* (Minneapolis, MN, 1998), James Crabbe, ed., *From Soul to Self* (London, 1999), Gregory R. Peterson, *Minding God: Theology and the Cognitive Sciences* (Minneapolis, MN, 2003).

[17] Herzfeld, *In Our Image*, p. 22.

[18] Ibid., p. 24.

[19] Stephen Garner, "Transhumanism and the *Imago Dei*: Narratives of Apprehension and Hope" (PhD Dissertation, The University of Auckland, 2006), pp. 111–12. For a

This leads Garner to Philip Hefner's notion of human beings as "created co-creators." At the core of this interpretation of the *imago dei* is an emphasis on human agency as representative of and analogous to divine agency—a functional approach. Hefner writes that "to be created in the image of God implies that humans can be the vehicle for grace toward the creation, in a way that is somehow reminiscent of God's graciousness."[20] Human beings may serve as the vehicles of God's grace toward creation in this way because of the way in which human nature is analogous to God's nature as "free creator of meanings, one who takes action based on those meanings and is also responsible for those meanings and actions."[21]

To be a "created co-creator," however, is to be both conditioned and free, and the character of human freedom as co-creator is rooted in the conditioned character of humanity as created by God. Hefner firmly insists upon the necessity of both terms, and in particular, upon the function of the conditioned, created aspect of human being as the context of the exercise of human agency as co-creator. The freedom to co-create is "the essential character of the human," and refers to "the condition of existence in which humans unavoidably face the necessity both of making choice and constructing the stories that contextualize and hence justify those choices."[22] This decision-making freedom, exercised most dramatically within the locus of human culture, is unavoidably technological: "In technological civilization, decision-making it universal and unavoidable; it is the foundation for that civilization. Since technological civilization has altered the circumstances of living so radically, this necessity of decision-making and story-construction is intensified."[23] Yet this freedom is exercised within the context of creatureliness which emphasizes, Hefner says, belonging: "we can no longer tolerate understandings of human nature that insist on separating us from our fellow human beings, from the natural ecosystem in which we live, or from the evolutionary processes from which we have emerged." Thus, "any concept of *Homo faber*, aggressive technical operator, that overlooks these basic qualities [of receptivity and belonging] is clearly inadequate and even perverse."[24]

*Relational Interpretations*

In this emphasis on belonging within Hefner's created co-creator proposal, one can detect an appreciation of the importance of relationality in defining the human being, even as it remains a functional interpretation. Interpreting the image

---

similar perspective see Willem B. Drees, "'Playing God? Yes!': Religion in the Light of Technology," *Zygon* 37/3 (2002).

[20] Philip Hefner, *The Human Factor: Evolution, Culture, and Religion* (Minneapolis, MN, 1993), p. 238.

[21] Ibid., p. 239.

[22] Ibid., pp. 38–9.

[23] Ibid., p. 38.

[24] Ibid., p. 37.

of God as itself relational, however, rather than substantive or functional, is a significant shift, for it redefines the concept of the human person as constituted in relationship, rather than as an autonomous, independently existing individual. That is, relationship is not simply an act that one engages in, nor an innate capacity; these definitions of relationship are present in many substantive and functional interpretations of the *imago dei*. The difference, therefore, between the relational interpretation and the other categories is that relationship is constitutive, not contingent, for human being.

F. LeRon Shults argues that a philosophical "turn to relationality" has reframed the contemporary theological task, and many theologians have rearticulated core theological and anthropological insights in the Christian tradition to reflect this. Though relationality is not a new concept for Christian theology, the reciprocity between theological concepts and the philosophical and scientific ideas has obscured the nature and importance of relationality in the formation of Christian doctrine; this is, Shults writes, "one of the reasons it is important for us to understand the *philosophical* turn to relationality and its impact."[25] Beginning with Aristotle, Shults offers a brief review of the philosophical tradition of the West, highlighting Kant and Hegel as the turning points reorienting philosophical concepts away from categories of substance to categories of relation.[26] Further, Shults argues that the ontological categories of substance that informed the Christian tradition's early grappling with anthropological and Christological identity shaped the interpretation of doctrine into forms that no longer make sense after the philosophical turn to relationality. Shults therefore makes the case that substance metaphysics, as a specific contextual influence on the formation of early Christian doctrine, can and should in some instances be discarded, and that the turn to relationality actually offers "a new opportunity for presenting a Christian understanding of humanity in a way that upholds some key biblical intuitions that have sometimes been obscured or lost."[27]

A primary example of relational interpretation is the work of neo-orthodox theologian Karl Barth. According to Barth, the image of God does not consist in what human beings are (substantive) or what human beings do (functional), but in the identification of the human being as "a counterpart to God."[28] Like the functionalists, Herzfeld observes, Barth begins with textual exegesis of Genesis 1:26–27, but focuses on different portions of the text, leading to a relational rather than functional interpretation. Barth sees the plural in "let us make" as indicative of the Trinitarian nature of God, and therefore, a God whose very being is constituted by a divine relationality, an "I" that can issue a call and a "Thou" which responds. The image of God in which human beings are created, therefore, is an image of this divine relationality:

---

[25] Shults, *Reforming Theological Anthropology*, p. 11.
[26] Ibid., pp. 11–36.
[27] Ibid., p. 5.
[28] Herzfeld, *In Our Image*, p. 25.

> In God's own being and sphere there is a counterpart: a genuine but harmonious self-encounter and self-discovery; a free co-existence and co-operation; an open confrontation and reciprocity. Man is the repetition of this divine form of life; its copy and reflection. He is this first in the fact that he is the counterpart of God, the encounter and discovery in God Himself being copied and imitated in God's relation to man.[29]

Herzfeld writes, "The copy is in the relation itself, not in human capacity for relationship. Thus the *imago dei* is not a quality for Barth, nor is it held by human beings as individuals. It exists first in our relationship to God."[30] Secondarily, it exists in human relationships with each other; here, the phrase "male and female" is lifted up by Barth as programmatic for human beings in relation to one another.[31] Thus, for Barth, "a human being is only fully human insofar as he or she is in relationship with another." There is, also of course, an essential Christological dimension to Barth's relational interpretation of the *imago dei* as well, for Barth's anthropological starting point is the person of Jesus Christ, who is "true man." In Christ, humanity as it was intended to be is evident; Jesus is "man for God and God for man," an example of the relationality intended between God and human beings, and between human beings for each other.[32]

Miguel H. Díaz identifies relationality as one of the central anthropological themes picked up by U.S. Hispanic theologians, calling recognition of and existence with others "the *sine qua non* of personhood." To be human in the image of God, he writes, is to be-for-the-other, a phrase reminiscent of Barth's formulation.[33] Roberto S. Goizueta's anthropology of accompaniment, for example, places relationality at the heart of what it means to be human, and is constructed as a deliberate alternative to the prevailing concept of human persons as autonomous individuals. Goizueta writes, "For modern liberal individualism, then, the individual (or 'socially unsituated self')

---

[29] Ibid., p. 26.

[30] Ibid.

[31] The template of male and female for human relationship creates a principle of differentiation within relationship for Barth, a divine intent that human beings should be in relationship with another who is both like and unlike themselves; this, too, mirrors both divine relationship within the Trinity as well as the divine–human relationship, in which human beings are differentiated from God, both like (in that God chooses humanity as God's "counterpart"), and unlike (in that God remains wholly other to humanity). For feminist critique of this move, see Rosemary R. Ruether, "Imago Dei: Christian Tradition and Feminist Hermeneutics," in Ted. K.E. Børresen (ed.), *The Image of God: Gender Models in Judaeo-Christian Tradition* (Minneapolis, MN, 1991). Lisa P. Stephenson, "Directed, Ordered and Related: The Male and Female Interpersonal Relation in Karl Barth's Church Dogmatics," *Scottish Journal of Theology* 61/4 (2008).

[32] Herzfeld, *In Our Image*, p. 26.

[33] Miguel H. Díaz, "Theological Anthropology," in Edwin David Aponte and Miguel A. De La Torre (eds), *Handbook of Lantino/a Theologies* (St. Louis, MO, 2006).

exists prior to his or her relationships with others, which relationships the particular individual may or may not choose to enter. Relationality is thus not essential to the individual person."[34] In contrast, Goizueta argues that the human person is always *intrinsically* relational, an observation he characterizes as both biological and anthropological, noting that "the individual is, quite literally, given birth by and through the parents' relationship to each other and to the newborn."[35] Goizueta's anthropology of accompaniment, therefore, pays attention not just to the social dimension of personhood but to the importance of human embodiment as well, a theme he develops in his characterization of the human person as "sacramental" (a concept which, of course, potentially resonates with Haraway's cyborg materialism).

An important decision for theologians engaging the posthuman, therefore, is how to interpret the Christian tradition itself on the central concept of the *imago dei*. This theological decision crucially determines what shape a theological anthropology of the posthuman will take. While functional interpretations, such as Hefner's "created co-creator" proposal, have an obvious affinity for posthuman dialogue, it is a relational interpretation which will inform the constructive theological proposal of the next chapter, for reasons to be explored further there.

The ambiguity of the scriptural witness and the plurality of interpretations of the doctrine of creation in the *imago dei* make it clear that the doctrine of the *imago dei* is, for all its antiquity and centrality, a surprisingly plastic one. Van Huyssteen describes the long history of its interpretation as a "mosaic, checkered history," which has sometimes elucidated important dimensions of original scriptural texts but also, sometimes, has "soared free from the deepest intentions of these texts."[36] The lack of an explicit, concrete definition for this elusive concept leaves a wide-open playing ground, as much now as in the past, and thus interpretations of the *imago dei* typically reflect the prevailing philosophical and anthropological assumptions of the day. This very plasticity in interpretation might perhaps function as an indication to theologians that rigid notions of human nature are not, in fact, intrinsic to the theological tradition or necessary in the construction of Christian theological anthropologies. In many ways, the concept functions as a placeholder, the image of God becoming whatever it needs to be in order to articulate the theological affirmation of human uniqueness and moral worth. The related idea of human uniqueness, therefore, bears discussion in its own right as an important theological anthropological benchmark.

### Alone in the World?

The centrality of the notion of human uniqueness within the Christian tradition's articulations of theological anthropology makes the posthuman challenge to

---

[34] Roberto S. Goizueta, *Caminemos Con Jesús: Toward a Hispanic/Latino Theology of Accompaniment* (Maryknoll, NY, 1995), p. 59.
[35] Ibid., p. 50.
[36] van Huyssteen, *Alone in the World?*, p. 315.

human uniqueness seem all the more threatening. As Haraway observes, "The last beachheads of uniqueness have been polluted if not turned into amusement parks—language, tool use, social behavior, mental events, nothing really convincingly settles the separation of human and animal."[37] The very possibility of the posthuman presumes a functional and ontological similarity between humans and machines, and indeed, as Haraway defines posthuman, between humans and other animals as well. If human uniqueness must be articulated theologically as an ontological distinctiveness not shared with other creatures, it seems that faithfulness to the Christian witness must dictate a wholesale rejection of the posthuman. The presumption that human uniqueness must be articulated in this exclusive ontological manner, however, is precisely what is at issue in the posthuman.

J. Wentzel van Huyssteen's recent interdisciplinary investigation into the topic of human uniqueness demonstrates how robust notions of human uniqueness are, not only within Christian theological anthropology but within other disciplines as well. Significantly, however, van Huyssteen's task is to construct a concept of human uniqueness that takes into account the continuity of human beings with the rest of creation; van Huyssteen takes for granted that humans are wholly embedded in the natural world, and as such, should be understood as part of the material and historical evolution of the natural world. In light of this strong affirmation of continuity with the rest of creation, the theological question becomes, what kind of ontological uniqueness for humanity can be posited? It is no accident, therefore, that the title of van Huyssteen's investigation is punctuated with a question mark: *Alone in the World?*

Van Huyssteen engages the work of paleoanthropologists, archaeologists, evolutionary epistemologists, and neuroscientists as well as the long history of Christian theological reflection on the *imago dei* in constructing a theological notion of human uniqueness which intends fidelity both to the witness of Christian scripture and to the best of our human scientific knowledge of ourselves. The result is a concept of human uniqueness that does not require denial of our kinship with the rest of creation, our animality or materiality, or rely on a supernatural concept of a natural, creaturely humanity possessing something "extra." Rather, human embeddedness in material creation and continuity with nonhuman animals is presupposed, and the concept of the *imago dei* itself is interpreted as "emerging from nature itself."[38]

The key to this revision is the seriousness with which van Huyssteen takes human embodiment, which forms the locus of the overlap between theological anthropology and the various sciences. Van Huyssteen writes, "This move is validated by the significant discovery that the focus by some contemporary theologians on the radical embodied nature of our human condition stunningly

---

[37] Donna J. Haraway, "A Cyborg Manifesto: Science, Technology and Socialist-Feminism in the Late Twentieth Century," in *Simians, Cyborgs and Women: The Reinvention of Nature* (New York, 1991), p. 152.

[38] van Huyssteen, *Alone in the World?*, p. 322.

intersects with transversally converging arguments about embodied human uniqueness from evolutionary epistemology, from paleoanthropology, and from the neurosciences. In all these very diverse disciplines, embodied human existence has emerged as crucial for defining human uniqueness in the sciences, as well as for the *imago dei* in theology."[39] Human uniqueness, therefore, is located not in soul, or mind, or disembodied concepts of rationality, but in the human body itself as the source of the uniquely human, symbolic propensities which give rise to relationality with God. It is in this sense that van Huyssteen proposes to affirm both continuity with the natural world and human uniqueness. Humans are unique, not because of disembodied capacities or qualities, but because they are *uniquely embodied* within the context of other bodily creatures.

Thus, though van Huyssteen does not address the posthuman as such, the significance of humanity's unique embodiment as a central insight to his project on human uniqueness within theology and the sciences provides an entry point into discussions of the posthuman. Such a proposal also points to a potential criterion for evaluating which aspects of our unique human embodiment we may wish to carry forward in our ongoing evolution into the posthuman. Moreover, while potentially converging with constructions of the posthuman, such as Haraway's cyborg, van Huyssteen's scientifically informed theological anthropology simultaneously offers a theological counter to transhumanist constructions which ignore or seek to transcend human embodiment in the pursuit of the posthuman.

While it is true that human uniqueness has historically been interpreted as ontological discontinuity within the Christian theological tradition, proposals like van Huyssteen's demonstrate that interpretations of the biblical notion of the *imago dei* and articulations of human uniqueness need not depend upon maintaining this strict ontological divide. To presume, as theologian Brenda Brasher does, that Christianity is inherently unable to answer this particular posthuman challenge is to misunderstand the nature of the Christian tradition as monolithic and static, rather than historically conditioned, diverse, and continually dynamic. Such a presumption also overlooks the internal resources of the Christian tradition itself as the source out of which constructive theological proposals well equipped to respond to the challenge of the posthuman, such as van Huyssteen's, are faithfully articulated.[40]

An interdisciplinary theological anthropology such as van Huyssteen's, then, makes it quite clear that the challenge the posthuman represents to the theological notion of human uniqueness is, more accurately, a challenge to a certain articulation

---

[39] Ibid.

[40] Brenda E. Brasher, "Thoughts on the Status of the Cyborg: On Technological Socialization and Its Link to the Religious Function of Popular Culture," *Journal of the American Academy of Religion* 64/4 (1996). For a response, see Garner, "Transhumanism and the *Imago Dei*," p. 239. Specifically, Garner sees the notion of hybridity potentially at work specifically within perichoretic models of the Trinity, in the dual affirmation of body and soul in the Christian tradition's holistic dualism, the Chalcedonian Formula of the dual natures of Christ, and the eschatological emphasis on proleptic Christian living.

of uniqueness, one which depends upon maintaining and emphasizing the ontological boundary between human and nonhuman at the expense of recognizing ontological continuity. The theological response to this particular posthuman challenge, however, is divided; while some theologians welcome the ontological continuity with the nonhuman that the cyborg hybridity represents, others find this aspect of the cyborg threatening to the central theological affirmations of the *imago dei*.

*Limited Dominion and Ontological Disjunction*

Brent Waters, for instance, argues passionately that this posthuman challenge requires the formulation of "a counter discourse ... that is genuinely Christian and theological."[41] Defining the posthuman as an anti-human discourse, a rejection of all human limitations (biological, intellectual, and moral), Waters's Christian counter-discourse asserts the necessity of acceptance of divinely ordained natural human limits and normative location within the created order. This theological refusal of this anti-human posthuman vision rests on maintaining the ontological discontinuity of the human and the nonhuman, which here categorically includes the posthuman.

While noting that it is impossible to pinpoint a precise definition of the term posthuman, Waters uses the term to refer to "a loose confederation of writers and intellectuals who envision a day when humans will virtually merge with their technology, thereby creating a new and superior posthuman species."[42] Defining the posthuman in this way isolates two salient characteristics: 1) humans merging with technologies and 2) a new and superior posthuman species. While the first characteristic might point to either transhumanist enhancement technologies or to Haraway's notions of cyborg hybridity, the second characteristic is clearly a transhumanist aspiration. These elements of the posthuman are firmly linked in Waters's analysis; the anticipated future biotechnological merger is the means by which the human will be transcended and succeeded by the posthuman.

In defining the posthuman in this way, Waters fails to distinguish the cyborg and transhumanist constructions of the posthuman; the cyborg is treated as a subset of transhumanism. This leads Waters to interpret the merging of humans and their technologies solely within the context of the transhumanist ambition to transcend the human: "there is no real boundary separating nature and artifice, only patterns or lines of information that can be erased and redrawn; *no real limit that cannot be overcome*."[43] The repudiation of biological limitation which characterizes transhumanism is the defining characteristic of the posthuman

---

[41] Brent Waters, *From Human to Posthuman: Christian Theology and Technology in a Postmodern World* (Burlington, VT, 2006), p. ix.

[42] Ibid., p. x.

[43] Ibid. Italics mine.

for Waters, and it functions as the interpretive context for the notion of cyborg biological–technological mergers.

Making a programmatic distinction between modern and postmodern science, Waters claims that modernity was about mastery of nature, but postmodern technoscience is about its transformation. In contrast to modern science, the goal of which is "ameliorative rather than transformative," "postmodern mastery attempts to transform nature and human nature in accordance with human goals and desires."[44] At the heart of postmodern technoscience is the cybernetic vision, in which all "natures" are seen as equally artifactual and essentially malleable, subject to human manipulation. As a result, Waters sees "posthumanists" as "by necessity committed postmodernists," arguing that "to cross the postmodern divide is also to enter the posthuman terrain."[45] Posthumanism is further characterized as a direct heir of Nietzschean philosophy, as the boldest explication of the moral and intellectual implications of a postmodern, historicist ethos. The posthuman is the technological expression of the Nietzschean hope of the *Übermensch*, the result of a radically postmodern historicist rejection of teleology in either religious or secular form, aided by the advent of technologies which seek to move humanity beyond mere mastery of nature to transcendence of the wretched, finite, mortal human condition.[46]

In direct contrast to this rejection of human limitations, Waters makes the theological argument that it is "by way of their position within creation that humans learn their proper role for participating in created order, and thus the normative location that has been assigned to humankind."[47] The normative location and proper role for human beings is defined as "the creatures that God has elected to oversee the providential unfolding of God's creation," a functional interpretation of the *imago dei*, but one which qualifies dominion as "limited" and freedom as "obedient."[48] Tellingly, Waters's interpretation of limited dominion specifies that, while there is

---

[44] Ibid., pp. 47–9. Not coincidentally, this distinction parallels the distinction between restorative and enhancement technologies in the field of bioethics. Waters makes this distinction based primarily on an interpretation of intent; though he grants "it may be objected that the mastery described above inevitably alters both nature and human nature," these changes "are the results, not the goals" of modern scientific practices. In contrast, Waters sees the transformation of nature and human nature as the explicit goal of postmodern/posthuman technoscience.

[45] Ibid., pp. x, 30–1. Because Waters does not make a distinction between cyborg and transhumanist discourses, I will follow his terminology and use "posthumanists" in elucidating his argument.

[46] Ibid., pp. 23, 50. As we noted in Chapter 2, the degree of Nietzsche's influence on transhumanism is a matter of some internal and external debate, and the dominant consensus seems to be that transhumanism is better characterized as an extension of Enlightenment rational humanism.

[47] Ibid., pp. 109–10.

[48] Ibid., p. 117.

a biblical mandate authorizing humans to use "natural resources," that is, plants and animals, in their fulfillment of the command to "be fruitful and multiply" and thereby subdue the earth, there is "no mandate to exercise dominion over *oneself or other humans*."[49] Humanity is not, here, viewed in ontological continuity with the rest of creation. Rather, humanity's normative location and role places humanity, as exercisers of dominion, over and against the rest of the created order even while simultaneously existing as a part of it. Insisting upon this ontological discontinuity becomes a necessary part of the strategy for refusing to countenance the application to humanity itself the kind of mastery or transformation of nature that Waters sees as mandated in the concept of limited dominion.

That this unique ontological status is dependent upon the proper functioning of the human being, rather than proposed as an innate substantive characteristic, does not negate its definitive importance. Rather, the sense that human beings can choose, and indeed have chosen, to function otherwise leads to anxiety regarding confusion about human ontology and the possible loss of the image of God.[50] That is, when human beings cease to exercise dominion over the nonhuman, they become nonhuman themselves; to be human is to exercise dominion over the nonhuman. The *imago dei* interpreted as the act of human dominion, then, functions as a boundary which is simultaneously given and vulnerable, divinely ordained but potentially forsakeable. Fiona Coyle's research into attitudes among Christians regarding the dissolution of boundaries between human and nonhuman nature leads her to conclude: "the designated role of humans brings as stewards, caregivers and guardians of nature carries with it the responsibility of maintaining life on this planet. However, the creation of 'transgenics', 'amalgams', 'hybrids' and 'vampires' by posthuman engineering were conceived to be deviations from this role." Dominion thus conceived necessarily includes the notion of policing this ontological boundary between human and nonhuman in the form of maintaining natural limits and existing kinds without confusion.

The theological and moral imperative in Waters's argument for obedient acceptance of humanity's "normative location" within the created order is therefore also an affirmation of "natural or inherent limits or borders."[51] Waters's theological response to the posthuman not only rejects the transhumanist ambition of transcending biological limitations but embraces the ontological boundaries which Haraway, Hayles, and other feminists seek to reconfigure as part of an ironic, liberating, feminist construction of the cyborg. The ontological discontinuity presumed in Waters's interpretation of limited dominion results in an inability to recognize or accept the kinship between human, nonhuman, and posthuman that the cyborg represents. Waters's final conclusion on posthumanism is firm and unmistakeably negative. Human beings may indeed continue to pursue

---

[49] Ibid., pp. 136–42.

[50] F. Coyle, "Posthuman Geographies? Biotechnology, Nature and the Demise of the Autonomous Human Subject," *Social & Cultural Geography* 7/4 (2006): p. 516.

[51] Waters, *From Human to Posthuman*, p. 135.

the posthuman, but to do so is in itself a rejection of humanity, and therefore a rejection of God and God's intent for human creatures. Waters states this in the strongest possible terms: "The issue at stake is not that in pursuing the postmodern or posthuman projects humans may cease to be human, but that they will cease to be creatures bearing the *imago dei* in effectively rejecting their election."[52]

*At Home in TechnoNature*

Other theologians, however, have found the posthuman affirmation of ontological continuity with nonhuman creation a much needed and useful insight. The historical prevalence of the assumption of ontological discontinuity with the rest of creation in the Christian tradition prompts Anne Kull's observation that Christian theology has often been demonstrably inadequate to the task of theorizing "the complexity of the contemporary (techno)cultural and (techno)natural situation."[53] Aware of the inadequacy of inherited theological constructions which depend on the maintaining the purity and integrity of "nature" and "culture" as separate categories, Kull is equally aware that this need not define faithful Christian witness in the face of this posthuman challenge. Bringing Paul Tillich's theology of culture into conversation with Haraway's cyborg, Kull sees the implosion of nature and culture as represented by the cyborg as the contemporary "situation" to which Christian theology must faithfully respond, by beginning to "think nature and culture simultaneously, as the present circumstances seem to demand."[54]

What the cyborg most fundamentally represents, for Kull, is the fusion of the categories of "Nature" and "Culture." The breach of the particular boundaries between species, and between organism and machine, which the cyborg effects in Haraway, are generalized to signal a more abstract categorical breakdown between the larger categories of Nature and Culture. While Haraway spends relatively little time on this level of abstraction, moving quickly to the political and ethical dimensions of the cyborg, Kull correctly interprets this as a philosophical and theological implication of Haraway's cyborg, and correctly anticipates the need for theological reassessment in response to the dismantling of categories so ubiquitous in Western thought and so well-integrated into the Christian tradition. This means shifting away from theological notions of nature which imply that "nature supplies patterns, boundaries, and essences for us to respect," to notions of nature as "dynamic process," in which "there is no single form of 'the natural.'"[55] Moreover, "If human beings, human work and imagination, are part of nature in

---

[52] Ibid., p. 144.

[53] Anne Kull, "A Theology of Technonature Based on Donna Haraway and Paul Tillich" (PhD Dissertation, Lutheran School of Theology, 2000), p. 9.

[54] Ibid.

[55] Anne Kull, "Mutations of Nature, Technology, and the Western Sacred," *Zygon* 41/4 (2006): p. 791.

some significant way, technologies are a part of that nature, too ... The artificial and the natural are bound together in the coevolving technonature."[56]

Here, Kull follows the lead of Philip Hefner, whose created co-creator anthropology intentionally incorporates a cultural and technological dimension into its theological definition of the human. Kull's introduction of the cyborg amplifies this connection between nature, culture, and technology as articulated in Hefner's original created co-creator anthropology. Not only is culture technological, but nature itself is cultural and technological; subsequently, in a slim volume entitled *Technology and Human Becoming*, Hefner, too, describes these domains as imploded: "Now that we have broken down the walls that separate humans from both nature and technology, now that we are crossing the boundaries between these domains, we see that humans and their technology are a set of nature's possibilities."[57]

Confronting the posthuman challenge to human uniqueness with a complementary strategy, Elaine Graham suggests that though the posthuman may confront Western culture with "a technologically mediated 'crisis' of human uniqueness ... definitive accounts of human nature may be better arrived at not through a description of essences, but via the delineation of boundaries."[58] Graham therefore tracks the construction and deconstruction of identity boundaries through a Foucauldian strategy of a "*genealogy* of boundary-creatures" and using the resources of popular culture (science fiction), through the presentation of liminal figures as monsters, aliens, and, of course, cyborgs.[59] This strategy provides the advantage of emphasizing the plurality of visions at play within posthuman discourse, allowing Graham to engage not only with various "boundary creatures" from the representative practice of science fiction that craft our cultural notions of the human, nonhuman, and posthuman, but also to recognize the specificity of various posthuman constructions within science fiction and technoscience as well. This enables Graham to distinguish between the transhumanist constructions of the posthuman and Haraway's cyborg—one of the few Christian theologians to make such a distinction.

Despite voicing substantive criticism of Haraway as overly optimistic and anti-religious, Graham perceives ample room for dialogue with Haraway's cyborg from a religious and theological perspective. Graham, like Kull, understands "the very hybridity of human being" as an indication of human embeddedness in material creation, "a reflection of the fact that human beings have always, as it were, 'co-evolved' with their environment, tools and technologies."[60] Here, hybridity functions as a sign of embeddedness within the surrounding natural and

---

[56] Ibid.

[57] Philip Hefner, *Technology and Human Becoming* (Minneapolis, MN, 2003), p. 77.

[58] Elaine Graham, *Representations of the Post/Human: Monsters, Aliens and Others in Popular Culture* (New Brunswick, NJ, 2002), p. 11.

[59] Ibid., pp. 12–13.

[60] Elaine Graham, "In Whose Image? Representations of Technology and the 'Ends' of Humanity," *Ecotheology* 11/2 (2006): p. 177.

technological environment, a matrix which provides the meaningful context for a notion of human uniqueness.

This theological interpretation of the significance of cyborg hybridity, of course, draws on Philip Hefner's description of the embeddedness of the human created co-creator within creation, a point also taken up by Stephen Garner. Garner's explication of Hefner's created co-creator emphasizes both the relational aspects embedded within the functional interpretation of the *imago dei* as co-creatorship, as well as Hefner's use of the concept of hybridity in connecting Haraway's cyborg to his concept of created-co-creator. Hefner's anthropology affirms that human beings, having emerged from natural evolutionary processes, are embedded within the material creation and possess a biological, genetic nature as well as a cultural, creative, meaning-making nature. In this affirmation are the seeds of both Hefner's emphasis on human beings as part of the larger material universe, implying an ethical responsibility not limited to anthropocentric concerns, and his emphasis on the "dual nature" of humanity as heirs to both biological and cultural evolution. These two emphases are of course also related in Haraway's own development of the cyborg, as the hybridity of the cyborg highlights the materiality, embeddedness, and connectivity of the posthuman.

Thus, what we see in all of these theologians' engagements with the cyborg is a continuity with van Huyssteen's rearticulation of the notion of an evolved and embodied human uniqueness. Human uniqueness, in these proposals, does not disappear, but is deliberately reconfigured to take into account, not only ontological continuity with the nonhuman, but also the distinctive human capacity for technological creativity. Adding notions of the posthuman to this already rich interdisciplinary conversation on theological and scientific notions of human uniqueness gives specific attention to the importance of technological dimensions of human being, and to the question of what sort of humans or posthumans we seek to become.

The mixed reactions within Christian theology to the perceived posthuman challenge to theological notions of human uniqueness demonstrate the complexity of this interdisciplinary dialogue. The differences between Waters, Kull, and Graham on the topic of human uniqueness are traceable in part to the different constructions of the posthuman which are being addressed; while Kull and Graham respond specifically to the feminist cyborg, Waters responds to a construction of the posthuman which interprets cyborg hybridity solely within the context of transhumanist transcendence. Thus Kull and Graham embrace a notion of cyborg hybridity and kinship with the nonhuman that remains definitively at odds with Waters's advocated embrace of normative limits and natural boundaries. Finally, it is evident that theological articulations of human uniqueness and interpretations of the *imago dei* which recognize human embeddedness, continuity, and kinship with the nonhuman are not only possible but inevitable within an interdisciplinary context that takes human embodiment seriously as part of what it means to be human.

## Original, Technological Sin

Like the notion of human uniqueness, the Christian doctrine of sin deserves special consideration, particularly with regard to the way the doctrine of sin intersects with the interpretation of the *imago dei* and the notion of human nature, and dictates attitudes about technology as an expression of human nature. At this point, the notion of humanity as inherently technological, *Homo faber,* intersects with Christian theological understandings of human nature and agency. Simply put, a pessimistic view of human nature in which the doctrine of sin is dominant will produce a pessimistic view of human activity, including technologies; correspondingly, an optimistic view of human nature produces an optimism regarding human innovation and technological possibility. This issue of the nature of human agency is the critical theological and philosophical issue in theological responses to transhumanism, which, as we have seen, is unabashedly "techno-optimistic."

*Hope Without Techno-Optimism*

To take this dimension of human activity into account in our theological discussions of human agency means recognizing the necessity of interpreting technology theologically, within a context that emphasizes the ethical dimensions of human technological activity. Philip Hefner's created co-creator proposal, once again, provides the most influential articulation of a theological anthropology which intentionally incorporates an explicitly technological dimension of human being and becoming. Gerald McKenny observes, "a theologian may (as some have done) take the *hubris* found in technology as a kind of impiety, a lack of gratitude for the goodness (or simply the existence) of creation or a sinful self-assertion of a humanity unable to accept its limits and therefore bent on achieving a godlike mastery over all that is other ... Alternatively, this same rejection of the given may appear in a positive light as an expression of the *imago dei.* Precisely by not resting content with nature as it is, human beings participate in the *creatio continua*, the ongoing divine act of creation."[61] Hefner's created co-creator anthropology seeks to hold these opposing alternatives in a creative and necessary tension (in Hefner's words, a polarity, following Tillich).[62]

Much of the theological critique of Hefner's proposed anthropology, in fact, voices suspicions that emphasis wrongly falls on the co-creator element, undermining the theological implications of createdness.[63] Brent Waters's explicit rejection of Hefner's anthropology in his theological response to the posthuman

---

[61] Gerald P. McKenny, "Technologies of Desire: Theology, Ethics, and the Enhancement of Human Traits," *Theology Today* 59/1 (2002): pp. 92–3.

[62] Hefner, *The Human Factor*, pp. 36–7.

[63] See, for example, Ron Cole-Turner, *The New Genesis: Theology and the Genetic Revolution* (Louisville, KY, 1993), Celia E. Deane-Drummond, *Biology and Theology Today: Exploring the Boundaries* (London, 2001).

rests on such a conclusion. Waters finds Hefner's theology to rely on an overly generic concept of divine creativity rather than a recognizably Christian Creator God; without any clear theological content for the notion of Creator, describing humans as "created" therefore lacks theological force. This further implies, Waters charges, a "weak Christology," since any notion of Christ connected to this overly-generic notion of divine creativity can only in the end point back to the endlessly self-referential posthuman self-creator.[64]

Waters finds specific evidence of this lack of normative theological content in Hefner's definition of "created" as simply the "conditionedness of human being."[65] This, in addition to Hefner's recognition of the implosion of the categories of nature, culture, and technology, leads Waters to conclude that co-creatorship as Hefner describes it "is really the self-created creator; the being that is now transcending and directing the evolutionary processes from which it has emerged," a formulation that lacks any reference to a Creator or created context. Co-creatorship not only loses its appended adjective, created, but collapses into an endlessly self-referential self-creatorship as well, which lacks any normative moral standards for adjudicating the posthuman future.

For Waters, as we have noted, this constitutes the rejection of God's election and even endangers the *imago dei* itself; there seems to be no scenario in which the pursuit of a posthuman future might turn out to be an expression of God's will for humanity. Left to our own devices, choosing to follow our own technological and existential inclinations, in other words, will always turn out badly. Implicit in this diagnosis is a view of human agency which draws heavily on notions of the depravity of human nature.

Hefner, however, characterizes the technological dimensions of our humanness as part of God's intent for humanity to "participate in God's own work of making all things new and fulfilling the creation."[66] It is a mistake, however, to interpret Hefner's anthropology as overly sanguine or as promoting a self-directed posthuman future. Rather, Hefner characterizes the challenge of transhumanism as presenting humanity with a "numinous moment," in which we must simultaneously recognize both our call to envision the possibilities of creation's future and that our visions of the future will be flawed, "for there is no human sense of the future that can somehow escape the flaws of finiteness and sinfulness." Indeed, Hefner goes on to say, the danger is that we will, as Waters describes, "be closed around ourselves, self-directed rather than other-directed," thereby forgetting the numinous theological dimension of contemplating and constructing a posthuman future.[67]

---

[64] Waters, *From Human to Posthuman*, pp. 102–3. The specific structure of Waters's argument seems to be that both Arthur Peacocke's and Hefner's anthropologies incorporate Gordon Kaufman's "symbolic 'God' of creativity."

[65] Hefner, *The Human Factor*, p. 36, Waters, *From Human to Posthuman*, p. 102.

[66] Philip Hefner, "The Animal That Aspires to Be an Angel: The Challenge of Transhumanism," *Dialog: A Journal of Theology* 48/2 (2009): p. 166.

[67] Ibid.

To be other-directed in this way, for Hefner, means to be mindful of humanity's created status, conditionedness, and embeddedness within creation. This is the fundamental meaning of the appended adjective "created" in Hefner's created co-creator anthropology, which, from the outset, Hefner insists upon as the indispensable context for co-creatorship.[68] Unpacking the implications of createdness in terms both scientific and theological, empirically, by "created" Hefner signals the "conditionedness" of human being in the sense that human beings have emerged through a long biological and historical process of evolution, and that we are dependent upon and embedded within a complex ecological and cultural/technological environment that sustains human life. However, Hefner's definition of createdness does not stop with these observations, as Waters implies, but includes a turn to specifically theological dimensions as well.[69]

Theologically, to be created means affirming "that God is the source of all things and that God continues to undergird creation as its source." If God is the source of all things, in the sense of the Christian tradition's doctrine of *creatio ex nihilo*, then, Hefner concludes, human nature as created co-creator is God's intention, and the appropriate follow-up question is, "what is God's intention for the human being so conceived?" The answer to this fundamental question for Christians, Hefner further suggests, is found in the figure of Jesus Christ, as the definitive clue to what God intends. These two dimensions of human createdness come together for Hefner, as the intentions of God for the created co-creator are "embodied in Jesus Christ and have to do with serving and building up the creation itself and its human communities."[70] Far from humanity existing as a willfully self-directed creator, Hefner's created co-creator exists within a theological context of createdness which affirms divine purposes for humanity, and which serves "as a criterion for determining and assessing the work of the co-creator."[71]

A positive appropriation of Hefner's created co-creator proposal in response to the posthuman can be found in Stephen Garner's work. Garner regards Hefner's proposal as the most useful interpretation of the *imago dei* for engaging transhumanism, as it provides a formulation of a functional *imago dei* tied explicitly to themes of creativity and technological activity. The usefulness of this functional emphasis, explicated through co-creation, is its construction of human agency as redemptive. In contrast to transhumanist characterizations regarding human passivity as the requisite response of faith to God and divine agency, the concept of co-creation elucidates a doctrine of active and creative human initiative

---

[68] Hefner, *The Human Factor*, p. 36.

[69] Ibid. Hefner writes, "the image becomes genuinely theological when we include the assertion that humans have been created and given their place in the process by God."

[70] Hefner, "The Animal That Aspires to Be an Angel: The Challenge of Transhumanism," pp. 163–4.

[71] Hefner, *The Human Factor*, p. 37.

in the material world.[72] Indeed, "the human being as created co-creator and image-bearer is called to agency in the world."[73]

Garner sees the inevitable theological follow-up question to be, "If being technological is part of being human, as functional models of the *imago dei* assert, then the issue becomes how optimistic or pessimistic should we be about human technological agency."[74] Garner views transhumanism as "extremely optimistic" in this regard. Garner notes critiques of Hefner's anthropology as "optimistic," but concludes that Hefner's construction, as well as the modifications of it by other theologians, adequately addresses the anthropological dimension of human sin. Ultimately, Garner argues, as Hefner himself does, that emphasis must fall equally on both sides of Hefner's proposal, for an uneven emphasis on the "co-creator" aspect leads to a transhumanistic techno-optimism, while an uneven emphasis on the "created" aspect leads to a rejection of proper uses of human agency through negative perceptions of technology.[75]

Garner therefore seeks to construct a *via media* between the techno-optimism of the transhumanists and a technophobic pessimism that negates the redemptive possibilities of human agency. Garner argues that his functional interpretation of the *imago dei* offers insight into how human agency is properly put into practice, "in a medium that highlights human finitude and dependence," incorporating the themes of representation of God, embodiment, solidarity, and interconnectedness with the natural world.[76] What this means, pragmatically, is a mandate for careful ethical consideration of our creation and use of specific technologies. Determination of what constitutes "appropriate technology" is necessary, as well as an appreciation of the moral imperative of beneficence, and awareness of social justice and risk.[77]

The theological issue of human agency is also front and center in Ted Peters's engagement with transhumanism. In his 2006 *Anticipating Omega*, Peters defines transhumanism as "a vision of a posthuman future characterized by a merging of humanity with technology as the next stage of our human evolution."[78] Though the form of the posthuman Peters engages is specifically transhumanism, like Waters he seems to conflate the posthuman construction of the cyborg with the posthuman constructions of the transhumanists, seeing no difference in the

---

[72] Garner, "Transhumanism and the *Imago Dei*," p. 188.
[73] Ibid., p. 244.
[74] Ibid., p. 245.
[75] Ibid., pp. 257–8.
[76] Ibid., p. 259.
[77] Ibid., pp. 245–6. Here, Garner references Ian Barbour's definition of "appropriate technology" as "creative technology that is economically productive, ecologically sound, socially just, and personally fulfilling." Ian Barbour, *Ethics in an Age of Technology: The Gifford Lectures 1989–1991*, vol. 2 (San Francisco, CA, 1993), p. 25. Garner follows Ted Peters's argument for beneficence as a primary motivation for technology.
[78] Ted Peters, *Anticipating Omega: Science, Faith and Our Ultimate Future* (Göttingen, 2006), p. 110.

"merging of technologies" proposed in these discourses.[79] However, unlike Waters, Peters is less concerned with the ontological issue of the potential merger of humanity and technology than with the teleology implicit in the transhumanist conviction that the posthuman is the necessary and inevitable next stage of human evolutionary progress.

Judging transhumanism to be "theologically and ethically misdirected," Peters contends that the transhumanist vision of the future fails to distinguish "what belongs in the domain of science from what belongs in the domain of divine promise."[80] Though Peters willingly recognizes the role of scientific and technological achievement in human efforts to contribute to human flourishing, Peters makes a distinction between these proleptic human efforts and the full transformation of the Christian eschaton. The full theological reasoning behind this distinction is that the techno-optimism inherent to transhumanism indicates a naïveté regarding human nature that ignores the doctrine of sin.

Unlike Brent Waters, who interprets transhumanism (and posthuman thought more generally) as quintessentially postmodern and Nietzschean, Peters interprets transhumanism as a continuation of Enlightenment belief in progress. Making a distinction between two types of futurist thinking, *futurum*, a belief in growth or progress, and *adventus*, anticipation of the new, Peters argues that transhumanism fits the first of these types, while Christian eschatology fits the second.[81] Peters sums up the difference: "Whereas *futurum* provides an image of the future that can result from present trends, *adventus* provides a vision of the future that only God can make happen."[82] Transhumanism, with its basic contention that human technologies—current, emerging, and future—are the mechanisms by which human beings will transcend biological limitation, is an example of *futurum*. Peters writes, "New and startling things await us in the future, but the way from here to there is growth, technological advance. Human and posthuman flourishing

---

[79] Ibid., p. 111. Peters does not refer to Haraway directly, but quotes Anne Kull's theological work on the cyborg, clearly placing it in a context of transhumanism. As a result, Peters deliberately turns aside from the major theological insights of hybridity and connectedness gleaned from Kull's engagement with Haraway and the cyborg.

[80] Peters, *Anticipating Omega*, 124.

[81] Here, Peters disagrees with the position of Robert M. Geraci in identifying the AI movement as apocalyptic (*adventus*); see Robert M. Geraci, "Apocalyptic A.I: Religion and the Promise of Artificial Intelligence," *Journal of the American Academy of Religion* 76/1 (2008). The same eschatological distinction has been made by Janet M. Soskice, "The Ends of Man and the Future of God," in John Polkinghorne and Michael Welker (eds), *The End of the World and the Ends of God* (Harrisburg, PA, 2000).

[82] Ted Peters, "Transhumanism and the Posthuman Future: Will Technological Progress Get Us There?" *The Global Spiral* 9/3 (2008), http://metanexus.net/magazine/tabid/68/id/10546/Default.aspx.

will be the result of step by step advances. This understanding of the posthuman future depends on a related concept, namely, progress."[83]

Peters regards transhumanist reliance on Enlightenment notions of cultural and scientific progress as evidence of an anthropological naïveté, an uncritical confidence in the goodness of human agency which, from a Christian theological point of view, is unwarranted and potentially dangerous. Turning to the Christian realism of Reinhold Niebuhr and Langdon Gilkey, Peters offers a theological critique of the modern notion of progress, centered on the ambiguity inherent in human endeavor and historical processes. Niebuhr writes, "The 'idea of progress,' the most characteristic and firmly held article in the *credo* of modern man, is the inevitable philosophy of history emerging from the Renaissance. This result was achieved by combining the classical confidence in man with the Biblical confidence in the meaningfulness of history."[84] Significantly, however, the idea of progress "did not recognize that history is filled with endless possibilities of good and evil ... It did not recognize that every new human potency may be an instrument of chaos as well as of order; and that history, therefore, has no solution of its own problem."[85]

As Peters puts it, "transhumanist assumptions regarding progress are naive, because they fail to operate with an anthropology that is realistic regarding the human proclivity to turn good into evil."[86] While acknowledging the efforts of some transhumanists to address the possible catastrophic risks that may accompany human technological advancement, Peters contends that the techno-optimism inherent to transhumanism indicates an insufficient appreciation of the propensity for evil within human nature: "What we see in transhumanism is a vague awareness of this ever lurking threat; but is it being taken with sufficient seriousness?"[87]

---

[83] Ibid.

[84] Reinhold Niebuhr, *The Nature and Destiny of Man*, 2 vols, vol. 2 (New York, 1941–2), p. 240.

[85] Ibid., pp. 154–5.

[86] Peters, "Transhumanism and the Posthuman Future."

[87] Ibid. Russell Blackford's response to this question is, yes: transhumanists "often devote much of their energy to identifying risks and considering ways to reduce them," citing specifically Nick Bostrom's work (see Nick Bostrom, "Existential Risks: Analyzing Human Extinction Scenarios and Related Hazards," *Journal of Evolution and Technology* 9/1 (2002)). Blackford also rejects what he sees as unrealistic pessimism: "If destructiveness, malevolence, spiteful glee in others' discomfort, and so on are asserted by Peters to be hallmarks of human nature—in the sense that humans are always, or typically, like that—then he is just wrong. He is operating with a philosophical anthropology that is unrealistically blind to the strong human propensities for sympathy, cooperation, and compromise." Moreover, Blackford argues, it is wrong to characterize all self-interested human action as "sin," as "people who are motivated by self-interest can still flourish side by side in reasonable and mutually-productive cooperation." Russell Blackford, "Trite Truths About Technology: A Reply to Ted Peters," *The Global Spiral* 9/9 (2009), www.metanexus.net/magazine/tabid/68/id/10681/Default.aspx.

Peters's critique of transhumanist notions of progress relies upon a theological anthropology in which "a sinner in need of divine grace is the starting point."[88] This starting point leads to an anthropology in which human moral agency is seen as deeply and inevitably compromised; human technologies, as an expression of human agency, are therefore equally deeply and inevitably compromised. Thus Peters's conclusion is that human technological advancements may augment human intelligence but cannot change basic human nature and its propensity to turn good into evil. As sinners, Peters writes, "we are unable to transform ourselves. Only God can deliver us."[89]

This theological conclusion, consistent with Peters's anthropological starting point, necessitates a decisive rejection of the techno-optimism of transhumanism, in which human agency and the possibilities of *futurum* are seen as sufficient, and awaiting the eschatological fulfillment of divine agency in *adventus* is at best unnecessary, and at worst, delusional. Peters's critique of transhumanism, therefore, resting as it does on a pessimistic anthropology, plays into, albeit unintentionally, the caricatures of religious faith current in transhumanist thought: while transhumanists bravely forge ahead with the Promethean task of making a better world through human innovation and creativity in technology, the religious faithful will sit passively and wait for God to deliver them, belittling their own capabilities. Despite Peters's own technophilic tendency, and his conclusion that "a Christian theologian can only encourage continued scientific research into genetics and nanotechnology when the goals are improved human health and well-being," the theological emphasis on the doctrine of sin remains the final judgment on the techno-optimism of transhumanism.

*The Ambivalent Cyborg*

It seems safe to conclude, then, that there exists a theological consensus that transhumanist visions of the posthuman future are deeply flawed in their assumptions regarding human agency, both in terms of its effective scope and its basic character. Though the theologians discussed above do have significant internal disagreements, the judgment on transhumanist techno-optimism is surprisingly univocal, and univocally negative. But what, if any, is the theological diagnosis of the cyborg posthuman vision on the matter of human agency?

Anne Kull's engagement with the cyborg, restricted to the philosophical categories of Nature and Culture and the implications of their implosion for the Christian tradition, only lightly addresses the matter of human agency. Elaine Graham, however, perceives in Haraway a level of techno-optimism which she finds problematic, for much the same reasons that Hefner, Garner, and Peters find transhumanism so troubling. Graham argues that Haraway's reinvention of the cyborg underestimates "the enduring power of the *Terminator-Robocop*-style omnipotent

---

[88] Peters, "Transhumanism and the Posthuman Future."
[89] Ibid.

killing machine of science fiction."[90] Given Michelle Bastian's contention that the political, ethical, feminist dimensions of Haraway's "coalition cyborg" are precisely those characteristics which have been discarded, leaving only the "technoborg," Graham's critique may indeed be well-placed.[91] Yet Haraway herself is demonstrably aware of the cyborg's compromised origins as the militarized "man in space," which suggests that Graham's critique may not apply so much to Haraway as a thinker, as to a deficient reception and interpretation of her cyborg writing. In fact, as Joseph Schneider comments, "the militarist, space-race, reductionist, and control-focused apocalyptic visions from which the cyborg emerged can't and shouldn't be separated from it, in Haraway's view."[92] Without this specific historical context, the cyborg cannot function as an ironic or subversive hopeful figure; therefore, far from being techno-optimistic, a deliberate ambivalence regarding the possibilities of human technology is necessary to Haraway's cyborg vision.

Such an ambivalence easily resonates with the dual message of the Christian tradition regarding human agency. Philip Hefner's contention that we must approach the challenge of constructing the posthuman future in the full recognition of ourselves as both saints and sinners captures this duality. We cannot, and should not, shrink from or deny our existence as created co-creators called to participate in the construction of the future; but neither can we forget that this is a fraught enterprise, not least because our visions of the future are limited, partial, and altogether too often narrowly self-serving and sinful.

This brings us back to Wentzel van Huyssteen's interpretation of Genesis 3:22 as offering an additional notion to the *imago dei* as an "epistemological likeness," one which is ambivalent in its description of humanity of becoming, in one act, both like God in the knowledge of good and evil, and fallen. Human moral self-awareness, the recognition of both good and evil within ourselves, is at the heart of what it means to be created in the *imago dei*, and it marks the unique nature of human agency within God's creation. Technological triumphalism is as unwarranted as technophobic despair.

In the next chapter, the insights of these various theological engagements with the posthuman, both positive and negative, will form the basis for taking up the task of constructing a posthuman theological anthropology, one which emphasizes the importance of hybridity as a concept which brings together the themes of embodiment and kinship. The concept of hybridity provides the transversal connection between posthuman and theological discourses, as it functions not only as the key concept for the cyborg, but as a central insight in feminist, queer, disability, and postcolonial theologies. These transversal connections provide a substantive answer to the "so what" question: what difference does the cyborg make for Christian theology?

---

[90] Graham, *Representations of the Post/Human*, p. 228.

[91] Michelle Bastian, "Haraway's Lost Cyborg and the Possibilities of Transversalism," *Signs: Journal of Women in Culture & Society* 31/4 (2006).

[92] Joseph Schneider, *Donna Haraway: Live Theory* (New York, 2005), p. 62.

# Chapter 5
# Constructing a Theological Post-Anthropology

Before dialoguing with the posthuman, theologians must first determine which form of the posthuman to engage. In Chapter 3, I argued at length that the transhumanist posthuman vision and the cyborg vision of feminist Donna Haraway are not only different, but competing, posthuman constructions, with differing anthropological assumptions. In Chapter 4, the responses of various theologians to the posthuman challenges to theological anthropology, specifically with regard to notions of human uniqueness and moral agency, evidence various theological commitments and concerns as well as various forms of the posthuman currently at play, and implicitly demonstrate the importance of recognizing the complexity of the posthuman discourse and the differences between the cyborg and transhumanist posthuman visions.

This brings us to an important point, which I hope will contribute to the ongoing theology and posthuman encounter in terms of clarification of the conceptual terrain. Failure to distinguish between the posthuman visions of the feminist cyborg and the transhumanist upload leads ultimately to both a mischaracterization of transhumanism and to a loss of the ethical, political, feminist aspects of Haraway's cyborg. In many instances Haraway's work is either ignored, or characterized as a subset of transhumanist discourse. The latter poses two distinct but related problems: first, it implies a misinterpretation of Haraway's cyborg; second, it attributes cyborg attitudes to transhumanism, which I have argued are actually antithetical to transhumanist anthropology. Choosing which form of the posthuman to theologically engage means, first, that we must more adequately interpret posthuman discourses to begin with.

In Brent Waters's response to the posthuman, both of these related problems are evident. Seeing posthumanism as the conjunction of a radical postmodernism with the "cybernetic vision" that treats material reality as endlessly reconfigurable informational pattern, Waters conflates the transhumanist and the cyborg visions into a single Nietzschean vision of unlimited will-to-power through biotechnological merger. In interpreting the posthuman as a radically postmodern, Nietzschean development, Waters overlooks almost entirely the transhumanists' Enlightenment philosophical heritage and ascription to narratives of scientific objectivism, and historical and evolutionary progress, and the way in which the transhumanist upload is simply the Enlightenment human writ large (humanity, plus).[1]

---

[1] Though Waters acknowledges that in identifying the essence of human identity with the mind transhumanism "is informed by the humanistic and liberal traditions with their

In addition, and no less significantly, Waters overlooks Haraway's insistence on forging a middle way between the radical postmodernism Waters mistakenly ascribes to all posthumanism, and the Enlightenment objectivism of the transhumanists. In fact, Haraway is only referenced once by Waters, emphasizing only her use of the cybernetic vision in the image of the cyborg: "Moreover to perceive the world in terms of underlying information is already to think and perceive oneself as a cyborg."[2] This says nothing at all about the significance of the cyborg in its feminist, political, or ethical dimensions, and is thus another example of what Michelle Bastian terms "the lost cyborg."[3] Presuming that Haraway represents only a subset of transhumanist discourse necessarily obscures these dimensions of the cyborg which resist the transhumanist posthuman and focuses solely on the broad, abstract, ontological level at which they only superficially agree in their rejection of rigid notions of human nature. This means, further, missing that the salient reasons for objecting to notions of human nature are substantially different, as Haraway is rejecting precisely the anthropological notions of the Enlightenment that transhumanism seeks to expand.

Stephen Garner offers a more nuanced treatment of the posthuman, identifying transhumanism as one representative of a "broad spectrum of ideas about human development in light of potential technological advances," and further, distinguishing between the libertarian orientation of the extropians and the social democratic emphasis of the democratic transhumanists, and positing more than one working anthropology within the broad movement of transhumanism.[4] Garner analyzes the tension between the materialistic and dualistic anthropological orientations simultaneously present in the movement as particular anthropological biases within different strands of transhumanism, depending upon which technologies serve as the focal point: "artificial intelligence asserts a materialistic anthropology, while virtual reality is more Cartesian in emphasis and asserts the primacy of the mind."[5]

However, while criticizing the unreconciled tension between the materialistic and dualistic emphases in transhumanist anthropology is apt, Garner overstates the case for a "materialistic anthropology" within transhumanism, not least because he conflates the Haraway cyborg with transhumanism. Garner places Haraway's

---

emphases on autonomy and freedom," he contends that "transhumanism takes a postmodern turn away from its humanistic and liberal forebears by insisting that no fate can be loved other than one that is self-created" (Brent Waters, *From Human to Posthuman: Christian Theology and Technology in a Postmodern World* (Burlington, VT, 2006), pp. 50, 51).

[2] Ibid.

[3] Michelle Bastian, "Haraway's Lost Cyborg and the Possibilities of Transversalism," *Signs: Journal of Women in Culture & Society* 31/4 (2006).

[4] Stephen Garner, "Transhumanism and the *Imago Dei*: Narratives of Apprehension and Hope" (PhD Dissertation, The University of Auckland, 2006), pp. 35–7.

[5] Ibid., p. 32. This construal ignores that it is transhumanist AI experts who are also most often the most visible public proponents of notions of the Singularity and uploading.

cyborg figure within the context of transhumanist AI, despite Haraway's explicit distancing of herself from transhumanism.[6] Garner similarly describes N. Katherine Hayles as promoting a "kinder, gentler transhumanism," despite Hayles's characterization of her critical relationship to transhumanism as "like a relationship with an obsessive and very neurotic lover. Knowing it is deeply flawed, I have tried several times to break off my engagement … I naively thought that I had dismissed it once and for all, exposing its misapprehensions to my satisfaction and delivering a decisive blow to its aspirations."[7]

As a result of reading the cyborg as part of transhumanist AI, Garner not only sees a greater emphasis on materialism in transhumanism than actually exists, but also attributes the boundary-transgressive aspects of Haraway's cyborg to the transhumanist vision, writing, "At the heart of the transhumanist vision is this potential to reshape the world, including human beings, in such a way as to fuse or ignore traditional categories that are used to order the world. The barriers between human and non-human, organic and inorganic, natural and synthetic, creature and machine cease to exist, creating a situation where the frameworks ordinarily used to make sense of the world become stressed or impotent."[8] It is Haraway's cyborg which emphasizes the permeability and flexibility of ontological boundaries, whereas transhumanism actually maintains sharp ontological distinctions even within its proposals to augment and enhance human beings technologically. The end result of interpreting Haraway, and also N. Katherine Hayles, within the umbrella of the transhumanist movement—despite their explicit and vocal criticisms of transhumanism—is, again, not simply a misread of their own distinct constructions of the posthuman but a misreading of transhumanism as well.

As theologians continue to engage the posthuman, it will become increasingly important not to make this mistake. Particularly as Garner identifies the cyborg as the "hopeful posthuman," the importance of accurately attributing these hopeful aspects to Haraway's posthuman discourse and not to transhumanism is underscored.[9] Presuming that transhumanism possesses the potentially hopeful, liberating aspects of the cyborg, when it actually does not, carries consequences for

---

[6] Ibid., pp. 64, 67. Haraway explicitly distances herself from transhumanism in a 2006 interview: "human/posthuman is much too easily appropriated by the blissed-out, 'Let's all be posthumanists and find our next teleological evolutionary stage in some kind of transhumanist technoenhancement.' Posthumanism is too easily appropriated to those kinds of projects for my taste. Lots of people doing posthumanist thinking, though, don't do it that way. The reason I go to companion species is to get away from posthumanism." N. Gane and D. Haraway, "When We Have Never Been Human, What Is to Be Done? Interview with Donna Haraway," *Theory Culture & Society* 23/7–8 (2006): p. 140.

[7] N.K. Hayles, "Wrestling with Transhumanism," *The Global Spiral* 9/3 (2008): p. 1.

[8] Garner, "Transhumanism and the *Imago Dei*," p. 37.

[9] Ibid., pp. 236–59, Stephen Garner, "The Hopeful Cyborg," in Ron Cole-Turner (ed.), *Transhumanism and Transcendence: Christian Hope in an Age of Technological Enhancement* (Washington, DC, 2011).

the wider social engagement of posthuman issues far beyond academic nitpicking over accuracy of interpretations within interdisciplinary engagements; at stake, as Haraway consistently reminds us, is the possibility of constructing liveable worlds, for everyone.

**The Hopeful Cyborg**

Bearing this in mind, this chapter specifically engages Haraway's cyborg as the positive construction of the posthuman, one which resonates with, and can serve as a prompt to recover, useful concepts present (even if historically marginalized) within the Christian tradition. Among those who see a positive potential in theologically engaging the posthuman, there is indeed a firm consensus emerging regarding the cyborg as the "hopeful posthuman" (Hefner, Kull, Graham, and Garner). Having argued, as well, that the cyborg and transhumanist upload visions of posthumanity are in significant ways opposed to each other, naming the cyborg as the hopeful posthuman also means firmly rejecting transhumanism.

Here, the emerging theological consensus is not simply firm, but practically unanimous: transhumanism as it is currently articulated invites multiple theological and ethical critiques from a Christian perspective. In addition to the critique set forth in the previous chapter on transhumanism's techno-optimism as anthropologically naïve, Ted Peters's initial theological appraisal of transhumanism concludes that transhumanism can be dismissed because "it is scientifically and philosophically unrealistic as well as theologically and ethically misdirected."[10] Peters's assessment of transhumanism as "scientifically and philosophically unrealistic" centers on issues of embodiment and personal identity, especially as represented in the transhumanist upload scenario. Peters, much like N. Katherine Hayles, makes the case that transhumanist anthropology identifies personhood with a disembodied intellect as an informational pattern. This is scientifically problematic, because, as discussed in Chapter 3, the upload scenario simultaneously presupposes a reductionistic materialism and an anthropological dualism. Peters writes: "The science of the brain and the technology of the brain, curiously, are dysfunctional. They are contradictory, at least in part. The tendency in the science is toward reductionism, toward reducing our minds and our souls to biological activity. The contrary tendency in transhumanist technology is to view the mind or soul as immaterial, as something that can become dis-embodied and re-embodied. The first tends toward a substance monism or materialism, the second toward a substance dualism."[11] And, like Hayles, Peters argues that the anthropological assumptions undergirding this view of personhood are untenable philosophically and scientifically, as the role of embodiment in the development

---

[10] Ted Peters, *Anticipating Omega: Science, Faith and Our Ultimate Future* (Göttingen, 2006), p. 125.

[11] Ibid., pp. 130–1.

of intelligence is seen to be fundamental, in the neurosciences as well as AI research. The dualism Peters identifies in transhumanist anthropology is therefore interpreted as an ideological departure from prevailing scientific assumptions of reductionistic materialism.

Theologically, Peters argues that the Christian tradition has recently reaffirmed the importance and goodness of embodied human existence, rejecting substance dualism, resulting in "a contemporary Christian anthropology that celebrates our physical nature and emphasizes a relational and integrated understanding of human selfhood and personhood."[12] Peters expands upon this point in the second of his two chapters on transhumanism, arguing that this is the result of both external and internal pressures on Christian anthropology and the doctrine of the soul. Externally, advances in the neurosciences demonstrate that mental abilities do not require the existence of a supernatural soul; internally, theologians not only have internalized the discourses of philosophers of religion on the mind–body problem but have retrieved the positive biblical valuing of the body.[13] In moving away from classical substance dualism, contemporary Christian anthropologies emphasizing the importance of embodiment offer a distinctively theological objection to the disembodied anthropology enshrined in the transhumanist upload scenario.

Elaine Graham's articulation of this theological critique is unpacked as an analysis of transhumanism as a discourse of transcendence. Transhumanism's explicit ambition "to overcome some of our basic biological limits" is interpreted by Graham as a desire "for *transcendence* of the flesh as an innate and universal trait, a drive to overcome physical and material reality and strive toward omnipotence, omniscience and immortality."[14] Thus, following Ed Regis's early assessment of the movement, Graham suggests that despite the transhumanists' claim of continuity with secular Enlightenment principles, transhumanism is as much a metaphysical system as it is a scientific outlook.[15]

Such a characterization is, of course, likely to raise the ire of transhumanists who regard their worldview as simply the result of a hardheaded appraisal of scientific truths regarding human nature and technological capabilities; Bostrom, for instance, regards this desire for transcendence of biological limits as simply the logical extension of secular humanism: "Transhumanism has roots in secular humanist thinking, yet is more radical in that it promotes not only traditional means of improving human nature, such as education and cultural refinement, but also direct application of medicine and technology to overcome some of our basic biological

---

[12] Ibid., pp. 119–20.

[13] Ibid., p. 130.

[14] Elaine Graham, *Representations of the Post/Human: Monsters, Aliens and Others in Popular Culture* (New Brunswick, NJ, 2002), p. 165.

[15] Ibid. Ed Regis, *Great Mambo Chicken and the Transhuman Condition: Science Slightly over the Edge* (New York, 1990).

limits."[16] Graham too acknowledges the overtly secular nature of transhumanist discourse, characterizing it as a "secular narrative of salvation through technology," descended from "unalloyed faith in the primacy of the Enlightenment subject—rational, autonomous, self-determining."[17] Thus what is at issue is whether the concept of transcendence is itself an inherently metaphysical, spiritual, or religious concept, whether it appears in the context of explicitly religious discourse or in the secular context of transhumanism. Graham argues that both critics and proponents of technological transcendence recognize it as such.[18]

For Graham, however, the significance of the appeal to transcendence is not so much that it reveals transhumanism as covertly metaphysical, though perhaps it does, as it conceals the value judgments involved in the construction of the transhumanist vision of the posthuman. Graham builds on the work of David Noble and Grace Jantzen to demonstrate that the particular construction of the concept of transcendence at work in transhumanism parallels what Jantzen calls the "necrophilic" preoccupation of Western religion, valorizing immortality and fear of death and constructing theologies of omniscience, omnipotence, and immateriality. This "imaginary of death" contrasts sharply with an "imaginary of natality," which emphasizes materiality, embodiment, birth, and interdependence.[19] Graham judges that the appeal to transcendence of biological limits, which is so central to transhumanism, "betrays not so much a love of life as, paradoxically, a pathological fear of death, vulnerability and finitude."[20]

Further, Graham argues that transhumanism, in particular extropian and libertarian articulations of transhumanism, is politically and ethically deficient in its vision of technological advancement for humanity as a whole. Graham's ethical critique centers on her distrust of the extropian assumption that social issues such as sexism, racism, and poverty will simply work themselves out as technology enables improvements to the human condition. Such an attitude is exemplified in Simon Young's casual remarks in his transhumanist manifesto: "Yes, initially some people more than others will be able to afford bioenhancement beyond the level of 'normal' good health. It's called living in the free world."[21] Graham argues that such attitudes can only serve to perpetuate an already demonstrably unequal global economy, in which the current techno-elite may enhance their status at the expense of a cyber-underclass: "The dream of transhumanism depends for its fulfillment on the ability to have access to the appropriate resources. To privileged first-world citizens, the digital and biotechnological developments bring with them an expansion of

---

[16] Nick Bostrom, "Transhumanist Values," World Transhumanist Association (Humanity+), http://transhumanism.org/index.php/WTA/more/transhumanist-values/.

[17] Graham, *Representations of the Post/Human*, p. 159.

[18] Ibid., p. 174.

[19] Ibid., pp. 171–3.

[20] Ibid., p. 230.

[21] Simon Young, *Designer Evolution: A Transhumanist Manifesto* (Amherst, NY, 2006), p. 63.

selfhood beyond the limits imposed by bodies and minds. To those unable to participate, however, it means further exclusion, compounded by the possibility that due to globalisation, the wealth of Western cyborgs rests on the cheap labour of their third-world sweatshop fellows."[22] This critique shares obvious affinities with Haraway's critique of Western technoscience, and her insistence on placing the question, *Cui bono?*, at the center of a re-envisioned technoscientific practice; who it is that gets included in the "humanity" that is destined for "posthumanity" cannot simply be taken for granted.

Both Peters's and Graham's assessments of the deficiencies of transhumanism point toward corresponding strengths in the cyborg posthuman vision, as a relational, embodied, and hybrid vision. Graham, as we have seen, interprets Haraway's cyborg vision as potentially over-optimistic; she also perceives Haraway's anti-religious stance as problematic, arguing that Haraway "undervalues a post-secular critique of her particular brand of Marxist-feminism."[23] Nonetheless, despite her critiques, it is clear that Graham receives the cyborg as a positive vision of the posthuman, one which highlights the political and ethical concerns of human and nonhuman wellbeing. Graham ultimately reads the cyborg as "a heuristic figure that suggests the rejection of solutions of either denial or mastery in favour of a post/human ethic grounded in complicity with, not mastery over, non-human nature, animals and machines."[24] Theologically and ethically, then, the cyborg teaches us that "we cannot afford to be afraid of our complicity with technologies, or fear our hybridity, or assume that proper knowledge and access to God can only come through a withdrawal from these activities of world-building."[25]

This echoes, of course, Anne Kull's theological conclusions regarding the usefulness of the cyborg in reconfiguring our notions of Nature into technonature/culture and reworking our notions of ontological relationship through cyborg hybridity, and anticipates Stephen Garner's identification of the cyborg as the "hopeful posthuman." The cyborg's hybridity has been well thematized by these

---

[22] Elaine Graham, "'Nietzsche Gets a Modem': Transhumanism and the Technological Sublime," *Literature & Theology* 16/1 (2002): pp. 69–70. Graham contrasts the technophilic visions of Ray Kurzweil and Michio Kaku with the United Nations Human Development Program (UNHDP) goals: "In contrast to the prospect of smart houses, microprocessors, and gene therapies, the UNHDP has set various targets for global development by 2015: goals to combat illiteracy, reduce child mortality, eradicate poverty and to promote primary health care. While the readers of *Scientific American* can look forward to smart jewelry ... the technologically rudimentary ambition of furnishing every man, woman and child on the planet with clean water goes unnoticed" (p. 71). Cf. Brenda E. Brasher, "Thoughts on the Status of the Cyborg: On Technological Socialization and Its Link to the Religious Function of Popular Culture," *Journal of the American Academy of Religion* 64/4 (1996): p. 817.

[23] Graham, *Representations of the Post/Human*, p. 228.

[24] Ibid., p. 229.

[25] Elaine Graham, "In Whose Image? Representations of Technology and the 'Ends' of Humanity," *Ecotheology* 11/2 (2006): pp. 179–80.

theologians as indicative of a technonatural, interconnected, embodied anthropology. Graham's theological application of the cyborg is a broad appeal connecting the hybridity of the cyborg to a theology of sacramentality that joins the spiritual and material. Likewise, Garner's exploration of theological hybridities focuses on the material and spiritual, and the divine and the human, and Kull's explorations focus on the metacategories of nature and culture. The theological conclusions generated by these theologians' appreciation of the cyborg's embeddedness within material creation are significant, and provide a foundation for an ethics of relationship that is radically inclusive, positing as it does hybrid kinship with both the "natural" and the "technological" creatures we inhabit the world with. These theological engagements with the cyborg, therefore, turn to the ecotheological implications of the cyborg's hybridity, materiality, and interconnectedness.[26] These explorations carry theological anthropological implications with regard to notions of human uniqueness, but the implications of hybridity stop with the recognition that theological notions of uniqueness can and must be restructured.

Thus, systematic theological work on the ways in which a cyborg anthropology restructures notions of human subjectivity and relationality, particularly within the context of Christian theological anthropologies which employ relational interpretations of the *imago dei*, remains to be done. This constitutes this chapter's first constructive theological task. In addition, the connection between the hybridity of the cyborg and concepts of hybridity already present and at work within the Christian tradition, in feminist, disability, postcolonial, and queer theologies, has not been explicitly and systematically made; making these connections, then, is the second constructive theological task. Finally, we take up again the ecotheological implications of cyborg hybridity, work initiated by Graham, Garner, and others, and extend it both into the realm of bioethics and animal studies through a specific thematic focus on posthuman, hybrid bodies.

**Decentered Subjects and Extended Selves**

The reconstructed notion of the posthuman self carries significant implications for theological anthropology and, in particular, significant implications for relational anthropologies. Elaine Graham asks, "If *homo sapiens* are to be succeeded by *techno sapiens*, what happens to our accounts of human subjectivity?"[27] Precisely how do

---

[26] Other ecotheological explorations of Haraway's cyborg include Peter M. Scott, "We Have Never Been Gods: Transcendence, Contingency and the Affirmation of Hybridity," *Ecotheology* 9/2 (2004), Kevin J. O'Brien, "An Ethics of Natureculture and Creation: Donna Haraway's Cyborg Ethics as a Resource for Ecotheology," *Ecotheology: Journal of Religion, Nature & the Environment* 9/3 (2004), Rita Lester, "Ecofeminism and the Cyborg," *Feminist Theology: The Journal of the Britain & Ireland School of Feminist Theology* 19 (1998).

[27] Graham, "In Whose Image?" p. 166.

the partial, shifting, temporary, incomplete, multiple, relational cyborg subjectivities connect with theological notions of the human articulated as *imago dei*?

Here, we pick up the thread of our argument from Chapter 4, where I suggested that relational interpretations of the *imago dei* prove superior to substantive and functional interpretations when engaging in interdisciplinary dialogue with the posthuman. LeRon Shults argues, as we noted, that substance metaphysics, as a specific contextual influence on the formation of early Christian doctrine, no longer describes the current philosophical context for theology after the "turn to relationality," and further, that this turn offers an opportunity to recover biblical insights marginalized by theological anthropologies dependent on substance metaphysics.[28]

It is easy enough to see that posthuman challenges to notions of stable, fixed, and essential self represent an obstacle to theological anthropologies which depend upon notions of a soul. Functional interpretation of the *imago dei*, however, seems much more promising as a posthuman conversation partner, and indeed, is the choice of more than one theologian engaging the posthuman. Stephen Garner argues that "within the Christian tradition the most robust understanding of the *imago dei* appears to be a form of functional interpretation." For Garner, the doctrine of the image of God means "firstly, to declare that the earth is the Lord's, secondly, to represent God within this world in a capacity of vice-regent or steward, and thirdly, to demonstrate that human agency is intimately tied to God's agency."[29] Philip Hefner's functional interpretation of the *imago dei* as "created co-creator," specifically intended to address the technological dimension of human creativity as part of the *imago dei*, therefore seems tailor-made for an interdisciplinary engagement with the posthuman.

However, functional interpretations tell one very little about the actual theological commitments driving a particular theologian's dialogue with the posthuman, as the incredibly divergent theological responses of Brent Waters and Stephen Garner well demonstrate. Waters's functional interpretation of the *imago dei*, as we noted in Chapter 4, defines human beings as "the creatures that God has elected to oversee the providential unfolding of God's creation," but the exercise of this oversight, however, significantly and specifically excludes dominion over humanity as part of the natural world; in Waters's words, there is "no mandate to exercise dominion over *oneself or other humans*."[30] This functional interpretation of the *imago dei*, then, includes the theological presupposition of human uniqueness as ontological discontinuity with the natural world.

Garner's interpretation, in contrast, emphasizes continuity with and embeddedness within the natural world, and even finds the hybrid cyborg to be a theologically hopeful construction of the posthuman. This crucial difference is

---

[28] F. LeRon Shults, *Reforming Theological Anthropology: After the Philosophical Turn to Relationality* (Grand Rapids, MI, 2003), p. 5.

[29] Garner, "Transhumanism and the *Imago Dei*," p. 174.

[30] Waters, *From Human to Posthuman*, pp. 117, 136, 142.

explained by Garner's deliberate modification of Hefner's functional created co-creator interpretation. While ostensibly maintaining the primacy of the functional interpretation, Garner also argues that to rely upon the functional model alone would be shortsighted, and therefore proposes to modify the functional model through the addition of relational and substantive aspects, such that the *imago dei* indicates relationship to God and other creatures, and awareness of relationship to God points perhaps to a "*capax Dei*" within human nature. Thus, in the end, "the call to represent God and to reflect God's glory within creation is in turn supported by substantive and relational dimensions."[31]

Garner's interpretation of Hefner, and his emphasis on what he sees as the "relational dimension" of Hefner's functional interpretation, actually constitutes a compelling argument for choosing a relational interpretation of the *imago dei* over a functional one. Both Garner and Hefner rely on the concept of relationality to unpack what it means to represent God and to provide content for the claim that human agency is tied to divine agency in specific ways. Without this "relational dimension," the claim that humanity images God as God's representative can be interpreted very differently, as the example of Waters's functional interpretation shows. It is the relationality of the created co-creator that allows this theological construction to resist both the techno-optimistic transhumanist quest for biological transcendence, and the theological refusal to acknowledge humanity's embeddedness within and kinship with the technonatural world. And, of course, it is this relationality that therefore allows both Hefner and Garner to see the cyborg as a useful and fruitful theological symbol.

As Haraway observes, cyborgs are posthuman creatures "needy of connection," a creature with no substantive pedigree and therefore possessing an ontology of hyper-relationality.[32] Elsewhere she utilizes the metaphor of hypertext to make this point, a technology all about making connections and establishing relationships.[33] Moving decisively away from categories of nature, disembodied essence, and substance, the cyborg's ontology is instead defined in categories of relationality, albeit partial, temporary, and constantly negotiated relationality. This ontology of hyper-relationality is one in which the posthuman subject is embedded in multiple, overlapping, shifting relationships, with both human and nonhuman partners. N. Katherine Hayles writes, "The posthuman subject is an amalgam, a collection of heterogenous components, a material-informational entity whose boundaries undergo continuous construction and reconstruction."[34]

---

[31] Garner, "Transhumanism and the *Imago Dei*," pp. 174–5.

[32] Donna J. Haraway, "A Cyborg Manifesto: Science, Technology and Socialist-Feminism in the Late Twentieth Century," in *Simians, Cyborgs and Women: The Reinvention of Nature* (New York, 1991), p. 151.

[33] Donna J. Haraway, *Modest_Witness@Second_Millennium.Femaleman©_Meets_Oncomouse™: Feminism and Technoscience* (New York, 1997), pp. 125–30.

[34] N.K. Hayles, *How We Became Posthuman: Virtual Bodies in Cybernetics, Literature, and Informatics* (Chicago, IL, 1999), p. 3. See also N.K. Hayles, "Refiguring

As Graham's question highlights, the posthuman reworking of our notions of subjectivity means that the concept of relationality itself must be somewhat refigured in light of the posthuman, as there are no longer presumed stable, autonomous, and well-bounded selves to do the relating. This does not mean, however, that the cyborg is a harbinger of the "death of the subject." When, in Hayles's words, "the human subject is envisioned as an autonomous subject with unambiguous boundaries, the human-computer interface can only be parsed as a division between the solidity of real life on one side and the illusion of virtual reality on the other ... This view of the self authorizes the fear that if the boundaries are breached at all, there will be nothing to stop the self's complete dissolution."[35] But the displacement of the liberal human subject, as Calvin Schrag notes, "does not entail a dissolution of the subject and consciousness in every manner conceivable ... one still has to end with the subject, duly decentered and refigured ... without loss of either the speaking or the acting subject."[36]

Here, Cary Wolfe's contention that posthumanism as the "decentering of the human" should carry us beyond simply decentering the human in relation to evolutionary, ecological, and technological coordinates, into "how thinking confronts these dynamics," is particularly illuminative. Wolfe's simultaneously epistemological and ontological investigation of this decentering of the human unearths the ways in which humanism's presumptive normative subjectivity is destabilized by the necessary embeddedness and openness of the self to the environment. Subjectivity or self does not, however, disappear or dissolve into an unbounded environment; instead, it is precisely the construction of boundaries between self and environment that produce openness and therefore subjectivity. To decenter the human in this way, Wolfe argues, "enables us to describe the human and its characteristic modes of communication, interaction, meaning, social significance, and affective investments with *greater* specificity once we have removed meaning from the ontologically closed domain of consciousness, reason, reflection, and so on."[37] The "fundamentally prosthetic creature" which is the human being is, in other words, can only be described in terms which include the environmental forms with which the human has co-evolved and without which it cannot exist.

Wesley Wildman's notion of human beings as "walking ecologies in the microbial world" offers one example of just such a decentered theological anthropological construction. Wildman contrasts the idea of "distributed identity" with more traditional notions of "concentrated identity," which views human identity as ontologically simple and unified, rooted in the direct, first-hand experience of personal consciousness. This simplicity, however, ignores the way in which human identity is "complex, and distributed across a variety

---

the Posthuman," *Comparative Literature Studies* 41/3 (2004).

[35] Hayles, *How We Became Posthuman*, p. 290.

[36] Calvin Schrag, *The Resources of Rationality: A Response to the Postmodern Challenge* (Bloomington, IN, 1992), p. 151.

[37] Cary Wolfe, *What Is Posthumanism?* (Minneapolis, MN, 2010), p. xxv.

of neurological, biological, social, ecological, cultural, and axiological systems." Ultimately, Wildman says, human identity is always constructed "as a corporate venture," in which a huge number of living organisms are networked together in relationships of mutual dependence.[38] Thus, what we see in Wildman's "walking ecologies" proposal is a posthuman, in Wolfe's sense of decentering the human, proposal which radically reconfigures and simultaneously amplifies the notion of relationality as the defining aspect of (post)human identity. Not coincidentally, Haraway's own recent description of her own identity resonates with Wildman's: "I love the fact that human genomes can be found in only about 10 percent of all the cells that occupy the mundane space I call my body; the other 90 percent of the cells are filled with the genomes of bacteria, fungi, protists, and such, some of which play in a symphony necessary to my being alive at all, and some of which are hitching a ride and doing the rest of me, of us, no harm … To be one is always to *become with* many."[39]

The metaphor of "walking, thinking ecologies," of course, is a highly organic image, and one which might benefit from an explicit coupling with the technological image of the cyborg—for humans, of course, do not exist in a purely natural environment constituted only by other organisms, but a world of artifacts and technologies upon which we also intimately depend. Decentering the human, therefore, takes place in both contexts, as Wolfe explicitly recognizes.[40] Human beings are "walking, thinking ecologies" in a world in which our walking, thinking, and being intimately depends upon the environmental scaffolding of our technologies.

In a more explicitly technological vein, N. Katherine Hayles dubs this the "posthuman's collective heterogeneous quality," which "implies a distributed cognition located in disparate parts that may only be in tenuous communication with one another."[41] In contrast to constructions of subjectivity which require humans to define their relationships to machines in ways that preserve conscious agency as the exclusive characteristic of human beings alone, denying the role that machines and other nonhuman components actually play in human decision-making, from a posthuman perspective, "the prospect of humans working in partnership with intelligent machines is not so much a usurpation of human right and responsibility as it is a further development in the construction of distributed cognition environments, a construction that has been going on for thousands of

---

[38] Wesley J. Wildman, "Distributed Identity: Human Beings as Walking, Thinking Ecologies in the Microbial World," in Nancey Murphy and Christopher C. Knight (eds), *Human Identity at the Intersection of Science, Technology and Religion*, Ashgate Science and Religion Series (Burlington, VT, 2010), pp. 165–6.

[39] Donna J. Haraway, *When Species Meet*, ed. Cary Wolfe, Posthumanities (Minneapolis, MN, 2008), p. 4.

[40] Wolfe, *What Is Posthumanism?*, p. xvi.

[41] Hayles, *How We Became Posthuman*, pp. 3, 4.

years."⁴² Further, "when the human is seen as part of a distributed system, the full expression of human capability can be seen precisely to *depend* on the splice rather than being imperiled by it."⁴³

Andy Clark and David Chalmers's "extended mind" thesis is a concrete exploration of this kind of cyborg subjectivity and distributed cognition. Clark and Chalmers begin by suggesting that the general tendency of human reasoners is "to lean heavily on environmental supports": the use of pen and paper for multiplication, the rearrangement of Scrabble tiles, the use of a slide rule, and the visual rotation of shapes in the game of Tetris with the use of a rotation button, for example, constitute "epistemic actions," actions which alter the world so as to aid and augment cognitive processes.⁴⁴ Clark and Chalmers suggest that an extended mind also implies an extended self: "Most of us already accept that the self outstrips the boundaries of consciousness; my dispositional beliefs, for example, constitute in some deep sense part of who I am. If so, then these boundaries may also fall beyond the skin."⁴⁵ In *Natural-Born Cyborgs*, Clark pursues this insight, arguing that the tendency to "off load" cognitive processes onto the environment is precisely what makes human beings unique, and that the term "posthuman" is a misnomer; rather, "my goal is not to guess at what we might soon become but to better appreciate what we already are: *creatures whose minds are special precisely because they are tailor-made for multiple mergers and coalitions*."⁴⁶ New waves of technology, Clark believes, will bring this age-old process to a climax, as our minds and selves become ever more enmeshed within the nonbiological matrix of our technologies, but this is continuous rather than discontinuous with our evolutionary past and our current existence. The difference is that our emerging technologies "actively, automatically and continually tailor themselves to us just as we do to them—then the line between tool and user becomes flimsy indeed. Such technologies will be less like tools and more like part of the mental apparatus of the person."⁴⁷

---

⁴² Ibid., pp. 289–90. See also Andy Clark, *Natural-Born Cyborgs: Minds, Technologies, and the Future of Human Intelligence* (Oxford, 2003).

⁴³ Hayles, *How We Became Posthuman*, p. 290.

⁴⁴ David Chalmers and Andy Clark, "The Extended Mind," *Analysis* 58/1 (1998).

⁴⁵ Ibid., p. 19. The first clause lays down an important condition for the plausibility of the extended mind thesis, namely that "the self outstrips the boundaries of consciousness"; and, as the opening clause suggests, "most," but not "all," accept this proposition.

⁴⁶ Clark, *Natural-Born Cyborgs*, p. 7.

⁴⁷ Ibid. It is worth noting that Clark's version of "extended mind" is contestable; Mark Rowlands argues, for instance, that the extended mind hypothesis is distinct from "embeddedness," whereas Clark seems to view the extended mind as the logical consequences of embeddedness. See Mark Rowlands, "Extended Cognition and the Mark of the Cognitive," *Philosophical Psychology* 22/1 (2009), Mark Rowlands, "The Extended Mind," *Zygon* 44/3 (2009). Lynne R. Baker disagrees with a more fundamental point when she argues that "there is no tool use without a user," and therefore that "persons cannot have

What difference does this decentering of the human, in relation to both ecological and technological coordinates, make theologically? As a first observation, posthuman subjectivity not only dismantles the anthropology of the liberal humanist subject, but the theology of the God to whom that subject was presumably in relation. F. LeRon Shults writes, "we may still ask whether the Bible describes a God whose highest goal is glorifying himself as a single self-conscious Subject."[48] Shults argues that a lack of attention to the Trinitarian personal relations of the three persons of God "led to a picture of an infinitely intelligent and powerful Subject who is intent on self-glorification"—a description eerily reminiscent of Haraway's description of the (im)modest witness of the gentleman scholar in the narratives of the scientific revolution (here, God is not just an old man in the sky, He is a man in a lab coat in the sky; and scientific objectivity is indeed a god-trick).[49] Shults's observation is salutary: if that single self-conscious subject is not who we are, it's not who God is, either.

Secondly, and this has profound implications for Christian spiritual practices and disciplines, this reconfigured posthuman subjectivity creates new space for the articulation of doctrines of prayer, spiritual growth, and the discernment and desiring of "God's will." Kull writes, "Dismantling the centered and masterful subject is an affirmative project, ending not in the absence of the subject or its incorporation into the body of nature ... but in new and positive conceptions of subjectivity. The cyborg demonstrates that things get to be the way they are—whether good, bad, or indifferent—by being put together a bit at a time."[50] Cyborg subjectivity is not loss of subjectivity or agency; indeed, for Haraway, the cyborg is a means of reclaiming agency and relationship, not losing them to technological determinism. But it is an agency whose boundaries are incorporative, not fortified; an agency which invites collaboration rather than insisting on autonomy. This is true on multiple levels: material, ontological, epistemological, social, and political; and here, I believe we may fairly add, theological: as we desire, seek out, and perfect the relationship with God which defines the *imago dei*, we invite the collaboration of divine agency to intertwine with our own. Thus, the Christian

---

extended minds in the sense of EM; shifting and transitory hybrids can hardly be persons"; Baker's "modest proposal" is that "persons can have partly (or perhaps wholly) inorganic, bionic bodies, and some persons currently do have bodies with bionic parts that play essential roles in cognitive and motor activity" (p. 656). Central to Baker's disagreement with Clark is an insistence on the importance of maintaining a sense of permanence, and therefore boundary, between bodies and transient cognitive aids in the environment. Lynne R. Baker, "Persons and the Extended-Mind Thesis," *Zygon* 44/3 (2009).

[48] Shults, *Reforming Theological Anthropology*, p. 240.

[49] Donna J. Haraway, "Modest_Witness@Second_Millenium," in *Modest_Witness@ Second_Millennium.Femaleman©_Meets_Oncomouse™: Feminism and Technoscience* (New York, 1997), pp. 23–33.

[50] Anne Kull, "A Theology of Technonature Based on Donna Haraway and Paul Tillich" (PhD Dissertation, Lutheran School of Theology, 2000), p. 138.

notion of conforming to God's will moves from being a zero-sum prospect, in which the proper human response is to negate the self in order to become holy, to a notion of (post)human identity which incorporates the divine as one component of identity which contributes to the whole. This openness to the divine no longer comes at the expense of the self, but contributes to the ongoing construction of the self.

**Glorified Bodies**

Nikolas Rose makes a compelling argument that advances in medical technologies and biology have increasingly prompted us to think of ourselves as "somatic individuals." This is a shift from previous conceptions of the individual self as defined by "a deep interior psychological space," or what Wildman refers to as the "ontological simplicity of immediate self-awareness."[51] Rose writes, "New sciences of brain and behavior forge links between what we do—how we conduct ourselves—and what we are. These games of truth work at a molecular level, the level of neurons, receptor sites, neurotransmitters, and the precise sequences of base pairs at particular locations in what we now think of as the human genome. Those molecular phenomena, rendered visible and transformed into the determinants of our moods, desires, personalities and pathologies, become the target of new pharmaceutical techniques."[52] In short, we are no longer able to sustain the assumption that our bodies are irrelevant in determining who we are; we are somatic individuals.

In Christian theology, too, we are increasingly becoming aware that we are "somatic individuals." Renewed attention to embodiment within Christian theology, and the repudiation of dualistic anthropologies which emphasize soul or spirit as the essential locus of human identity, first took the form of "body theology." James Nelson offers a definition of "body theology" in his book of the same title: it is not primarily a theological description of the body, nor an ethical prescription for expressing ourselves physically, but rather, "it is doing theology in such a way that we take our body experiences seriously as occasions of revelation."[53] The proposal to take the body seriously as occasion for revelation is multi-faceted; not only, as Nelson specifically explicates, does this reintroduce bodily issues such as gender and sexuality into theology proper, but it also demands a reconsideration of the nature of revelation itself; no longer an abstract matter primarily of "Word," revelation itself becomes embodied.

Elizabeth Moltmann-Wendel, like Nelson, begins her project with the acknowledgment that "the topic of the body confronts us above all with the distinctive

---

[51] Nikolas Rose, *The Politics of Life Itself: Biomedicine, Power, and Subjectivity in the Twenty-First Century* (Princeton, NJ, 2007), p. 26, Wildman, "Distributed Identity," p. 164.
[52] Rose, *The Politics of Life Itself*, p. 26.
[53] James Nelson, *Body Theology* (Louisville, KY, 1992), pp. 9, 50.

character of the Christian tradition: God's becoming body."[54] Moltmann-Wendel thus constructs the Incarnation as the definitive feature of Christianity, yielding a theology which mistrusts abstract spirituality which is dissociated from the body, life, earth, and social relationships; mistrusts self-made fantasies of the beyond which are engaged in at the expense of healing people here and the realization of the kingdom of God on earth; seeks to give people the courage to use their senses, to accept themselves with their bodies; prefers a concrete body language which incorporates symbols, myth, and fairy tales to a disembodied language.[55] Unlike Nelson, however, who highlights sexuality as a constant and crucial aspect of embodiment, Moltmann-Wendel's focus, rather, is on bodily processes and experiences which are germane to both sexes: childhood, youth, sickness, and aging.[56]

Nelson and Moltmann-Wendel's wish to retrieve the body is echoed and intensified by the work of feminist theologians whose critique of the Christian tradition is not simply that the body per se has been ignored, but that the body assumed as normative has always been identifiably male. In this critique, the significance of the body as a locus for theology is deepened as it becomes clear that bodily differences affect how one does theology. The association of maleness with rationality and femaleness with bodiliness in the Christian tradition has led to the exclusion of female bodies as legitimate sites for doing theology (conceived of as a purely rational task).[57] Adele McCollum observes, "It is no accident that it is women theologians and religionists attempting to redeem body and its differences as a focus of debate … women have been disproportionately maligned, decentered, and impaired by anti-body philosophies of Cartesian schizophrenia."[58] Lisa Isherwood and Elizabeth Stuart, therefore, make the programmatic declaration in *Introducing Body Theology* that their "first break with tradition is that we take the female body as normative throughout this work."[59]

While this work on "body theology" has been a significant first step in making embodiment a topic of theological discussion, there remains, however, a final and problematic layer of abstraction covertly at work in the terms "embodiment," "the body," or even "the female body." These terms, all singular, point to a concept of normative, homogenous, human embodiedness. To talk of human embodiment or

---

[54] Elizabeth Moltmann-Wendel, *I Am My Body: New Ways of Embodiment*, trans. John Bowden (London, 1994), p. xiii.

[55] Ibid., pp. 104–5.

[56] Ibid., p. xiv.

[57] See Judy Tobler, "Beyond a Patriarchal God: Bringing the Transcendent Back to the Body," *Journal of Theology for Southern Africa* 106 (2000), Rosemary R. Ruether, *Sexism and God-Talk: Toward a Feminist Theology* (Boston, MA, 1983).

[58] Judith Plaskow and Elizabeth S. Fiorenza, "Women with Disabilities: A Challenge to Feminist Theology," *Journal of Feminist Studies in Religion* 10 (1994): p. 126.

[59] Lisa Isherwood and Elizabeth Stuart, *Introducing Body Theology*, ed. Mary Gray et al., vol. 2 Introductions to Feminist Theology (Sheffield, 1998), p. 9.

the human body, rather than human bodies, is itself a move from the concrete into the abstract.[60]

This same problematic usage of embodiment is employed by N. Katherine Hayles, in her initial exploration of the posthuman; in Hayles's analysis, valuing embodiment and its associated finitude functions as the resistance to transhumanist constructions of the posthuman.[61] It is finitude which constitutes the difference between the hopeful posthuman Hayles invites us to collectively construct, and the transhumanist "cybernetic posthuman," with its disembodied and infinite aspirations. Yet in Hayles as well, despite her explicit intent, talk of abstract embodiment and associated finitude moves away from the concrete, specific, hybrid bodies that Haraway symbolizes in the cyborg, into a discourse that seeks to articulate a general and universal aspect of humanness, a definitive commonality. For Hayles, this move functions as a counter to the universalizing anthropology of transhumanism, but it also sidesteps the consideration of actual (post)human bodies, in favor of emphasizing the ontological necessity of having a body.

This is all the more curious, since Haraway's cyborg is less about the ontological categories of "Man and Machine" than it is about the championing of embodied hybridity in both its gendered and social-cultural contexts.[62] To miss this about the cyborg is to get it only half-right, for the breakdown of ontological barriers the cyborg signals do not take place in the abstraction of academic philosophical or theological discourse about technoscience and anthropology, but within actual bodies and lived experiences. While embodiment is acknowledged as important, the actual body seems to be taken for granted; what matters is the phenomenon of embodiment and what it signifies, whether finitude (Hayles), material sacramentality (Graham), or interconnectedness with the natural world (Kull, Garner). Yet as Haraway insists, actual bodies matter, for it is the material reality of the bodies of women that demonstrates the falsity of the idealized construct of Woman; it is the hybrid body of the cyborg that demonstrates the falsity of ontological purity and disembodied essences. Living as cyborg means recognition that the boundaries constructed to delineate the self cut across the predetermined categories, not as an act of will but as an acknowledgment of the material reality of actual (post)human bodies.

Theological work remains to be done, therefore, explicitly connecting the cyborg to theological articulations of hybridity, as expressed within the theologies of those living out the material dimensions of cyborg existence. In making

---

[60] As Elizabeth Grosz observes: "Indeed, there is no body as such; there are only *bodies*." Elizabeth Grosz, *Volatile Bodies: Toward a Corporeal Feminism* (Bloomington, IN, 1994), p. 19.

[61] Hayles chooses the term embodiment specifically arguing that it is more resistance to abstraction than "the body." Hayles, *How We Became Posthuman*, pp. 196–9.

[62] Donna J. Haraway, "Femaleman©_Meets_Oncomouse™. Mice into Wormholes: A Technoscience Fugue in Two Parts," *Modest_Witness@Second Millennium.Femaleman©_Meets_Oncomouse™* (New York, 1997), p. 51.

hybridity, rather than embodiment, the focal concept in a theological anthropology of the posthuman, there is a decisive move away from abstraction into the techno-flesh concreteness of multiple, plastic (post)human bodies.

*Disability Theologies as Cyborg*

The connection between disabled bodies and the cyborg bodies is easily made; not only do these bodies demonstrably repudiate notions of natural wholeness metaphorically, but disabled bodies are often also technologically augmented bodies. Thus an obvious starting point for connecting the cyborg image with Christian theological anthropology is what we might call "medical cyborg theologies." The so-called "medical cyborg" is, of course, any human person whose physical body incorporates a medical device in physical functioning; this might be as commonplace and invisible as the presence of a pacemaker, as eye-catching and cutting-edge as the recent prosthetics which incorporate brain–computer interface technologies, or as accepted and (more or less generally) accommodated as a wheelchair for mobility.

Elaine Graham's brief mention of the connection between the differently-abled and differently-configured bodies of many human beings to the cyborg indicates her awareness of the importance of taking into account the diversity of human and posthuman bodies in the construction of theological anthropology.[63] To presume that one sort of bodily experience is normal, and therefore all others marginal, actually abstracts from lived, human, bodily experience to an extent that it grossly misrepresents what it means to be embodied. As a corrective, Graham proposes that narratives of disability and bodily suffering, as well as other narratives that challenge ideas of bodily naturalism, fixity, and uniform ability, such as the hybridity of the cyborg, be lifted up alongside of those which have been assumed normative. What this means is a shift in our definition of the body from a singular norm to a range of definitions of embodiment, wide enough "to encompass prosthetic limbs, use of wheelchairs, diverse physical sensations and accomplishments."[64]

As outlined above, "body theology" seeks to recover the importance of the embodiment, not simply as a signal of historical, social, and epistemological location, but as itself a source of theologizing. Yet this retrieval of "the body" as theological source glosses over the real and significant differences of multiple human embodiments. In particular, both Nelson and Moltmann-Wendel describe the experience of illness as a deviation from the norm, which may both simultaneously assert the embodiedness of the human experience and serve to distance our sense of self from the body. Though both Nelson and Moltmann-Wendel consider illness a specific mode of embodiment, avoiding explicit talk of norms, both theologians

---

[63] Elaine Graham, "Words Made Flesh: Women, Embodiment, and Practical Theology," *Feminist Theology* 21 (1999): p. 117, note 28.

[64] Ibid., p. 119.

treat the experience of illness in counterpoint to an assumed normative mode of health and wholeness. Moltmann-Wendel interprets illness as one of the "limit situations" in which we come up against "our real existence, namely that we are in a body."[65] We do not, these theologians presume, experience health in the same body-conscious way we experience illness.[66]

In contrast, theologians with disabilities emphasize the importance of bodily differences—pointing out that the (normative) human body is presumptively male, whole, and healthy.[67] Nancy Eiesland argues, "Unless the notion of embodiment is deliberately deconstructed, the cultural norms of 'body as natural' seep into the subtext ... the real, lived experiences of people with disabilities ... explicitly deconstruct any norms which are part of the unexpressed agenda of 'normal embodiment.'"[68] Like Moltmann-Wendel and Nelson, Eiesland works to recover the body as the starting point for theological reflection; she writes, "The corporeal is for people with disabilities the most real ... we become keenly aware that our physical selves determine our perceptions of the social and physical world."[69] Unlike Moltmann-Wendel and Nelson, however, the particularities of her own body enable Eiesland to perceive a distorting universal assumption of normative experience at work in the abstract notion of embodiment. Outside that presumed normativity, Eiesland's own experience of her body belies the universality of "normal embodiment" and produces an awareness of the theological importance of particular embodiments.

There is, therefore, more variation than consensus to be found among disabled theologians on the topic of bodies as loci for theological reflection, though certain key themes emerge. Eiesland is representative in voicing an affirmation of the central importance of the body as "the origin of constructed reality."[70] It is acknowledged and expected that the reality constructed from disabled bodies will be different in certain respects from that of the assumed norm, and this is legitimized and celebrated rather than denied or marginalized.

The significance of this, already evident in feminist assertions of the importance of gendered bodies, is heightened by the acknowledgment of disabled bodies, which deviate in a different way from the assumed able-bodied male norm. Thus the same challenge which feminist theologies of the body offer to the

---

[65] Ibid., p. 22.

[66] Moltmann-Wendel notes as an exception the experience of recovery from a serious illness in which one experiences health "like a new garment" (Moltmann-Wendel, *I Am My Body*, p. 22.) I would also add that pregnancy is a state of physical being in which one is constantly aware of one's body(ies), without being in any way ill (despite this categorization of pregnancy by American health insurance agencies).

[67] Plaskow and Fiorenza, "Women with Disabilities," p. 126.

[68] Nancy Eiesland, *The Disabled God: Toward a Liberatory Theology of Disability* (Nashville, TN, 1994), p. 22.

[69] Ibid.

[70] See also Plaskow and Fiorenza, "Women with Disabilities," p. 127.

conceptualization of the male body as normative, theologies of disability offer to a feminist theology which assumes a static concept of health or ability, an idealized "perfect body," as norm. Valerie Stiteler's criticism of feminist theology in this regard is harsh and to the point: "The feminist movement did not adopt patriarchal attitudes toward the human body so much as it created theologies of embodiment rejecting anything representing our oppression by patriarchy or interfering with the pursuit of wholeness. Since women with disabilities do not embody the feminist notion of wholeness, this leads us to reject our disabilities as integral aspects of our embodiment."[71] Stiteler's words echo Haraway's cyborg critique of the goddess as a feminist ideal, in that both scholars perceive that actual women's bodies belie the natural, whole, universal ideal symbolized by the construction of the goddess.

Beyond this basic consensus, however, the particularities of embodiment produce multiple perspectives on the experience of disabilities. As Eiesland points out, the category of "disability" itself is falsely homogenous, a categorical identity created by the construction of boundaries drawn by those whom she names "the temporarily able-bodied."[72] People with disabilities may have a wide variety of physical, psychological, and intellectual impairments, which may produce vastly different types of functional impairment; there are differing degrees of impairment, leading to dramatically different experiences of disability; disabilities may be static or progressive, congenital or acquired.[73] Eiesland juxtaposes the narratives of two women to illustrate the degree to which perspectives on disabled bodies may differ. Diane DeVries, born without arms or legs, "never internalized able-bodiedness as the norm to which she should aspire. Thus she was able to see her own body as different, but not defective." In contrast, Nancy Mairs experienced the onset of multiple sclerosis as "the diminishment of her body, which she described as her body going away." However, "neither of these women more authentically represents the experience of people with disabilities; rather, they depict the multiple realities that constitute ordinary existence in our nonconventional bodies."[74] Thus, one important theological insight to glean is that the multiple experiences of variable human embodiments will include both positive and negative narratives, experiences of suffering as well as flourishing.

Like DeVries, Valerie Stiteler and Adele McCollum both exemplify a positive vision of the body and the disabled body as the place from which to begin theologizing. Stiteler states, "I feel each woman's disabilities enhance

---

[71] Ibid., p. 119.

[72] Eiesland, *The Disabled God*, pp. 24–8. For Eiesland's discussion of media stereotypes, "Poster Child Syndrome," and Du Bois' "double consciousness," see also Nancy Eiesland, "What Is Disability," *Stimulus* 6 (1998): pp. 28–9.

[73] Eiesland, *The Disabled God*, p. 24. Eiesland specifically alludes to the need for avoiding the "false universalism" of 1970s feminism, and the necessity of political action as coalition, rather than identity-based support group, politics (pp. 28–9). This of course strongly echoes Haraway's political cyborg perspective.

[74] Ibid., p. 32.

her embodiment differently ... I regard my blindness as an aspect of my unique embodiment ... emancipation requires 'embracing' our disabilities. Embracing our disabilities means accepting them as part of our uniqueness; acknowledging them as a source of our embodied power and allowing a sense of holiness to flow through our disabilities."[75] McCollum echoes this perspective: "I don't call myself disabled because it is clear that I am able and capable ... I prefer being physically challenged."[76]

Characterizing disability as "unique embodiment," in Stiteler's phrase, opens the door to conceiving the body as plastic and mutable, rather than a given which can be described as a static norm. Eiesland writes, "My own body composed as it is of metal and plastic, as well as bone and flesh, is my starting point for talking about 'bones and braces' bodies as a norm of embodiment."[77] This obviously cyborg starting point challenges the notion of a bodily norm of natural wholeness, not simply in asserting the normativity of differently abled bodies, but of technologically augmented bodies as well. Eiesland's description of her body as composed of metal and plastic, as well as bone and flesh, is by no means unusual; Chris Hables Gray cites one of the first major studies of prosthesis wearers, in which 61 percent claimed to forget being an amputee "most of the time," and most respondents considered themselves able-bodied.[78]

The example of Aimee Mullins underscores in a dramatic way the possibilities opened up by conceiving of "disability" as unique embodiment; a double amputee as an infant, Mullins "has become the fashionable face of disability and a spokeswoman for the promise of high-tech prosthetics."[79] Mullins owns over a dozen pairs of prosthetic legs, including sprinting legs modeled after the hind legs of a cheetah, and an ornately carved pair of wooden legs; with these prosthetics, Mullins comments, "I have different negotiations of the terrain under my feet. And I can change my height—I have a variable of five different heights."[80] Indeed, in her contention that the conversation about "disability" is no longer a conversation about overcoming a deficiency, but a conversation about augmentation and

---

[75] Plaskow and Fiorenza, "Women with Disabilities," p. 120.

[76] Ibid., p. 128.

[77] Eiesland, *The Disabled God*, p. 22.

[78] Chris H. Gray, "Medical Cyborgs: Artificial Organs and the Quest for the Posthuman," in Chris Hables Gray (ed.), *Technohistory* (Malabar, FL, 1996), p. 157.

[79] Aimee Mullins, "Prosthetic Power," *The Utne Reader*, July–August 2009, p. 54. Note: this description of Mullins comes from the editors' preface of her article, an excerpt from a speech entitled, "How My Legs Give Me Superpowers," originally presented at the 2009 TED (Technology, Entertainment, Design) Conference.

[80] Ibid., p. 55. For a picture of Aimee Mullins's carved wooden legs, see the preceding article, Graham Pullin, "Design Meets Disability," *The Utne Reader*, July–August 2009, p. 51.

potential, Mullins makes explicit the way in which posthuman and disability discourses overlap.[81]

This plasticity of body image is not necessarily uncomplicated, however, as Gray's analysis of medical studies, particularly the research of Joseph Kaufert and David Locker, demonstrates.[82] Kaufert and Locker followed the progress of 10 poliomyelitis victims from the 1950s, discerning distinct shifts in the patients' attitudes regarding the medical technologies upon which they were more or less dependent. Gray writes,

> The patients followed a number of different "careers." First came the "acute" phase, the fight to survive. It involved tremendous physical effort and reliance upon the iron lung for survival. Then came "rehabilitation" where dependence on the iron lung was seen as an impediment to independence. Then came "stability" which also meant constant exercise and conscious breathing to minimize or eliminate reliance on medical machinery. As many of these patients grew older and entered a "transitional" stage marked by medical setbacks, newer equipment, especially portable respiration machines which could fit on wheelchairs, were developed. Because of this technological change, patients who could not maintain themselves without machinery could still increase their independence with the help of portable machines; although before, reverting to the machine meant losing independence ... The extreme work ethic of the rehabilitation and stability phase also had to be overcome, since it was linked with a rejection of machine dependence.[83]

The portable respirators require the acceptance of a permanent tracheal airway, which provides a "direct physical connection to a machine" and therefore a dramatic change in body image. Further, the patient must also adapt to the machine, and develop a constant awareness of its rhythms and vibrations, even, as one patient related, during sex. This close integration of body and machine requires, beyond the pragmatic aspects of adjustment, the modification of "culturally grounded beliefs about dependence on technology," that is, a rejection of whole, natural bodily norms in order to embrace a cyborg existence and its physical, social, and psychological benefits.[84]

---

[81] Mullins, "Prosthetic Power," p. 55. Nor is Mullins the only prosthetic-limbed sprinter; see Jeré Longman, "An Amputee Sprinter: Is He Disabled or Too-Abled?" *The New York Times*, May 15, 2007, Alan Schwarz, "An Injured Soldier Re-Emerges as a Sprinter," *The New York Times*, August 13, 2009.

[82] Gray, "Medical Cyborgs," pp. 154–9. In addition to Kaufert and Locker's research on polio victims and "the iron lung," Gray cites the suicidal response of artificial heart recipients to the clicking sound of the pump and numerous studies on the connection between long-term dependence on kidney dialysis and the refusal of CPR.

[83] Ibid., p. 155.

[84] Ibid., pp. 156–7.

The plasticity of body image demonstrated by Eiesland, Miller, and the polio patients in Kaufert and Locker's long-term study underscores the fluidity of the boundaries between able and disabled bodies, as an awareness of mutability and flux, rather than stasis, characterizes the experience of bodily existence. McCollum describes the experience of her body as one of constant change: "Body is ever present though changeable and unpredictable ... Notions of fixed reality, permanent ideas or identities, unchanging gods, predictable archetypes or patterns find no match in my present experience."[85] Instead of taking for granted an undisrupted, background experience of wholeness or health—the experience which Nelson and Moltmann-Wendel thematize as "background," allowing the body and the consciousness of self as body to slide into subconscious expectation—disability promotes an awareness of the body as a constantly changing aspect of personal experience. The presupposition of a fixed norm of wholeness, McCollum notes, against which all else is judged mutant, variant, or deviant is what leads people to react with amazement when those with disabilities turn out to be as capable as anyone else.[86] Elaine Graham takes this insight to heart when, in dialogue with both James Nelson and Nancy Eiesland, she points out that everyone, even the supposedly able-bodied and whole, "are all prone to cyclical fluctuations of bodily well-being and that any kind of demarcation—most especially an ontological distinction—between able/disabled actually polarizes and distorts lived experience."[87]

This brings us to an important intersection between the posthuman, theology, and bioethics, on the common bioethical distinction between therapy and enhancement. Often operative in theological and bioethical considerations of emerging technologies and their effects on human bodies, this distinction rests on a notion of bodily normativity that is becoming increasingly difficult to define clearly. If, indeed, our anthropology includes Eiesland's "bones and braces" cyborg bodies as well as "natural," whole bodies, the line between therapy and enhancement cannot be drawn according to the restoration of disabled bodies to an approximation of wholeness and normalcy.

Nikolas Rose, therefore, issues a call to create a "somatic ethics," which he firmly distinguishes from bioethics, which currently functions as a cultural, political, and academic institution that legitimates the movement of biocapital.[88] As Rose's analysis makes clear, one of the ways in which bioethics falls short of the somatic ethics he envisions is the way in which it depends upon clear-cut ontological distinctions that are increasingly undermined in our knowledge of ourselves as somatic individuals: "the classical distinction made in moral philosophy between that which is not human—ownable, tradeable, commodifiable—and that which is human—not legitimate material for such commodification—can no longer do the

---

[85] Ibid., p. 128.
[86] Plaskow and Fiorenza, "Women with Disabilities," p. 128.
[87] Graham, "Words Made Flesh," p. 117.
[88] Rose, *The Politics of Life Itself*, p. 256.

work that is required to resolve the issue: that distinction is itself what is at stake in the politics of the contemporary bioeconomy."[89] Troubling entities such as embryos and stem cells, whose position on the boundaries of human/nonhuman and life/nonlife make them subject to political and bioethical dispute, illustrate vividly the sense in which these questions are at play, and unable to be resolved in noncircular fashion without a revisioning of our bioethical categories. These cyborg figures function to illuminate precisely what is missing in bioethical discourse—the sort of close attention to material particularities, as well as their embeddedness within political and economic networks, that Haraway urges. The shift in subjectivity to the somatic, which we have called "posthuman," and the ways in which new biomedical technologies have opened to question previously given ontological boundaries (between life/nonlife and human/nonhuman), require, he argues, the development of an ethics "not in the sense of moral principles, but rather as the vales for the conduct of a life—that accords a central place to corporeal, bodily existence."[90]

Here, once again, the choice of which form of the posthuman to engage becomes highly significant for theologians, for transhumanism intersects with bioethical considerations of enhancement in an entirely different way than the cyborg.[91] Enhancement, of course, is closely intertwined with the posthuman vision of the transhumanist movement, and many transhumanists are strong advocates for the human right of enhancement of the body. On a surface level, the cyborg's dismantling of notions of natural body norms, and transhumanist advocacy of enhancement, seem to lead to the same skepticism regarding the philosophical and ethical distinction between therapy and enhancement. It is significant, however, that once again the differing anthropological assumptions at work in these two posthuman discourses produce very different reasons for rejecting natural bodily norms. Transhumanism rejects these norms in order to pursue a future bodily (or in some cases, disembodied) vision of perfection and invulnerability, whereas cyborg hybridity appeals to the material realities of bodies, and in this context, "imperfect" bodies, to demonstrate that the norm does not exist, focusing on the social implications of existing bodily differences.

In disability theology, narratives of the suffering body also have their place, and represent an important point of resistance to the reassertion of bodily norms through the pursuit of a perfected bodily ideal. Eiesland sees "the myth of bodily perfection" as a negative cultural and philosophical influence on Christian theology, and as decisively repudiated by the experience of disability, which forces a recognition of finitude and mortality: "Whether we have come to disability recently, or come to the

---

[89] Ibid., p. 38.

[90] Ibid., p. 6. Rose resists the term "posthuman," seeing in an implication of historical and ontological discontinuity with the human (see, for example, pp. 7, 252–3).

[91] For theological engagements with transhumanism on this topic which make use of the therapy/enhancement distinction, see Celia E. Deane-Drummond, "The Future of the Human: Transhuman Evolution or Human Identity as *Imago Christi*?" in *Christ and Evolution: Wonder and Wisdom* (London, 2009), Peters, *Anticipating Omega*.

world with disability, we have by necessity faced finitude, the limits of mortality. In so far as we dared to acknowledge our own lives we've had to look full in the face of the human condition. We are not gods who by the force of our will, cunning or goodness can make situations we know should be righted, right. Try as we may, we cannot produce paradise, we cannot abide in this place of ultimate transcendence."[92] This is a clear repudiation of the transhumanist quest for transcendence and bodily perfection, but Eiesland's target is the way in which this myth of bodily perfection has become integrated into Christian theology and eschatology, with dire consequences. First, it results in the symbolic exclusion of persons with disabilities from the Christian community and tradition. Promises of "being made whole," framed as eschatological hope, simply emphasized to Eiesland that "in heaven I would have to be someone else entirely if I didn't have the knowledge of my disability. I simply didn't know myself without my disability."[93] Second, it provides a theological rationale for social inaction. Eiesland writes, "Disability is one of those few remaining areas where theologians and religious professionals in good conscience tell people to defer their flourishing until the afterworld. This theological utopianism is a siren song that drowns out our real and necessary calls for justice and the possibility of human flourishing in our real bodies, in our real communities, in the here and now."[94]

Finding herself shut out from the Christian narrative by these incursions of cultural norms of natural bodily wholeness into theology, Eiesland counters with a theological interpretation of the resurrected Christ as the disabled God, focusing specifically on the imperfections that mark the resurrected body precisely as marks of personal identity. Here, perhaps unexpectedly, along with the deconstruction of a notion of a singular norm of human embodiment, we find a second thematic overlap with Haraway's cyborg discourse, for Haraway, too, is fully aware of the necessity of acknowledging the material realities of suffering, limitation, and mortality, writing: "I want to focus on the discourses of suffering and dismemberment."[95] Indeed, one of Haraway's chosen icons of such a discourse is the crucified Jesus. Thus, here, the overlap between Haraway's cyborg and Eiesland's liberatory theology of disability specifically includes recognition of the experientially negative dimensions of material existence and a rejection of the pursuit of the "myth of bodily perfection." This theological acknowledgment of finitude and even mortality, along with hybridity, as an equally undeniable experiential reality of disabled bodies, incorporates notions of the cyborg while simultaneously sharply rejecting transhumanist visions of

---

[92] Eiesland, "What Is Disability," p. 29.
[93] Ibid., p. 25.
[94] Ibid., p. 29.
[95] Donna J. Haraway, "Ecce Homo, Ain't (Ar'n't) I a Woman, and Inappropriate/D Others: The Human in a Post-Humanist Landscape," in Judith Butler and Joan W. Scott (eds), *Feminists Theorize the Political* (New York, 1992), p. 86.

posthuman perfection and invulnerability.[96] Rather, these different bodies, in their full positive and negative material realities, are acceptable in a Christian narrative of the disabled God: "If, indeed, Christ resurrected still participated fully in the experience of human life, including the experience of impairment, we must be scandalized by our theological tendencies to perpetuate the myth of bodily perfection in our defense of paradise."[97]

Further, this suggests that the kind of somatic ethics called for by Rose should incorporate this perspective on the significance of unique, disabled, technologically augmented, suffering, and imperfect human bodies. Cary Wolfe suggests that "shared finitude" and vulnerability become the basis for the formation of an ethics which may then be "based not on ability, activity, agency and empowerment but on a *compassion* that is rooted in our vulnerability and passivity."[98] This closely aligns with Nancy Eiesland's theological insight that Christ's body, as a suffering body, invites us to accept, rather than reject, the vulnerability of the somatic self, and further, to perceive that all creatures, even the "temporarily able-bodied" are subject to this reality of embodied existence, each in their own ways, and are due compassion.

The questions we should be asking, therefore, are questions about particular bodies: what can *this* body do? And what does *this* body need? To frame the ethical task this way is to reiterate one of the basic insights of Haraway's cyborg vision, the need to pay close attention to the particularities of the cyborg bodies under consideration, as a decisive move away from not only abstract, categorical, natural bodily norms, but from an abstract pursuit of ideal bodily perfection as well.

Christian theological anthropologies wishing to incorporate the insights of the cyborg with regard to hybridity should therefore take into account the theological contributions of theologians with disabilities on the importance of human bodies as loci for doing theology, and moreover, the importance of bodily differences in the task of theological construction. Hybridity, therefore, leads not simply to an appreciation of materiality and embodiment in general, providing a starting point for the development of a more nuanced ecotheology, but also to a heightened attention to actual (post)human bodies and therefore to a critique and reconsideration of "body theology." Further, attention to the overlap between theologies of disability

---

[96] In particular, N. Katherine Hayles's focus on finitude as a necessary aspect of embracing material existence, precisely as a resistance to transhumanist anthropology, is brought to mind. Further, this specifically counters Brent Waters's theological suspicions of the impossibility of a finite cyborg.

[97] Eiesland, "What Is Disability," p. 29.

[98] Wolfe, *What Is Posthumanism?*, p. 141. Wolfe's posthuman analysis of the field of disability studies and activism notes a persistent "fetishization of agency" at work, in which the norms of the liberal subject (active not passive, subject not object, etc.) are invoked to validate the disabled subject; this, he notes, is understandable for all sorts of historical, institutional, and strategic reasons, but reinscribes the norms which have functioned to exclude the disabled in the first place.

and cyborg hybridity make clear that theological appreciation of the importance of bodily difference leads not simply to acceptance of a multiplicity of bodily norms, even those which may transgress ontological categories of human and machine, but also the realities of finitude and mortality experienced as part of bodily reality. Understanding that presumptions of naturalness, wholeness, and able-bodiedness do not comprehensively or normatively describe the embodiments of human beings is a lesson articulated not only by the figure of Haraway's cyborg, but within the Christian tradition itself in the voices of disabled, differently-abled, or "uniquely embodied" theologians.

*Queer Theologies as Cyborg*

In queer theology, the cyborg's emphasis on bodily difference is articulated in the ways in which specific bodies transgress the categorical boundaries of gender roles and sexual behaviors, a more metaphorical expression of the cyborg's hybridity than the literal integration of bodies and technologies demonstrated in "medical cyborgs" and thematized in the theologies of persons with disabilities. At the same time, of course, human gender and sexuality are themselves curiously hybrid concepts, intertwining the biological and the social in ways impossible to pull apart.

Marcella Althaus-Reid's "From the Goddess to Queer Theology" provides a starting point for defining queer theology and its relationship to feminist and liberation theologies that historically precede it. At the same time, Althaus-Reid's positioning of queer theology as a successor to feminist theology and goddess thealogy provides a demonstrable overlap between her theologizing and Haraway's cyborg repudiation of the goddess in feminist theory: what Haraway does in the "A Cyborg Manifesto" is recapitulated in the theological context in the work of Althaus-Reid and other queer theologians. Theological constructions of the human which ignore, or universalize, gender and sexuality miss the ways in which multiple human embodiments make a difference in our conceptions of the human. In this sense, then, queer theology is posthuman theology, or more specifically, cyborg theology.[99]

Althaus-Reid begins with the story of Charles Darwin's daughter Hetty, who "was distressed because she wanted to be so good that God would accept her amongst the male angels." Althaus-Reid writes, "strangeness, that feeling of being born as a permanent Other to God, was a decisive experience at the beginning of Feminist thinking and theology. The first feminist theological wave wanted inclusivity ... Like Hetty before them, but through historical re-reading and modern exegesis, feminist theologians have been trying to find a place for women amongst male

---

[99] Here, like Hayles, the "human" in this use of "posthuman" refers to the historically specific construction of the human which Hayles tags as "the liberal humanist subject." In this precise sense, queer theology is indeed posthuman.

angels."[100] Later, however, this feeling of "strangeness" yielded to the realization that inclusion in an essentially patriarchal system was not sufficient, and prompted a search for "a 'god' who is one of us: for women she was the Goddess."[101] The goddess movement offered an important critique to feminist theology, confronting the textual limitations of feminist theology and offering an interpretation of Christian tradition as thoroughly, and not incidentally, patriarchal.

Yet, for Althaus-Reid, the radical critique of the goddess movement also fell short, as she perceived its critique to, in the end, fail to challenge "heterosexuality as ideology" even while it spoke against patriarchalism.[102] Here, of course, Althaus-Reid's perception of the goddess movement as the validation of "heterosexuality as an ideology" parallels Haraway's critique of the goddess: in both instances, the problem identified is that the strategy of claiming a gender-specific goddess leaves the given categories of gender intact. The consequences of this are two-fold: first, as Althaus-Reid comments, the problematic aspects of heterosexual gender categories are integrated into one's own feminist thealogy; second, as Haraway analyzes, withdrawal leaves the patriarchal order itself intact, rendering women and their goddess a permanent stranger and outsider to the operative structures of power and technological prowess. Thus, the point is not to re-read the Christian tradition in order to recover the place of women within it, nor to claim a gender-friendly deity but to question the category of gender altogether; in other words, "the point in Queer Theology is a resistance to normativity and a subversion of the politics of representation which are essentialist and reductionist."[103]

Althaus-Reid thus perceives that the same fragmentation of identity analyzed by Haraway with regard to the feminist movement equally applies to thealogy, as "the fracture of identity (and systematic theological identities) can no longer be ignored." Thus, "the goddess may be re-inscribed in similarity instead of alternatives, unless she becomes Queer and learns to deconstruct herself, to be multitudes and to destabilize her sexuality and political stances."[104] The goddess may deify the category of Woman, leaving in place "heterosexuality as ideology" and a denial of the material reality of the differences between human bodies—or she may choose to become queer, and strive, instead, for differentiation and plurality.[105]

Althaus-Reid and Lisa Isherwood characterize this aspect of queer theology as "in this sense equivalent to a call for biodiversity in theology," another organic metaphor which could benefit from an experimental laboratory cross-pollination with Haraway's cyborg, yielding not simply an image of natural diversity but

---

[100] Marcella Althaus-Reid, "From the Goddess to Queer Theology: The State We Are in Now," *Feminist Theology* 13/2 (2005): p. 265.

[101] Ibid., p. 267.

[102] Ibid., p. 270.

[103] Ibid.

[104] Ibid., p. 271.

[105] Marcella Althaus-Reid and Lisa Isherwood, "Thinking Theology and Queer Theory," *Feminist Theology* 15/3 (2007): p. 304.

techno-bio-diversity. The natural Goddess must become cyborg goddesses: no longer the deified representative of Woman, but the divinities of women. As Ruth Mantin phrases the issue, "can Goddesses travel with nomads and cyborgs?" Mantin's answer is yes: "Goddesses like Medusa, Lilith and Tiamat would be happy to converse with cyborgs about the subversive power of monstrous hybrids. These are no passive Earth Mothers. They do not represent a soft, blobby matrix who invites us to merge into her all-embracing lap ... They are wisdom Goddesses who present embodied ways of knowing and epistemologies which reflect the multiple, fluctuating nature of subjectivity."[106] No less must the God of the Christian theological tradition acknowledge the techno-bio-diversity of the created world, and the human beings who live and love in it.

"More than anything else," Althaus-Reid and Isherwood write, "Queer Theology is an incarnated, body theology."[107] This means not simply celebrating a generic embodiment but a "plunge into flesh in its unrefined fullness in order to embrace and be embraced by the divine." Doing so impels the recognition that "we have constructed bodies within boundaries that could never contain them but have at times distorted and mutilated them."[108] Indeed, "heterosexuality [is] a construction which does not even properly apply to the real experiences of heterosexual people."[109] This theological emphasis on the specificity and materiality of the doctrine of incarnation, again, reiterates Haraway's cyborg insight that it is the material reality of our bodies that puts the lie to our ontological categories of Man and Woman and even Human—leading to the necessity of paying attention to the ways in which we construct our identities as posthuman.

Though the term hybridity itself makes no significant appearance in queer theology discourse, the concept of hybridity, as the material reality which belies pure ontological categories, including gender, is ubiquitously present. Althaus-Reid recognizes that such theological work is "boundary work," a phrase reminiscent of the cyborg.[110] It is precisely the "myth of heterosexuality as a natural or a given" that queer theology seeks to radically question. This willingness to forgo the sanctity of the categorically natural is indeed a cyborg characteristic; moreover, it is not the result of an embrace of the categorically unnatural, but of a deliberately hybrid positioning of the theologian with regard to the heteronormative categories of gender and sexuality. Althaus-Reid writes that independent of the sexual identity of the theologian as an individual, theology is the art of "a critical bisexual action and reflection on God and humanity."[111] This deliberate positioning of the

---

[106] Ruth Mantin, "Can Goddesses Travel with Nomads and Cyborgs? Feminist Thealogies in a Postmodern Context," *Feminist Theology* 26 (2001): p. 40.
[107] Althaus-Reid and Isherwood, "Thinking Theology and Queer Theory," p. 309.
[108] Ibid., p. 310.
[109] Ibid., p. 308.
[110] Althaus-Reid, "From the Goddess to Queer Theology," p. 272.
[111] Marcella Althaus-Reid, *The Queer God* (London, 2003), p. 15.

theologian as critically bisexual underscores the attention given to the construction and deconstruction of the boundaries of sexual identity in the doing of theology.

Finally, of course, it is Haraway herself who offers the cyborg as both a figure of hope for a "world without gender" and as a "junior sibling in the much bigger, queer family of companion species."[112] And while Haraway's critical stance with regard to the Christian tradition may be overtly hostile, she can, as I have argued, also be read in critical relation to Christian theology. The cyborg's material-spiritual hybridity, as well as its material specificity, are articulated in a queer theology that takes seriously our human bodies as sites of both revelation and difference.

Just as the work of theologians with disabilities highlights the necessity of recognizing the material differences among (post)human bodies as a theological and anthropological reality, queer theologians remind us that the heteronormative gender roles and sexuality accepted as "natural" and "given," are in fact specific social constructions which exclude the material bodily reality of many people. Willingness to recognize the permeability and hybridity of these constructed categories may be described in Althaus-Reid's terms, as a critical bisexuality, or in Haraway's term, cyborg.

*Postcolonial Theologies as Cyborg*

Human bodies are also sites for inscribing meaning and for contestations of power, a fact always in view for Haraway, as well as biological and material realities. Postcolonial theologians have made the connection between bodily hybridity and social/ethnic hybridity, highlighting the experience of hybridity as a distinctive theological resource. Here, again, the disjunction between the categories of homogeneous cultural identity and the material reality of hybridity provide a specifically embodied starting point for constructing theology, and a critical perspective on theological constructions of the human.

"Postcolonial" is a broad and somewhat contested term, as Kwok Pui-Lan's summary of recent debate over the term demonstrates. Despite the possible pitfalls of using a single term to designate a variety of perspectives generated from different historical and geographical particularities, as well as the possible temporal interpretation of the prefix "post-", the term postcolonial is widely employed in a variety of contexts and disciplines. Kwok notes that "for many postcolonial critics, postcolonial denotes not merely a temporal period or a political transition of power, but also a reading strategy and discursive practice that seek to unmask colonial epistemological frameworks, unravel Eurocentric logics, and interrogate stereotypical cultural representations."[113]

---

[112] Haraway, "A Cyborg Manifesto," p. 181, Donna J. Haraway, *The Haraway Reader* (New York, 2004), p. 300.

[113] Kwok Pui-Lan, *Postcolonial Imagination & Feminist Theology* (Louisville, KY, 2005), p. 2.

The concept of hybridity, variously signified, therefore takes center stage in postcolonial theologies in a way which destabilizes colonial cultural representations and the categories of identity that rely on them. Jung Young Lee's theological concept of marginality and Virgilio Elizondo's *mestizaje* stand as two exceptionally clear articulations of postcolonial hybridity within a theological context. Kwok Pui-Lan's autobiographical essay demonstrates the importance of her own experience of hybridity in the formation of her theology, and her "postcolonial feminist theology" pulls together the political and economic critiques of postcolonial theory with the gender and sexuality critiques of feminism and queer theory, in order to generate a theology which is aware of the multiple dimensions of its construction.

Jung Young Lee's use of the metaphors of marginality and centrality, applied to the Christian theological tradition, originates in his own experience of hybridity, and defined as "in-between and in-both." Lee writes, "I am situated ambivalently between two worlds—America and Asia," and experiences rejection from both because of his roots in the other. To be in-between, then, means also to be part of neither; marginality is the result of hybridity, and here, it is a negative experience. This is to view hybridity from the viewpoint of the center; however, Lee also sees hybridity and its consequent marginality as a positive location, from which one may be not in-between, but in-both, a view of hybridity from the margin. Both the positive and the negative aspects of the experience of marginality must be affirmed. Further, in affirming both aspects of marginality, the marginal theologian may then become, rather than the margin of the center, the "margin of marginality," a new space in which the old categories of identity may be challenged, and the necessity of a "center" subverted.[114] In identifying the "margin of marginality" as a place of empowerment, Lee, like Haraway, sees hybridity as a source of strength and vision, rather than a wholly oppressive reality. At the same time, Lee, like Haraway, does not shrink from acknowledging the negativities of the experience of the center's oppression of the margin.

Miguel H. Díaz's synopsis of U.S. Hispanic and Latina/o perspectives on theological anthropology provides a sense of the centrality of the notion of hybridity as a crucial experiential component of theologizing within this context.[115] Specifically, the theological anthropology of Virgilio Elizondo, as a pioneering and foundational theology, demonstrates the importance of hybridity as an

---

[114] Jung Y. Lee, *Marginality: The Key to Multicultural Theology* (Minneapolis, MN, 1995), pp. 29–76. Lee writes that despite his deliberately autobiographical style, his experiences of hybridity are echoed in the experiences of other Asian-Americans, especially Chinese-Americans, Korean-Americans, and Japanese-Americans (p. 29).

[115] Miguel H. Díaz, *On Being Human: U.S. Hispanic and Rahnerian Perspectives* (Maryknoll, NY, 2001), pp. 23–59. Díaz provides a brief synopsis of the theological anthropologies of Virgilio Elizondo, Roberto S. Goizueta, Orlando O. Espín, Ada María Isasi-Díaz, María Pilar Aquino, and Alex García-Rivera. In all of these theologians, the experience of hybridity is a theological reference point.

embodied and social experience. Elizondo's interpretation of Jesus emphasizes his socio-cultural identity as a Galilean: a hybrid identity which was at once powerful and subversive. Díaz writes, "Galilee was a crossroads of peoples, a place where cultures and religious traditions mingled. Elizondo claims that this cultural mixture, or '*mestizaje*,' became for other Jews 'a sign of impurity and a cause for rejection.' Yet what for others may have been the cause of rejection, Elizondo sees as the cause of divine election. For Elizondo, the logic of divine election implies the embrace of *mestizaje*—a 'both/and' rather than an 'either/or' anthropology."[116]

For both Lee and Elizondo, it is important to note that while it is ethic or socio-cultural hybridity that is the issue, this experience of hybridity is inevitably tied to bodily human reality. The experience of racial, ethnic, or cultural hybridity is at rock bottom an experience of particular bodies resisting imperial cultural interpretation; the material reality does not fit the established categories. In the task of constructing a theological anthropology, this experience of being a body which does not fit the dominant cultural categories is inevitably a formative one, and provides a perspective in which one's own flesh testifies to the inadequacy of reigning categories of the human.

Kwok Pui-Lan's feminist postcolonial theology, however, stands as perhaps the clearest example of how these various discourses may come together into a multi-faceted critical theology. Perceiving a gap between postcolonial theologies which analyze economic and political realities, and feminist and queer theologies which focus on gender, Kwok argues that "gender, religion and colonialism interplay in intricate and myriad ways, and scholars have to examine these triadic elements together."[117] She thus seeks to bring together postcolonial theory, feminist theology, and queer theology in order to construct a "postcolonial feminist theology" which revolves around three loci: resignifying gender, requeering sexuality, and redoing theology.[118]

In seeking an analysis which acknowledges the "implosion" of these categories of analysis, Kwok is already following in Haraway's cyborg footsteps. In resignifying gender, Kwok argues that the task at hand is one in which gender must be structured so as to avoid both the "essentialized gender binarism" and the loss of gender altogether "in the poststructuralist play of difference." This means asking the question, "What sort of female gendered bodies and subjects are produced by the globalization process in the households, workplaces, churches, academy, or military?"[119] Haraway, too, seeks to navigate this conceptual terrain, and the cyborg is introduced in large part as its answer.[120] Further, Kwok follows Chandra Talpade Mohanty and M. Jacqui Alexander in advocating a "transnational feminist

---

[116] Ibid., p. 27.

[117] Kwok, *Postcolonial Imagination & Feminist Theology*, p. 7.

[118] Ibid., p. 128.

[119] Ibid., p. 136.

[120] Ibid. Kwok's loci for consideration are quite similar to Haraway's in the "Cyborg Manifesto."

project," which requires contextual and geographical specificity in the construction of gender, rather than a false universalizing category, resulting in the possibility of political coalition-building on the basis of "common differences."[121] Here, one might say that Kwok has located Michelle Bastian's lost political cyborg, without consciously seeking her. In requeering sexuality, Kwok argues that "the manifold and entangled relations of homophobia and homoerotic desire to gender, race, religion and colonialism scarcely surface on the pages of white queer theology, either in the United States or Britain."[122] Kwok cites Althaus-Reid's "indecent theology" as making "the connection among sex, politics and liberation theology," pointing out that "sexuality has much to do with the globalized economic structures, political terror, and violence, as well as with maintaining colonial and neo-colonial power."[123]

These considerations lead Kwok to identify three issues for an emerging postcolonial feminist theology: first, the circulation of theological symbols and cultural capital in the colonial period and its permutations in late capitalism; second, the conceptualization of religious difference and the construction and maintenance of religious boundaries; third, environmental degradation and its impact on the lives of those (women) who bear the majority of its consequences.[124] The cyborg nature of all of these issues is apparent. Kwok writes, "an important theological agenda will be to analyze the use of theological symbols for the colonization of women's minds and bodies, as well as the reappropriation of such symbols for resistance, subversion and empowerment."[125] Just as Haraway perceived the need to reappropriate the cultural symbol of the cyborg and employ it as a feminist icon in order to subvert the power of the dominant construction of the hypermasculine, militarist technoborg, Kwok identifies a similar need to identify and reappropriate specifically theological symbols. And, just as Haraway defines the issue of differences in terms of the construction and maintenance of ontological boundaries, Kwok sees the same dynamic at work within the world of interreligious dialogue, regarding the construction and maintenance of religious boundaries; further, she suggests that "Asian feminist theologians" may contribute in this regard precisely "because they are known in the ecumenical circles for their 'syncretism' and their defying rigid and stable religious identities."[126]

Finally, of course, attention to the embodied and interdependent aspects of human lives echoes the cyborg's insight that hybridity implies connection. Yet

---

[121] Ibid. Kwok draws on Chandra T. Mohanty, *Feminism without Borders: Decolonizing Theory, Practicing Solidarity* (Durham, NC, 2003) and Chandra T. Mohanty and M. Jacqui Alexander, eds, *Feminist Genealogies, Colonial Legacies, Democratic Futures* (New York, 1997).

[122] Kwok, *Postcolonial Imagination & Feminist Theology*, p. 141.

[123] Ibid., p. 144.

[124] Ibid., pp. 144–5.

[125] Ibid., p. 144.

[126] Ibid., p. 145.

this last issue is only briefly identified, and in terms that echo the generality of Graham and Garner's ecotheological interpretation of the cyborg rather than queer theology's specific emphasis on transgressive hybrid embodiment. Here it may be that the conscious addition of the cyborg to Kwok's postcolonial feminist analysis might yield a greater degree of focus on women's bodies as the sites of both oppression and potential liberation. The cyborg also highlights an analytic dimension implicit in the categories of the global economy and the military, but which is sufficiently complex in its own right to require focused attention: technology. As a dimension of human agency intertwined with political, economic, and military interests, technology is one other specific locus at which religion, gender, and colonialism collide.

How will all of this be done? Kwok suggests that one might work either within the accepted traditional loci of Christian theology, reworking and rearticulating its categories through a postcolonial feminist perspective, or begin with postcolonial feminist analysis and articulate theological issues and themes from that perspective.[127] Kwok concludes, "Who will be interested in these theological hybrids, and for whom is postcolonial feminist theology written?" The answer is, unsurprisingly, an imagined hybrid community of intellectuals across various disciplines, composed of those "interested in the relation between theology and empire building and having the commitment to subvert the use of sacred symbols to oppress people," that is, a coalition of cyborgs.[128]

## When Species Meet

The cyborg's hybridity, extending across the human/nonhuman ontological boundaries in both ecological and technological directions, provides a provocative symbol for ecotheological work. Firmly embedded within evolutionary history and ecological environment, the (post)human becomes one creature among others—unique in its own species' distinctiveness, but not, for that reason, the sole representative of its own separate ontological category. This requires, as Hefner, Kull, Graham, and Garner have each acknowledged, a rearticulation of theological notions of human uniqueness within the Christian tradition, which often presume ontological discontinuity with the rest of God's creation. In this final constructive section, we will take up the ecotheological insight, voiced by Elaine Graham, that "ethically and experientially, the cyborg is heuristic figure that suggests the rejection of solutions of either denial or mastery in favour of a post/human ethic grounded in complicity with, not mastery over, non-human nature, animals and machines."[129] Further, Graham concludes, this "post/human ethic can be neither

---

[127] Ibid., p. 147.
[128] Ibid., p. 148.
[129] Graham, *Representations of the Post/Human*, p. 229.

an escape into technocratic invulnerability nor a retreat into the imagined purity of organic essentialism."[130]

The ecotheological implications of cyborg hybridity are spelled out succinctly by Kevin J. O'Brien. O'Brien points out that "while Haraway can accept no hard and fast distinction between humanity and the rest of the world, neither does she dismiss all claims to human uniqueness."[131] This nuanced negotiation of the notion of human uniqueness parallels J. Wentzel van Huyssteen's theological proposal in Chapter 4, as an affirmation of both embeddedness and uniqueness grounded in an appreciation of the importance of human embodiment. Haraway's recognition of this embedded and embodied human uniqueness, O'Brien further argues, provides the force of her environmental ethics, which comes partly from an insistence that human beings must be responsible for our particular agency and impact on the world.[132]

This emphasis on particularity is the next move within an ecotheological appropriation of the cyborg. Unpacking precisely what this posthuman reconsideration of human uniqueness means, however, has not yet happened in ecotheological consideration beyond the general affirmation of human embeddedness within creation. Here, Haraway's move into the explicit consideration of species boundaries, as well as Cary Wolfe's recent work on the connections between disability studies, animal studies, and the posthuman, provide a way to sharpen this theological insight that human uniqueness need not be theologically articulated at the expense of human belonging in the (techno) natural world. This move from generality to specificity, from the dismantling of the opposing categories of Nature and Culture and affirmation of embedded uniqueness to a consideration of active kinships, pushes theologians within the Christian tradition to consider more explicitly exactly what our ethical obligations to the nonhuman others around us may be, and how best to meet them.

Wolfe's analysis forges, through his emphasis on posthuman embodiment, a link between the fields of disability and animal studies, the aim of which is gleaning what these distinct fields of academic inquiry offer "about who or what comes 'after' the subject as it is modeled in liberal humanism"; Wolfe's hope is that, "in the wake of this 'after,' new lines of empathy, affinity, and respect between different forms of life, both human and nonhuman, may be realized," in ways not possible within the framework of liberal humanism's singular, normative, and unique construct of the human.[133] The new lines of empathy, affinity, and respect are generated from an appreciation of each human and nonhuman's specific embodied vulnerabilities.

Picking up the recent internal critique within the field of disability studies, as some scholars seek to move away from "the fetishization of agency" and the ways in which this reasserts the normative liberal humanist subject, Wolfe

---

[130] Ibid., p. 234.
[131] O'Brien, "An Ethics of Natureculture and Creation," p. 301.
[132] Ibid.
[133] Wolfe, *What Is Posthumanism?*, p. 127.

simultaneously affirms and critiques Rosemarie Garland-Thomson's application of "the vibrant logic of biodiversity to humans."[134] Her recognition that all bodies need care and assistance to live, a recognition which resists the cultural denial of vulnerability, contingency, and mortality, are, Wolfe argues, exactly right—but she fails to recognize that "these ethical imperatives extend *across* species lines and bind us, in our shared vulnerability, to other living beings who think and feel, live and die, have needs and desires, and require care just as we do."[135] Wolfe sees this failure to extend the posthuman insight into the nonhuman realm in Garland-Thomson's discussion of a magazine cover featuring a model accompanied by a service dog; while Garland-Thomson celebrates the shift in the image of disability represented by the image, in its juxtaposition of "a visually normative fashion model" with the "mark of disability" represented by the dog, Wolfe suggests, "wouldn't we do better to imagine this example as an irreducibly different and unique form of subjectivity—neither *Homo sapiens* nor *Canis familiaris*, neither 'disabled' nor 'normal,' but something else altogether, a shared trans-species being-in-the-world constituted by complex relations of trust, respect, dependence, and communication (as anyone who has ever trained—or relied on—a service dog would be the first to tell you?)."[136]

Despite Wolfe's posthumanist reinterpretation, his critique of Garland-Thomson's analysis demonstrates that this example of interspecies collaboration remains locked in its dominant cultural context of disability—as long as it stands alone. Here, Haraway's drilled-down, detailed examinations of multiple locations and dimensions of human and canine interactions contribute a necessary reminder that such "trans-species being-in-the-world" is a mark of all human life, not simply in the unconscious mode in which we as "walking ecologies" exist in symbiosis with all sorts of other critters, but also in the personal, social, economic, and even political dimensions of human life which so often exclude overt recognition of the nonhuman participants within them. Haraway moves from the locus of dog breeding to the experimental laboratory and from South African politics and the fate of wolfish hybrid security dogs, to her own personal training in the sport of agility with her dog, Cayenne. Such a wide-ranging set of examples of the ways in which any human's life in entangled with and dependent upon multiple nonhumans serves as a corrective to the assumption that such relationships and dependencies are the exceptions.

Further, Haraway's unflinching look at the ethical ambivalence that attends the realities of living as companion species once again forcefully brings narratives of shared suffering, vulnerability, and asymmetry into consideration. Haraway argues that instrumentality itself is not "the root of turning animals (or people) into dead things, into machines whose *reactions* are of interest but who have no

---

[134] Ibid., pp. 138–41.
[135] Ibid., p. 140.
[136] Ibid., p. 141.

*presence*, no *face*, that demands recognition, caring and shared pain."[137] Rather, Haraway claims, relationships of work, use, and instrumentality are intrinsic to bodily existence; the problems arise in automatically legitimating and/or denying the reality of instrumental relations which undergird bodily existence. Humans use other animals unequally, in experiments, directly or indirectly, in daily living, knowing, and eating; sorting through which instrumental relations should be ended, and which nurtured, requires "the kind of engagement that keeps the inequality from becoming commonsensical or taken as obviously okay."[138]

This is as true in the lab as it is at the dinner table, two specific locations where the harsher realities of interspecies relationship are straightforwardly interrogated, and, not coincidentally, with theological overtones. As Haraway remarks, in her revisitation of Lynn Randolph's *The Passion of the OncoMouse,* "it is tempting to see my sister OncoMouse as a sacrifice, and certainly the barely secular Christian theater of the suffering servant in science and the everyday lab idiom of sacrificing experimental animals invite that thinking," but to accept this is to accept the "transcendent excellence of the Human over the Animal, which can then be killed without the charge of murder."[139] Seeing OncoMouse and her Dial-a-Mouse descendants as victims only is to participate in the legitimation of this instrumental relationship through a baptism into innocence via the borrowed idiom of religious sacrifice. What happens, Haraway asks, if instead we do not regard or treat lab animals as victims, or as other to the human, or relate to their suffering and deaths as sacrifice? There is no once-for-all answer to this question, but when the human becomes posthuman, no longer opposed to the nonhuman, use of and killing of nonhuman bodies becomes a matter of confronting shared suffering, and acknowledging, further, that this suffering is asymmetrically borne. This leads Haraway to the conclusion, expressed with some degree of fear and trembling, that it is a misstep both "to separate the world's beings into those who may be killed and those who may not"—but equally a misstep "to pretend to live outside killing."[140]

In her final "parting bite," Haraway applies this insight to the practice of "eating well together." Observing that "maybe God can have a solitary meal, but terran critters cannot," Haraway comments, "in eating we are most inside the differential relationalities that make us who and what we are and that materialize what we must do if response and regard are to have any meaning personally and politically."[141] To make her point that "there is no way to eat and not to kill, no way to eat and not to become one with other mortal beings to whom we are accountable," she recalls a departmental party at which the roasting of a feral pig for the communal meal caused a ruckus among those attending. The crisis, she writes, was one that could not be solved by the partygoers by appeal to human exceptionalism, the oneness of

---

[137] Haraway, *When Species Meet*, p. 71.
[138] Ibid., p. 77.
[139] Ibid., pp. 76–7.
[140] Ibid., p. 79.
[141] Ibid., pp. 294–5.

all things, or to the calculus of suffering and choice, because "all the alternatives carry their own burden of assigning who lives and who dies and how."[142]

The Christological, eucharistic implications of these posthuman musings on human and nonhuman suffering, killing, dying, eating, and incorporation add a rich, new dimension to ecotheological appropriations of the cyborg. An ethic of complicity with, rather than mastery over, nonhuman nature is not a plea for an idealistic and inevitably delayed eschatological lion-and-lamb vision. Rather, as Haraway's dual description of the act of eating as both killing and incorporation reminds us, partaking of the sacrament is participating in a narrative in which both suffering and redemption are made equally present. To seek forgiveness is not the same as laying claim to innocence.

## The Cyborgs in the Garden

In this final musing on the possibilities of a cyborg theological anthropology, I dare to imitate Haraway's use of provocative figures to shape an answer that flatly contradicts her original assertion that the cyborg does not belong in the Garden of Eden: Adam and Eve as cyborg.[143] The Genesis narrative of humanity's first parents need not be read in the organic, originary, heteronormative, naturalized, and universalizing mode that has given us both a problematic original innocence and an even more problematic original sin. As interpreters of this biblical narrative of our cyborg origins—in which Adam is not born of Woman but is manufactured of material elements not unlike those of the flesh of humanity's monstrous cousin the golem, and in which Eve, too, is manufactured out of superfluous flesh in a strange foreshadowing of our own emergent biotech capabilities—how can we read such a myth as one of Nature, Man, and Woman in perfectly ordered, natural existence?

The elements of a posthuman relationality are also undeniably present. God marks this creature, the human, as unique in no way other than God's chosen relation to it; the human dwells, walks, and talks with the nonhuman—God, but also the nonhuman animals, including an extremely ontologically suspect serpent—the human is not "alone in the world." In the Garden of Eden, all manner of human and nonhuman creatures exist. Embedded within a nexus of strange boundaries of human and nonhuman relationships—human and divine, human and animal, human and human—the cyborg pair in the Garden are what they are because of the construction and contestation of these boundaries. What does it mean to be made a cyborg in the *imago dei*? Simply to have been made a creature who is simultaneously kin and other: to God, to other humans, and to nonhumans. The boundaries do not disappear in our acknowledgment of our construction and negotiation of them—they become conditions of relationship, not obstacles preventing it.

---

[142] Ibid., p. 299.
[143] Haraway, "A Cyborg Manifesto," p. 151.

This cyborg reconstruction suggests further that the Fall represents, not a loss of original innocence (which does not exist) nor a loss or deformation of the *imago dei* (which, as relationship, continues), but a poignant renegotiation of the ontological boundary between the human and the divine. Reaching for the knowledge of good and evil provides a "rather dramatic new dimension to the image or likeness of God," one which stands in apparent tension with God's intent of divine and human closeness. Nothing in the biblical narrative resolves this tension, the contradiction between the created likeness and the epistemological likeness; yet what, in our cyborg ancestors' bid for greater understanding and closeness to the divine, for greater incorporation of the divine into themselves (eating, after all, being a material and sacred act), is there that seems strange, out of character, or even necessarily blameworthy? Transgression of categorical boundaries in the living out of material embodied reality is, after all, what cyborgs and (post)humans are all about. The aspect of our unique humanness gained, and lamented in the Fall, is also the means by which we come to know, and relate, to each other and our nonhuman kin, including God.

This is not to suggest that this element of our humanness is unproblematic, an entirely "happy fault." Certainly the narrative itself spells out the consequences of this renegotiation of the human *imago dei*: a shift from gathering to agrarian labor, a painful and awkward descent for the oversized *Homo sapiens* cranium down the birth canal, an instinctive fear of aspiring too far towards divinity. But the cyborg has always been an ambivalent figure, capable of knowing and doing both good and evil, and is no less so here. There is no innocence to be regained for the cyborgs in the Garden; to be cyborg is to know good and evil, that is, to know that innocence is illusory, and what must be pursued is elusive forgiveness.

this "mix" hadn't happened before the Annunciater

# Chapter 6
# Christology and the Posthuman

In a brief article entitled "Cyborg Embodiment and the Incarnation," Anne Kull suggests that "the concept of the cyborg urges us to see in the Incarnation, and generally in embodiment of any kind, not a matter of fate and common sense but emancipation and choice."[1] Given Kull's emphasis on the cyborg as a reassertion of the material body, the extension of the systematic implications of the cyborg to the doctrine of the incarnation is almost inevitable. Following Haraway's interpretation of Jesus as a "trickster figure," and describing Jesus as "a hybrid creature," Kull points us in the direction of what we might call the cyborg Christ. At the same time, as Kull openly acknowledges, even as the cyborg upholds the logic of incarnation and embodiment, it troubles the category of the human. Destabilizing what it means to be human troubles what it means for God to become human; this might seem overtly threatening, but Kull sees it as a theological and Christological opportunity.

The hybridity of the cyborg Christ, in light of the traditional Christological definition of Chalcedon, prompts a reconsideration of the substantive notions of both humanity and divinity, and a rehabilitation of what was once anathematized as heresy. Reconstruction of not just the ontological category of the "human," but also concepts of personal identity from a posthuman perspective also opens up new possibilities for answering persistent age-old Christological questions regarding the possibility of the unity of Christ's person and divine/human status. Finally, the question of Christ's "ultimate humanity," as a divine figure who is not simply human, but who (re)defines the human, is considered in light of the posthuman.

Reintroducing the concept of hybridity into Christology is in some ways more theologically problematic than considering hybridity in the context of theological anthropology, for classical Christology explicitly rejects hybridity and mixture, upholding not only the concept of substantive dual "natures" but the necessity of their separation. Thus, this chapter opens with a brief review of the Christological doctrine and heresies negotiated in the years leading up to the Council of Chalcedon (451). This theological background will elucidate the reasons that the notion of mixture and hybridity were anathematized as heretical, and how this theological conviction, shared nearly universally, cuts across the boundaries of orthodoxy and heresy. Against this background, the reintroduction of hybridity into theology and Christology means a rehabilitation of a classically heretical

---

[1] Anne Kull, "Cyborg Embodiment and the Incarnation," *Currents in Theology and Mission* 28/3–4 (2001): p. 284.

notion, and a re-evaluation of the philosophical concepts that form the framework of classical Christology.

Further, Haraway's interpretation of Jesus as a "trickster figure" and Anne Kull's suggestion that the cyborg points us to the incarnation provide the connection to the already existing notion of a hybrid Jesus. Feminist, postcolonial, and queer Christologies prompt an acknowledgment of both the historical hybridity of the human Jesus, the inevitable hybridity of all Christological constructions, as well as specific reconsiderations of Christ's ethnicity and gender.

**A Cyborg Christ**

The central Christological problem negotiated by Chalcedon can be phrased simply: how can one talk about a single, unified subject who is both substantively human and substantively divine? The potential heretical errors are multiple: one may err by sacrificing the unity of Christ in order to affirm both substantive natures, or one may err by sacrificing either of the two natures in order to preserve unity. Or, even worse, one may err by holding on to the notion of unity so strongly that both the human and divine natures merged into a single nature, no longer fully human or fully divine. Indeed, all of these heretical mistakes were committed by one theologian or another, in the years leading up to and following Chalcedon.

Richard A. Norris's summary of the various Christological formulations, both orthodox and heretical, leading up to Chalcedon provides a succinct background for this discussion. Beginning with the New Testament's portrayal of Jesus, Norris identifies three important developments: first, that Jesus is proclaimed as "Lord," both of the Christian community and of the cosmos; second, Jesus' life and earthly ministry were understood as the expression of divine will and initiative; third, that Jesus is seen as the presence of God "with us."[2] These biblical proclamations, and their early exposition by church fathers, result in "a portrayal of Jesus as having a dual character—as embodying in himself the unity of two ways of being, spiritual and fleshly, divine and human." This, Norris writes, provides the essential paradigm and dictates the agenda for later patristic Christology.[3]

The rise of Logos-theology, beginning in the second century, provided a way of interpreting the dual character of Jesus as the incarnate divine Logos. However, "it was not clear exactly what that term 'divine' meant ... it might denote a quality of which there can be degrees, and on such an understanding it would be consistent to say that the Logos was divine and yet not God in the same sense, to the same degree, as the Father."[4] This indeed seems to be the formulation of Arius, whose doctrine of the Logos expressed two convictions based on his understanding of the

---

[2] Richard A. Norris, ed., *The Christological Controversy*, Sources of Early Christian Thought (Philadelphia, PA, 1980), p. 3.
[3] Ibid., p. 5.
[4] Ibid., p. 17.

unity of God and of divine transcendence: first, the Logos could not be God in the proper sense, and second, that the Logos mediates the relation of God to the world. Based on this doctrine of divine transcendence, in itself not heretical, Arians could logically argue that "the things said about Jesus in the gospels are not things one can say about the Logos if the Logos is truly God." Hunger, emotions, ignorance, and mortality could simply not be attributed to divinity.

Norris writes that the Arian position reveals two important assumptions: the first is that in the person of Jesus the Logos is the sole real subject; "the Logos is the 'self' in Jesus." The second assumption is that of a basic disjunction between the nature of humanity and the nature of divinity, such that "they are not merely different but logically irreconcilable."[5] The Bishop of Alexandria, Athanasius, refuted the Arians with a Christology which accepted an enfleshed Logos, or Logos-*sarx*, Christological construction; his disagreement with the Arians was not their view of the constitution of Jesus' person, but their deficient view of the divinity of the Logos. Thus, Athanasius challenged the Arians' solution to the theological problem of the impossible conjunction of the divine and the human, but left the first assumption, that the Logos constituted the "self" of Jesus, intact.

The Logos-*sarx* Christology of Athanasius was taken to its logical conclusion by Apollinaris of Laodicea: in a Christological model which presumed the Logos as the sole real subject, the doctrine that Jesus lacked an independent, human soul or intellect seemed a matter of logical necessity. Norris writes, "If the Logos had 'put on' a rational soul as well as flesh, the result would, [Apollinaris] thought, have been conflict. Either the Logos would simply dominate the human soul and thus destroy the freedom by which it was human, or the human soul would be an independent center of initiative and Jesus would be, in effect, schizophrenic."[6] The denial of a human soul in Jesus, of course, risks making Jesus less than fully human—a serious consequence, and one which, in the end, would result in the repudiation of Apollinarism at Chalcedon.

In contrast, the Antiochene school favored a Logos-*anthropos* construction, which insisted not only on the full humanity of the man Jesus, but strictly separated the human and divine natures. The emphasis of the Antiochene school on the two natures in Christ, the divine Logos and the complete human being Jesus of Nazareth, can be traced back to Paul of Samosata. The motivation for the Antiochene school's emphasis on the two natures appears to be twofold. First, the Antiochenes were concerned to protect the divine Logos from the misattribution of human passions, change, and corruption. Thus, in their response to the heresy of Arianism, rather than follow the Alexandrian bishop Athanasius in challenging the Arian solution to the problem of the conjunction of the divine and the human, the Antiochenes solved the problem by separating the natures and proposing two subjects of attribution in Christ. Second, this strong disjunction between the divine and the human also meant that the Antiochenes, unlike Athanasius and Apollinaris, could not regard the divine

---

[5] Ibid., pp. 19–20.

[6] Ibid., p. 22.

Logos himself as the model of humanity, but rather the human nature of Jesus of Nazareth. The Logos, as divine, was not the nature after which humanity could model itself, but rather than "Jesus the human being ... in his movement to a fulfilled life of immutable goodness."[7]

The language of indwelling, originating with Paul of Samosata, is characteristic of Antiochene Christology. Theodore of Mopsuestia viewed the incarnation as a special, unique case of divine indwelling, in which Jesus could be spoken of as a human being who shared the divine sonship of the Logos in a way no other human being might claim. The unity of Christ, for Theodore, is a "prosopic" union, a union which becomes perfected throughout the course of Jesus' life and struggle against evil, "until, in the resurrection, the human being and the Logos show that they have always been, so to speak, one functional identity—one *prosopon*."[8] Thus, one important aspect of Theodore's Christology is that "he conceives the relationship between God and humanity in the incarnation in terms of will," and the unity of Christ as the result of Jesus' willing and acting at one with the Logos.[9]

The Christological controversy leading to Chalcedon began with the collision of the Antiochene Christology of the monk Nestorius, and the Alexandrian Christology of Cyril of Alexandria. Shortly after becoming bishop of Constantinople, Nestorius preached a sermon suggesting that the Virgin Mary could not properly be called *theotokos*, since such a title implied the attribution of birth to the Logos, an affront to the Antiochene sensibility regarding the impropriety of attributing human characteristics to the divine Logos. Nestorius' in-your-face sermon invited quick response from Cyril of Alexandria, who affirmed the Alexandrian Christological position of "hypostatic union" between the two natures of Christ. A certain amount of mutual misunderstanding and semantic difficulty added to the controversy, as Nestorius claimed that Cyril's phrase signaled a "mixture" or "confusion" of the divine and human natures, though, despite his ambiguities of language, Cyril seems rather to have meant that "the one hypostasis and the one nature are the Logos himself, making a full human existence his own," rather than the "composite nature" Nestorius feared.

In the Formula of Reunion (A.D. 433), the Antiochenes conceded the propriety of the title *theotokos* for Mary; in their turn, Alexandrians conceded the use of the expression "two natures," and that one could distinguish attributes proper to divinity from attributes proper to humanity, as long as the Logos-*sarx* model was affirmed. This compromise was eventually taken up, along with other documents, by the Council of Chalcedon, and the "definition" composed by the council accepts these elements of both the Alexandrian and Antiochene schools.

Thus, what comes out of the Council of Chalcedon is a view of Christ which accepts two premises important in a posthuman consideration of Christology: first, that "mixture" or "confusion" of the divine and the human is theologically

---

[7] Ibid., p. 24.
[8] Ibid., p. 25.
[9] Ibid.

improper, and second, that there is a single unified subject in Christ. These coexist uneasily, of course, but craft a position in which "orthodoxy consists in the acknowledgment that Jesus is one subject, who is properly spoken of both as God—the divine Logos—and as a human being."[10]

Thus when Anne Kull writes that Jesus deliberately poses as "a hybrid creature," she is certainly employing a loaded description, given the context of Christological formulations that have declared it anathema to attribute not only hybridity but creatureliness to Jesus the Christ. The deliberate provocation of this phrase, however, points to the necessity of further consideration of the logic of orthodox formulations which eschew hybridity and creatureliness. It is interesting to note that the perceived theological necessity to protect the divine nature from mixture with the human is precisely that which produced both the heresy of Arius, who taught that Christ was a creature and therefore not fully divine, and Nestorius, who protected the divine nature by proposing two subjects of attribution in Christ. These heretical proposals were different solutions to the same theological problem, of how to conceptualize the incarnation of the divine without thereby losing or corrupting the divine nature.

Even more interesting is that this same theological assumption is present in the thought of Athanasius, who opposed the Arians and provided the Logos-*sarx* construction which would be the Alexandrian's theological counter to the Antiochenes. Despite the strain it placed on his Christology, particularly in providing an account of Christ's occasional ignorance, Athanasius taught that "tears, hunger, ignorance and the like do not belong to the Logos in himself; they belong to him by virtue of his incarnate state. They are proper to the flesh which is proper to the Logos."[11] Thus in both orthodox and heretical formulations, in both Alexandrian and Antiochene schools, the presumption that divinity and humanity could not truly mix was unquestionably present.

Why would this be the case? F. LeRon Shults argues persuasively that this is the result of the patristic theologians' reliance on philosophical categories of substance. The logic undergirding substantive notions of divinity and substantive notions of humanity means that, inevitably, no truly satisfactory account of how two things might become one can be found. Therefore, as Norris notes, the definition of Chalcedon is "essentially a rule of language. Its terms are not calculated to picture the way in which Jesus is put together. Rather, they are calculated to explain how it is proper to speak of him."[12] The orthodoxy of Chalcedon consists in juxtaposing two simultaneous yet essentially incompatible accounts of Jesus.

Thus the literally embodied and symbolic ontological hybridity of the cyborg presents an overt challenge to the theological repudiation of mixture enshrined in Chalcedonian Christology. Hybridity within the context of these substantive categories of humanity and divinity is logically and definitively heretical. The

---

[10] Ibid., p. 31.
[11] Ibid., p. 20.
[12] Ibid., pp. 30–1.

theological options are to reject the posthuman and hybridity altogether, as does Brent Waters, to interpret Chalcedon itself in terms of hybridity, as does Stephen Garner, or to rehabilitate the classical heresy of mixture, as does Anne Kull.

Waters contends that any "posthuman theology" definitively and necessarily lacks a redemptive Christology: "at best," he writes, "Jesus is a kind of divine virus stimulating an inherent human potential to aspire to self-divination."[13] His repudiation of the image of Jesus as "a kind of divine virus" is suggestive, as such an image hints at hybridity, in a decidedly invasive, anti-human metaphor. In any case, it is very clear that Waters deems it impossible to construct a faithful posthuman Christology, though this seems to be the result of Waters's rejection of anthropological hybridity more than a rejection of the possibility of Christological hybridity.

In arguing, in answer to Brenda Brasher, that the Christian tradition "has within it a range of sources that deal with ambiguity and possibility within the notion of the hybrid," Garner locates the notion of hybridity in a number of theological loci, including Christology, naming it as "perhaps the richest source of engagement."[14] Garner writes, "The assertion that God became 'enfleshed' in the person of Jesus of Nazareth, the incarnation, is a paradox of hybrid existence. In Jesus Christ, both human and divine natures were united in a hypostatic union that brought together two different realities and held them in tension as a unified identity."[15] Garner's "hybrid tension" attempts to maintain the Chalcedonian orthodoxy of the distinction between the two natures, yielding a notion of hybridity that is more about proximity than mixture. Interpreting Kull's comments on the cyborg and incarnation through the lens of Chalcedonian Christology, Garner maintains the categories of divine and human, supernatural and natural, spiritual and material, in a way that resists mixture and instead opts for "dynamic tension."

For Kwok Pui-Lan, however, hybridity is not simply juxtaposition, implying that the Christological definition of Chalcedon cannot be successfully interpreted as a construction of hybridity.[16] Further, Kwok's attention to the power dynamics of postcolonial hybridity hints at the inherent instability of juxtaposition as an interpretive strategy. This mirrors the instability of the juxtaposition of the divine and human natures of Christ; as is well attested by the history of the Christological controversy, the Chalcedonian formula easily tilts under pressure of systematic examination in several potential heretical directions, depending upon whether the human or divine nature is the dominant term. To construct Christ as the juxtaposition of two equally empowered natures is therefore a denial of the instability of the

---

[13] Brent Waters, *From Human to Posthuman: Christian Theology and Technology in a Postmodern World* (Burlington, VT, 2006), p. 106.

[14] Stephen Garner, "Transhumanism and the *Imago Dei*: Narratives of Apprehension and Hope" (PhD Dissertation, The University of Auckland, 2006), pp. 239–42.

[15] Ibid., p. 242.

[16] Pui-lan Kwok, *Postcolonial Imagination & Feminist Theology* (Louisville, KY, 2005), pp. 170–1.

power differential of binary constructions. Finally, of course, the concept of hybridity destabilizes the binary framework itself, as it questions the presumption of rigid boundaries, such as that drawn by Chalcedon between Christ's human and divine natures. Ultimately, Garner's approach fails to do justice to the notion of hybridity the cyborg represents, for the Chalcedonian emphasis on the distinction and separation of the two natures of Christ is precisely a rejection of hybridity.

Kull's embrace of Jesus as "hybrid creature," in contrast, begins with a description of the incarnation as "an attempt to articulate resistance to an otherworldly divine perfection."[17] As a reading of Chalcedon this may be lacking; certainly a notion of otherworldly divine perfection was at work in both orthodox and heretical impulses to maintain the boundary between Christ's human and divine natures. However, as a cyborg perspective on the importance of the doctrine of incarnation, Kull's interpretation underscores the way in which the boundaries between the spiritual and material, divine and human, are being redrawn in the figure of Christ. As a divine/human hybrid, the cyborg Christ "redefines each and every term."[18] As Kull's description of Jesus as "hybrid creature" indicates, an affirmation of hybridity also means a redemption of creatureliness, a healing of the unnecessary theological rift between materiality and spirituality. The cyborg Christ, the hybrid reality of divine humanity, is creature—a statement which, in a theological context which no longer needs to protect the divine nature from material corruption, can be heard in a wholly redemptive way; creature is no longer the opposite of God, or, to put it differently, we creatures are not doomed to relate to God as God's opposition.[19]

*Jesus as Trickster Figure*

Haraway's interpretation of Jesus and Sojourner Truth as figures of (post)humanity outside the narratives of humanism provides a glimpse into what Haraway herself calls the spiritual meaning of cyborg discourse.[20] Despite the fact that "humanity is a modernist figure," whose generic face and universal shape has been that of man, Haraway nonetheless contends that "we need something called humanity."[21] The struggle is to find "a speaker who might figure the self-contradictory and

---

[17] Kull, "Cyborg Embodiment and the Incarnation," p. 284.

[18] Ibid.

[19] This aspect of cyborg Christology reaches systematically toward an articulation of pneumatology that no longer depends upon the binary opposition of natural and supernatural, and thus ties back to the work of Elaine Graham and other ecofeminist theologies.

[20] Donna J. Haraway, "Ecce Homo, Ain't (Ar'n't) I a Woman, and Inappropriate/D Others: The Human in a Post-Humanist Landscape," in Judith Butler and Joan W. Scott (eds), *Feminists Theorize the Political* (New York, 1992), p. 88. While Haraway actually spends more time in this essay on Sojourner Truth, I am focusing solely on her interpretation of Jesus.

[21] Ibid., pp. 86, 88.

necessary condition of a nongeneric humanity."[22] For this, Haraway reinterprets the figures of Jesus and Sojourner Truth as "trickster figures in a rich, dangerous, old and constantly renewed tradition of Judeo-Christian humanism."[23]

Haraway first introduces the notion of the Trickster within the context of her epistemology of "situated knowledges," as a means of characterizing the material world as "witty agent," as opposed to natural resource: "Acknowledging the agency of the world in knowledge makes room for some unsettling possibilities, including a sense of the world's independent sense of humor. Such a sense of humor is not comfortable for humanists and others committed to the world as resource ... The Coyote or Trickster, embodied in American Southwest Indian accounts, suggests our situation when we give up mastery but keep searching for fidelity, knowing all the while we will be hoodwinked."[24] Interpreting Jesus as "trickster figure," then, is a way of articulating a sense in which Jesus is an active participant, rather than passive resource, in our theological and Christological constructions; moreover, an agent who is "a shape changer, who might trouble our notions—all of them: classical, biblical, scientific, modernist, postmodernist, and feminist—of 'the human,' while making us remember why we cannot want this problematic universal."[25] While Haraway does not invoke the cyborg as a symbol in this particular essay, it is helpful to remember that Haraway now situates the cyborg as one among many metaphors with and through which she writes, one of a large cast of "trickster figures": "Throughout ... I have tried to look again at some feminist discards from the Western deck of cards, to look for the trickster figures that might turn a stacked deck into a potent set of wild cards for refiguring possible worlds."[26] Haraway, then, does not call Jesus "cyborg," but as trickster figure, Jesus is an identifiable member of Haraway's "much bigger, queer family of companion species."[27]

Jesus, Haraway claims, has been a trickster figure from the very start, taking on multiple aspects as he is interpreted and reinterpreted throughout the Christian tradition: a figure who is simultaneously the suffering servant of Isaiah morphed into the Jesus of the gospel of John, who is both king and suffering servant, criminal and innocent, scapegoat and savior, God and man. Though, for Christians, Jesus came to signify "the union of humanity and divinity in a universal salvation narrative," the proclamation "Ecce homo!" can, and must, be read ironically by

---

[22] Ibid., p. 86.

[23] Ibid., p. 87.

[24] Donna J. Haraway, "Situated Knowledges: The Science Question in Feminism and the Privilege of Partial Perspective," in *Simians, Cyborgs and Women: The Reinvention of Nature* (New York, 1991), p. 199.

[25] Haraway, "Ecce Homo, Ain't (Ar'n't) I a Woman, and Inappropriate/D Others," p. 98.

[26] Donna J. Haraway, "Introduction," in *Simians, Cyborgs and Women: The Reinvention of Nature* (New York, 1991), p. 4.

[27] Joseph Schneider, *Donna Haraway: Live Theory* (New York, 2005), p. 58.

"post-humanists" who are aware that even while Jesus is interpreted as the universal figure of humanity, Jesus is also "the original mime, the actor of a history that mocks especially the recurrent tales that insist that 'man makes himself.'"[28] Jesus the trickster is not the universal Man of the Enlightenment, one of the "figures of coherent and masterful subjectivity, the bearers of rights, holders of property in the self, legitimate sons with access to language and the power to represent, subjects endowed with inner coherence and rational clarity, the masters of theory, founders of states, and fathers of families, bombs and scientific theories—in short, Man as we have come to know and love him,"[29] but, like the cyborg, is an illegitimate son with whom, as Sojourner Truth observed, Man had nothing to do with—Jesus, after all, came from God, and a woman.[30]

The story of this trickster figure, however, "has constantly to be preserved from heresy, to be kept forcibly in the patriarchal tradition of Christian civilization, to be kept from too much attention to the economies of mimicry and the calamities of suffering."[31] The boundaries of traditional Christology require constant doctrinal policing, because Jesus himself is a trickster who constantly escapes the categorical boundaries of humanity (and divinity). Traditional Christology concerns itself with the category of humanity, a universal category, but attention to Christ's problematic embodiment, its material particularity and brokenness, subverts a Christology which focuses on the abstract categories of humanity and divinity and their impossible union in this one, universal, man. Once again, it is fidelity to specific, material, hybrid reality that dismantles the notion of generic, pure, and universal humanity: a cyborg Christ, a "trickster figure," is a particular body, and a broken, suffering one, at that. Jesus, as a figure of humanity, is a (post)human who disrupts our assumptions about what it means to be categorically human, and (though Haraway keeps her distance from this twin affirmation) a God figure who disrupts our assumptions about God as well. And the ultimate point, in Kull's words, is that this cyborg Christ "can call us to account for our imagined humanity."[32]

## Quest for the Hybridized Jesus

Kwok Pui-Lan's second-order reflection on the hybridities of all Christological construction, including those traditionally accepted as orthodox as well as the self-

---

[28] Haraway, "Ecce Homo, Ain't (Ar'n't) I a Woman, and Inappropriate/D Others," p. 90.

[29] Ibid., pp. 90, 87.

[30] Donna J. Haraway, "A Cyborg Manifesto: Science, Technology and Socialist-Feminism in the Late Twentieth Century," in *Simians, Cyborgs and Women: The Reinvention of Nature* (New York, 1991), p. 151. Haraway, "Ecce Homo, Ain't (Ar'n't) I a Woman, and Inappropriate/D Others," p. 91.

[31] Haraway, "Ecce Homo, Ain't (Ar'n't) I a Woman, and Inappropriate/D Others," p. 90.

[32] Kull, "Cyborg Embodiment and the Incarnation," p. 284.

consciously hybrid Christologies from postcolonial and queer theologians, echoes Haraway's observations on the constructed nature of the trickster figure Jesus. Emphasizing the impossibility of originary theological purity, Kwok calls Jesus/Christ "the most hybridized concept in the Christian tradition."[33]

Orthographically pointing to the "borderland" between the human and divine, Kwok uses the slash in writing "Jesus/Christ" to indicate that the human/divine boundary is unfixed and fluid, contested and constructed, something which she regards as positive and necessary. She writes, "the richness and vibrancy of the Christian community is diminished whenever the space between Jesus and Christ is fixed, whether, on the one hand, as a result of the need for doctrinal purity, the suppression of syncretism, or the fear of contamination of native cultures, or, on the other hand, on account of historical positivism and its claims of objectivity and scientific truths about Jesus."[34] She, like Haraway, points out that there are no original and pure "first versions" of Christology, and following George Soares Prabhu, observes that "New Testament Christology is inclusive and pluriform ... The New Testament preserves all these christologies, without opting exclusively for any one among them, because it does not wish to offer us (as dogmatic theology pretends to do) a finished product, to be accepted unquestionably by all."[35] Kwok thus proclaims a forthright theological disregard for purity of categories, whether doctrinal, cultural, or philosophical, embracing rather than eschewing hybridity on multiple levels. In taking this stance, she sets herself deliberately counter to the Chalcedonian imperative to separate the divine and human natures; and is so doing, she notes, "it is important to remember that the Christological formulas crafted in Nicaea, Ephesus or Chalcedon were never accepted as normative by all Christians."[36]

Kwok then shifts her attention to the ways in which the notion of hybridity in postcolonial criticism intersects with "the quest for Jesus." She argues that, first, "the search for Jesus must be read against the search for 'natives' who could be conquered," and second, as the various hybridized constructions of Jesus offered by theologians from marginalized communities.[37] Kwok describes how the quest for the historical Jesus resulted from the anxiety regarding European self-identity generated by the cultural contact of imperialists and natives, noting that, even as the quest for Jesus expressed a yearning for purity in identity, such portraits of Jesus are examples of cultural hybridization, "attempts to interpret the Christ symbol through the lenses of the culture of imperialism."[38] Such hybridization takes place in the midst of denial, through the attempt at a scientific and objective historical portrait of Jesus, yielding a symbol that endorses the cultural and political status quo. In contrast, hybridity becomes a deliberate and central focus in

---

[33] Kwok, *Postcolonial Imagination & Feminist Theology*, p. 171.
[34] Ibid.
[35] Ibid., p. 172.
[36] Ibid.
[37] Ibid., pp. 172–4.
[38] Ibid., p. 173.

the construction of Christologies such as the Black Christ, Jesus as Corn Mother, Jesus as the Feminine Shakti, and Jesus as the Bi/Christ. What these constructions share in common is a theological impulse to locate Jesus within the marginalized community, but in such a way that rigid categories of identity are subverted rather than upheld.

Like these examples Kwok offers of hybrid Christological constructions from various marginalized communities, Virgilio Elizondo's autobiographical work, *The Future is Mestizo*, recounts his "inability to accept theoretical constructs related to Christ."[39] For Elizondo, the doctrine of incarnation necessarily implies an affirmation of Jesus' specific, socio-cultural identity; Christological constructions which ignored or glossed over the particularities of Jesus' identity are unhelpful and irrelevant. For Elizondo, the quest for the historical Jesus is then equivalent to the quest for the hybridized Christ; for as it turns out, the material, historical reality of Jesus' person, Elizondo argues, is socio-culturally hybrid.

Elizondo writes, "Humanly speaking, just who was this Jesus of Nazareth? It seemed like such an elementary question, but I had never asked it before, nor had I found it studied seriously in any of the works on Christ that I knew of. His socio-cultural identity was simply passed by or idealized into a heavenly existence. The fullness of the Incarnation was not appreciated, and in many ways we Christians are still scandalized by just how human our God became."[40] Perhaps it might be better stated that we are not scandalized by the degree to which God became human, but by which kind of human God became: in Elizondo's term, a *mestizo* Galilean, a human being embodying all sorts of categorical, cultural hybridities and impurities.[41]

Kwok's consideration of Althaus-Reid's "Bi/Christ" makes hybridity of gender categories a matter of Christological consideration; what we might call here the question of the FemaleMan and the God-man. Kwok writes, "the question of the gender of Christ has been so much a part of our common sense that 'engendering Christ' has seldom been the substance of serious theological debate."[42] As Kwok points out, Rosemary Radford Ruether's question, "can a male savior save women?" implicitly consents to the maleness of Christ. So, too, does the response of feminist post-Christians such as Mary Daly and Daphne Hampson, who do not dispute Christ's maleness but conclude that the categories of male and divine share in a profane *communicatio idiomatum*, and that the divinity of the male is written so strongly into the Christian tradition that the necessary answer to Ruether's question is "no."[43]

---

[39] Miguel H. Díaz, *On Being Human: U.S. Hispanic and Rahnerian Perspectives* (Maryknoll, NY, 2001), p. 25, Virgilio Elizondo, *The Future Is Mestizo: Life Where Cultures Meet* (New York, 1992).

[40] Elizondo, *The Future Is Mestizo*, p. 75.

[41] Díaz, *On Being Human*, p. 27.

[42] Kwok, *Postcolonial Imagination & Feminist Theology*, p. 169.

[43] Ibid.

Yet such a position accepts an ontological divide between male and female in a way that the cyborg discourse on gender dismantles. In contrast, Kwok wonders, "If we problematize the gender of the savior, what kinds of questions will we ask?"[44] The ontological boundaries at issue in this query are not simply the boundary between the human and the divine, but the male and the female. From a cyborg perspective, the "partial, fluid, sometimes" aspect of sex and sexual embodiment means the maleness of Christ may be accepted as historical and ontological fact, without Christ's maleness necessarily functioning as an obstacle in Christ's salvific relationality to women.

As the cyborg demands that we pay attention to the particularities and oddities of various human embodiments, the mismatch between our social constructs of gender and our actual embodiments are revealed. This is what attracts Haraway to Joanna Russ's SF novel, *The Female Man*: not only does Russ deconstruct Man, but Woman as well. Such attention also reveals that there is no common essentiality indicated by similar embodiment: "there is nothing about 'female' that naturally binds women."[45] At the same time that this admission fragments monolithic and mythic identities, and frustrates the politics of their expression, it enables connections between those of differing embodiments—that is to say, every body. Theologically and Christologically, it means, simply, that Jesus' penis is no obstacle to salvific relation.

Kwok draws the following conclusions: first, that the notion of Jesus/Christ has been a hybrid concept from the very beginning, and there is no original, privileged understanding of Christ that can be claimed as pure and foundational; second, the explosion of hybridized images of Jesus are the expressions of the struggle for the articulation of identity of formerly colonized and oppressed peoples, and further, that as the identity of a group becomes more fluid and diversified, a more nuanced and diverse Christology emerges.[46]

The question of who Christ was—the quest for the historical Jesus—is indeed then replaced by what Kwok calls "the quest of the hybridized Jesus," and this quest is a self-consciously constructive one, an expression of "creative theological imagination of Christ," utilizing not simply sacred and historical understandings of Jesus' identity, but also contemporary anthropological understandings of human identity and specific social constructions of identity as well.[47] Here, I think, is where the image of the cyborg Christ might helpfully be added to Kwok's list of hybrid Christologies. These cyborg Christologies are offered as partial, temporary, specific, and context-dependent constructions—ongoing negotiations of Christ's identity and relation to human beings and lives—rather than absolute constructions

---

[44] Ibid.

[45] Haraway, "A Cyborg Manifesto," p. 155.

[46] Kwok, *Postcolonial Imagination & Feminist Theology*, pp. 182–3. Kwok's analysis of the critical dialogue between black and womanist Christologies forms the basis for this observation.

[47] Ibid., pp. 170–1.

aimed to serve as the expression of a truth for all people independent of context. Thus, Kull writes, "[Christ] would be the one who comes in many guises, and cannot be represented once and for all, and for everybody's satisfaction."[48]

## Posthuman Subjectivity and the Mind of Christ

As Kull observes, however, even as the cyborg upholds the logic of incarnation and embodiment, it troubles the category of the human, "for the cyborg exemplifies the fact that we do not have a clearly defined, exhaustive concept of humanity, let alone divinity."[49] The posthuman, in signaling a need to move away from substantive, static, essential constructions of the human, provides not simply the overt challenge of hybridity to categories of pure substance and identity, but shifts the terms of theological anthropology, and therefore Christology, altogether.

While this may be the very aspect of the posthuman which some theologians find threatening, others find it provides a theological opportunity. Shults proposes that perhaps we theologians need to "overcome our addiction to 'substance abuse,'" moving away from categories of substance to categories of relation. In this proposal, he deliberately builds upon his prior arguments in theological anthropology.[50] Shults points out that the theological task at hand for us is the same task confronted by previous generations of theologians: the articulation of an understanding of the incarnation in dialogue with concepts of humanity current in the historical and philosophical contexts. The "turn to relationality" Shults discerns, then, forms part of the contemporary theological context; moreover, Shults argues that, "The turn to relationality can help us move beyond the assumptions that compel us to formulate the question in this way [in terms of substances]. We might learn to ask different kinds of questions such as: how is the life of Jesus related to the identification of God and identifiable with God?"[51]

Shifting from categories of substance to relationality within Christology means realizing that, in Shults's words, "divinity is not a substance that 'fills' other things by fitting into their boundaries and that humanity is not a substance whose boundaries are threatened by such 'filling.'"[52] Substances require definitive boundaries, but relationships are about the ongoing negotiation of boundaries; one way of phrasing a relational approach to Christology, then, is to ask how the permeable boundaries between divinity and humanity are renegotiated in Christ.[53]

---

[48] Kull, "Cyborg Embodiment and the Incarnation," p. 284.

[49] Ibid.

[50] F. LeRon Shults, *Reforming Theological Anthropology: After the Philosophical Turn to Relationality* (Grand Rapids, MI, 2003).

[51] F. LeRon Shults, *Christology and Science* (Grand Rapids, MI, 2008), p. 23.

[52] Ibid., p. 57.

[53] In talking of permeable boundaries, I do not intend to convey the dissolution of boundaries in what Rita N. Brock terms "fusion." (See Rita N. Brock, *Journeys by Heart:*

To talk of a cyborg Christ, then, is to talk about Jesus as a human being in a particular relationship to the divine; and the questions we ask of the cyborg Christ are questions about the uniqueness, significance, and consequences of that relationship. Moving decisively away from categories of nature, disembodied essence, and substance, the cyborg's ontology is instead defined in categories of relationality, even hyper-relationality, in which the posthuman subject is embedded in multiple, overlapping, shifting relationships, with both human and nonhuman partners. What does this decentered posthuman subjectivity imply with regard to the relationship between the human and the divine?

While we must be careful not to anachronistically project a modernist anthropology of the liberal humanist subject into the terms of Chalcedon, there is a similar presumption of the unity of the subject which should be noted; thus, just as the posthuman subverts the unity of the liberal humanist subject, it subverts the unity of the subject taken for granted in the definition of Chalcedon. The Logos-*sarx* Christology of Alexandria, in conjunction with the presumption of the unity of Christ's subjectivity, led to the historical heresy of Apollinarism; if Christ were the Logos enfleshed, then "the mind of Christ" was, simply, the Logos, and there was no room for a purely human mind, the coexistence of which would, in Norris's words, "render Jesus in effect schizophrenic." Here, it is not simply the Logos-*sarx* construction which forces the heretical conclusion, for, after all, it is this construction which wins the day at Chalcedon as the orthodox Christology. It is rather the combination of the presumed unity of subjectivity and the Logos-*sarx* construction that forces Apollinaris' logic to its consistent, heretical conclusion that Christ could have no human mind.

In moving away from the constraints of substance categories and the corresponding necessity of the unity of subjectivity assumed at Chalcedon, toward a posthuman subjectivity characterized by the collective, heterogeneous distributed cognition described by Hayles and others, the heresy of Apollinarism is no longer even coherent. In contrast, it becomes entirely possible to conceive of Christ's human subjectivity in a way which unproblematically includes a divine component which neither usurps nor threatens Christ's human identity. Hayles writes, "when the human is seen as part of a distributed system, the full expression

---

*A Christology of Erotic Power* (New York, 1995), p. 57.) Rather, relationship is about the overlap of the boundaries of self and other, and the cyborg indicates that this overlap may include others who are indeed other: nonhumans of all sorts, animal, machine, and divine. Similarly, F. LeRon Shults considers the role of the categories of sameness and difference within the context of Christology, noting that within classical Christologies reliant on substance metaphysics, sameness is the prerequisite for identification of substances; in contrast, Shults makes the point that relationality requires difference (Shults, *Christology and Science*, pp. 56–8). What Shults analyzes as a preoccupation with sameness, Brock calls "fusion," and in both cases, a substance metaphysics rather than a relational anthropology and Christology is the basis for this problematic version of unity which dissolves boundaries rather than renegotiating them.

of human capability can be seen precisely to *depend* on the splice rather than being imperiled by it"; to put this insight to work within a theological and Christological context, then, we might say Christ is seen as part of a distributed system that includes God and the man Jesus, the full expression of Christ's humanity and divinity can be seen precisely to depend on the splice, rather than being imperiled by it.[54] This indeed is a cyborg Christ, in ontological relation to the divine.

Richard Norris observes that the peculiarity of Theodore of Mopsuestia's Christological construction "seems to lie in the fact that he conceives the relationship between God and humanity in the incarnation in terms of will rather than in terms of substance."[55] For Theodore, the unity of Christ's person resulted as the unity of the divine and human wills; this not only meant that the Logos-*anthropos* construction preserved a full humanity in deliberate contrast to the Apollinarian heresy, but also creates a picture of Jesus maturing into this unity that does not threaten human identity and agency. Further, the language of "indwelling" is inherently relational, and, while Jesus' relationship to God may indeed have been ontologically unique, other human beings, too, are invited into this relational possibility of the indwelling of the Spirit of God. Thus, as we revisit Chalcedon as posthumans, the Antiochene Christology may be conceived of as an expression of the distributed cognition of a human being specially indwelt by God, offering us, too, the possibility of joining with the divine in a posthuman hybridity that includes a component of divine indwelling in our daily lives.[56]

Reconstructing Christology in dialogue with the posthuman, then, reveals some surprising opportunities for moving beyond age-old impasses enshrined in the two classical schools of Christological thought, juxtaposed but unresolved in the definition of Chalcedon. First, the hybridity of the notion of a "cyborg Christ" overtly challenges the dominant tendency of the Antiochenes to separate the "two natures" of Christ, a tendency not entirely absent from the Alexandrian school and enshrined in the definition of Chalcedon. This rehabilitation of the heretical notion of mixture hints at a monophysite Christology, historically a heresy located on the extreme Alexandrian end of the Christological spectrum. At the same time, however, in challenging anthropological and Christological categories of substance in favor of a hyper-relationality, the "cyborg Christ"

---

[54] N.K. Hayles, *How We Became Posthuman: Virtual Bodies in Cybernetics, Literature, and Informatics* (Chicago, IL, 1999), p. 290.

[55] Norris, *The Christological Controversy*, p. 25.

[56] A relational Christology such as Friedrich Schleiermacher's offers interesting possibilities for transversal connections to a notion of the cyborg Christ as sketched above. Kevin Hector's interpretation of Schleiermacher's Christology as offering one approach to a "post-essentialist" Christology, and moreover, one which arrives at a "high" Christology, in which Christ is God incarnate because of Christ's perfect expression of God-consciousness in the pure act of love, offers a starting place for such a consideration. See Kevin Hector, "Actualism and Incarnation: The High Christology of Friedrich Schleiermacher," *International Journal of Systematic Theology* 8/3 (2006).

may be explicated in Antiochene terms of the indwelling of God and the unity of wills. The classical Christological constructions thus become confused, producing (appropriately!) a hybrid of sorts, one which, in its confusion of the classical orthodox and heretical options, opens up possibilities for new configurations and new Christological questions. The hybrid nature of the cyborg Christ defies the need for a duophysite Christology, but rather than that monophysitism implying docetism, the importance of incarnation and embodiment implies a single nature which is indeed fully human.

One final note regarding the implications of the cyborg Christ for soteriology, certainly a strong motivating concern in patristic Christology, and one at the heart of Waters's rejection of even the possibility of such a thing as a posthuman Christology at all. Is a relational Christology, whether explicated in terms of indwelling such Theodore of Mopsuestia's, or in the hypertext, techno-metaphor of the cyborg's distributed cognition, "high" enough to ground the strong soteriological claim of the Christian tradition? Is not such a Christ simply an inspired, though perhaps a uniquely inspired, human being, and not God in the flesh? Ultimately, this theological objection is what is at stake between the Logos-*sarx* and Logos-*anthropos* constructions of the competing Alexandrian and Antiochene schools. Insofar as the tendency in subsequent Christian tradition has been to categorize Alexandrian Christology as "high," and Antiochene Christology as "low," the posthuman again confuses these designations: reinstating hybridity as a theological concept opens the door to a high Christology in which the divine and the human become one, with no need for maintaining rigid boundaries between the two categories; simultaneously, hybridity opens the door to a "low" Christology in which Jesus is seen as a complete human being, ontologically participating in the life of God. The concept of hybridity functions here as the key for constructing a "high" Christology "from below."

In shifting from a classical, Chalcedonian Christology to cyborg Christologies, the central Christological question shifts. The question is not, "how can two natures coexist in one person," but, in Kwok's words, "how is it possible for the formerly colonized, oppressed, subjugated subaltern to transform the symbol of Christ—a symbol that has been used to justify colonization and domination—into a symbol that affirms life, dignity, and freedom?"[57] Likewise, the symbol of the cyborg is not about the two natures of human and machine coexisting as one entity. Rather, the cyborg's hybrid ontology points us toward the fact of our kinship with the nonhuman (in all its forms: animal, machine, and divine) and the necessity of constructing a world in which the life, dignity, and freedom of all God's hybrid creatures may be affirmed; in Haraway's phrase, it is about the construction of "possible liveable worlds."[58]

---

[57] Kwok, *Postcolonial Imagination & Feminist Theology*, p. 168.
[58] Donna J. Haraway, "Modest_Witness@Second_Millenium," in *Modest_Witness@ Second_Millennium.Femaleman©_Meets_Oncomouse™: Feminism and Technoscience* (New York, 1997), p. 39.

## The Ultimate Human

If the posthuman is a future possibility or indeed a currently emerging possibility, the central Christian claim of a God to whom we relate, and who relates to us, through the act of becoming human seems, at least on the face of it, in danger of becoming obsolete. It is this, perhaps, which is so alarming; if, after all, the human race ceases to be "human" and becomes "posthuman," will a savior who is fully divine and fully, yet merely, human remain a salvific figure? If the possibility exists that humanity might evolve itself beyond the possibility of redemption, that is a truly alarming prospect, and perhaps is what lies behind Brent Waters's judgment that "in pursuing the postmodern or posthuman projects humans ... will cease to be creatures bearing the *imago dei* in effectively rejecting their election."[59]

For Waters, Christ the fully divine human stands in judgment of the emerging possibility of any form of the posthuman, leading to his theological rejection of posthuman theologies as necessarily lacking "any compelling Christology."[60] Interpreting the incarnation as an affirmation of "the created order," Waters writes, "It is in and through Christ that nature, which Christians properly name *creation*, discloses its vindicated order."[61] By discerning the vindicated order of creation as disclosed in Christ, "humans learn their proper role for participating in created order, and thus the normative location that has been assigned to humankind."[62]

This problem may be quickly evaded by an appeal to a more nuanced understanding of the term "posthuman," which does not, after all, necessitate the obliteration of the human but is simply another way of asking what "human" means to begin with. But it is better not to answer too quickly, for, as F. LeRon Shults points out, "The idea that being truly human means being a part of the ongoing adaptive differentiation of the species *Homo sapiens*, does indeed challenge some traditional Christological formulations."[63] The posthuman, as part of the ongoing evolution of the human species, challenges any anthropological or Christological formulations that rely upon static notions of human identity; however, as Shults also points out, the task at hand is no different than it has ever been, as we seek to articulate notions of the human and of Christ, the divine-human, in dialogue with the concepts of humanity (and posthumanity) prevalent in our context.[64]

Finally, then, in a posthuman context it may be helpful to consider Christ as the "ultimate human," the expression of humanity to which we aspire as the fulfillment of the potential and longing for goodness that characterizes us as creatures of God. In interpreting Christ not simply as posthuman but as the ultimate-human, that definitive expression of humanity beyond or after which there can be

---

[59] Waters, *From Human to Posthuman*, p. 144.
[60] Ibid., p. 95.
[61] Ibid., p. 109.
[62] Ibid., p. 110.
[63] Shults, *Christology and Science*, p. 31.
[64] Ibid., p. 23.

no more to say, the posthuman is clearly not anti-human, but inclusive of our notions of humanity. This is, indeed, the sense in which Haraway, in her single use of the term in the essay "*Ecce Homo*," employs the notion of posthumanity. Haraway chooses Jesus and Sojourner Truth as speakers for humanity outside the narratives of humanism: posthuman figures of humanity. Such a framing puts to rest the theological uneasiness produced by Brent Waters's interpretation of the posthuman as necessarily anti-human. Of course, we must be quick to concede that precisely what the posthuman will be is a matter of contention; there are multiple possibilities, and some visions of posthumanity are more human than others. This, however, as Haraway, Hayles, Graham, and Kull are ready to remind us, is an opportunity to collectively construct a posthuman future and a liveable world for every body, human and post- and non-, of all sorts.

Interpreting the cyborg Christ as the ultimate human leads systematically into the loci of pneumatology and eschatology, and reflexively doubles back to theological anthropology, deepening our understanding of ourselves as posthuman in the process. Tracing out these systematic implications fully falls well outside the scope of this work, and only this brief gesture toward articulating these implications is possible here. Yet we can say that, just as Christ's relation to God is part of his (post)humanity, so too we can hope to redraw the boundaries of our human subjectivity to include a relation to God in which our wills coincide and indeed become indistinguishable. This indwelling of the Spirit, this ontological relation, this desirable permeability between the boundaries of self and God, is modeled for us in the ultimate human, the cyborg Christ, who invites us, too, to participate in the life of God.

# Bibliography

Althaus-Reid, Marcella, *The Queer God* (London: Routledge, 2003).

Althaus-Reid, Marcella, "From the Goddess to Queer Theology: The State We Are in Now," *Feminist Theology*, 13/2 (2005): 265–72.

Althaus-Reid, Marcella, and Lisa Isherwood, "Thinking Theology and Queer Theory," *Feminist Theology*, 15/3 (2007): 302–14.

Andrews, Gillian, "Janelle Monae Turns Rhythm and Blues into Science Fiction," *io9* (2010): http://io9.com/5592174/janelle-monae-turns-rhythm-and-blues-into-science-fiction, date accessed April 19, 2011.

Andrews, Lori B., "My Body, My Property," *The Hastings Center Report*, 28 (1986).

Anissimov, Michael, "Ideas for Mitigating Extinction Risk," Accelerating Future, www.acceleratingfuture.com/michael/blog/2008/09/ideas-for-mitigating-extinction-risk/, date accessed October 2, 2008.

Anissimov, Michael, "Response to Cory Doctorow on the Singularity," Accelerating Future, www.acceleratingfuture.com/michael/blog/2007/06/response-to-cory-doctorow-on-the-singularity/, date accessed November 11, 2008.

Anissimov, Michael, "The Word 'Singularity' Has Lost All Meaning," Accelerating Future, www.acceleratingfuture.com/michael/blog/?p=504, date accessed May 22, 2008.

Bainbridge, William S., "The Transhuman Heresy," *The Journal of Evolution and Technology*, 14/2 (2005): 91–100.

Bainbridge, William S., "Burglarizing Nietzsche's Tomb," *Journal of Evolution and Technology*, 21/1 (2010): 37–54.

Baker, Lynne R., "Persons and the Extended-Mind Thesis," *Zygon*, 44/3 (2009): 642–57.

Barbour, Ian, *Ethics in an Age of Technology: The Gifford Lectures 1989–1991*. Vol. 2 (San Francisco, CA: HarperSanFrancisco, 1993).

Bartsch, Ingrid, Carolyn DiPalma, and Laura Sells, "Witnessing the Postmodern Jeremiad: (Mis)Understanding Donna Haraway's Method of Inquiry," *Configurations*, 9/1 (2001): 127–64.

Bastian, Michelle, "Haraway's Lost Cyborg and the Possibilities of Transversalism," *Signs: Journal of Women in Culture & Society*, 31/4 (2006): 1027–49.

Blackford, Russell, "Trite Truths About Technology: A Reply to Ted Peters," *The Global Spiral*, 9/9 (2009): www.metanexus.net/magazine/tabid/68/id/10681/Default.aspx, date accessed March 1, 2009.

Blackford, Russell, "Editorial: Nietzsche and European Posthumanisms," *Journal of Evolution and Technology*, 21/1 (2010): i–iii.

Bostrom, Nick, *Anthropic Bias: Observation Selection Effects in Science and Philosophy* (New York: Routledge, 2002).

Bostrom, Nick, "Existential Risks: Analyzing Human Extinction Scenarios and Related Hazards," *Journal of Evolution and Technology*, 9/1 (2002).

Bostrom, Nick, "Are We Living in a Computer Simulation?" *Philosophical Quarterly*, 53/211 (2003): 243–55.

Bostrom, Nick, "The Transhumanist FAQ: A General Introduction," The World Transhumanist Association (2003): http://humanityplus.org/learn/transhumanist-faq/, date accessed June 21, 2011.

Bostrom, Nick, "A History of Transhumanist Thought," *Journal of Evolution and Technology*, 14/1 (2005): 1–25.

Bostrom, Nick, "The Simulation Argument: Reply to Weatherson," *Philosophical Quarterly*, 55/218 (2005): 90–7.

Bostrom, Nick, "Transhumanist Values," World Transhumanist Association/ Humanity+ (2005): http://transhumanism.org/index.php/WTA/more/transhumanist-values/, date accessed April 14, 2009.

Brasher, Brenda E., "Thoughts on the Status of the Cyborg: On Technological Socialization and Its Link to the Religious Function of Popular Culture," *Journal of the American Academy of Religion*, 64/4 (1996): 809–30.

Brock, Rita N., *Journeys by Heart: A Christology of Erotic Power* (New York: Crossroad, 1995).

Brooke, John H., "Visions of Perfectibility," *Journal of Evolution and Technology*, 14/2 (2005): 2–12.

Brown, Warren S., Nancey Murphy, and H. Newton Malony (eds), *Whatever Happened to the Soul? Scientific and Theological Portraits of Human Nature* (Minneapolis, MN: Fortress Press, 1998).

Burton, Justin D., "Ipod People: Experiencing Music with New Music Technology," PhD Dissertation (Rutgers-The State University of New Jersey, 2009).

Campbell, Heidi, "On Posthumans, Transhumanism and Cyborgs: Towards a Transhumanist–Christian Conversation," *Modern Believing*, 47/2 (2006): 61–73.

Campbell, Heidi, and Mark Walker, "Religion and Transhumanism: Introducing a Conversation," *Journal of Evolution and Technology*, 14/2 (2005): i–xv.

Carrico, Dale, "Superlative Summary," http://amormundi.blogspot.com/2007/10/superlative-summary.html, date accessed May 4, 2009.

Castree, N., and C. Nash, "Posthuman Geographies," *Social & Cultural Geography*, 7/4 (2006): 501–4.

Cavalieri, Paola, and Peter Singer, "The Great Ape Project—and Beyond," in Paola Cavalieri and Peter Singer (eds), *The Great Ape Project* (New York: St. Martin's Griffin, 1993), 304–12.

Clark, Andy, *Natural-Born Cyborgs: Minds, Technologies, and the Future of Human Intelligence* (Oxford: Oxford University Press, 2003).

Clark, Andy and David Chalmers, "The Extended Mind," *Analysis*, 58/1 (1998): 7–19.

Clynes, Manfred, and Nathan Kline, "Cyborgs and Space," *Astronautics* (1960): 29–33.
Cole-Turner, Ron, *The New Genesis: Theology and the Genetic Revolution* (Louisville, KY: Westminster/John Knox Press, 1993).
Coyle, F., "Posthuman Geographies? Biotechnology, Nature and the Demise of the Autonomous Human Subject," *Social & Cultural Geography*, 7/4 (2006): 505–23.
Crabbe, James (ed.), *From Soul to Self* (London: Routledge, 1999).
Daly, Todd, "Life-Extension in Transhumanist and Christian Perspectives: Consonance and Conflict," *Journal of Evolution and Technology*, 14/2 (2005): 69–87.
de Grey, Aubrey, and Michael Rae, *Ending Aging: The Rejuvenation Breakthroughs That Could Reverse Human Aging in Our Lifetime* (New York: St Martin's Press, 2007).
de Thezier, Justice, "Mute: Why Reimaginative Democrats Should Ignore the Siren Songs of a Posthuman Future," *Re-public*, www.re-public.gr/en/?p=660, date accessed May 4, 2009.
Deane-Drummond, Celia E., *Biology and Theology Today: Exploring the Boundaries* (London: SCM Press, 2001).
Deane-Drummond, Celia E., "The Future of the Human: Transhuman Evolution or Human Identity as *Imago Christi*?" in *Christ and Evolution: Wonder and Wisdom* (London: SCM Press, 2009), 256–87.
DeLashmutt, Michael W., "A Better Life through Information Technology? The Techno-Theological Eschatology of Posthuman Speculative Science," *Zygon*, 41/2 (2006): 267–87.
Díaz, Miguel H., *On Being Human: U.S. Hispanic and Rahnerian Perspectives* (Maryknoll, NY: Orbis, 2001).
Díaz, Miguel H., "Theological Anthropology," in Edwin David Aponte and Miguel A. De La Torre (eds), *Handbook of Latina/o Theologies* (St. Louis, MO: Chalice Press, 2006), 67–74.
Dinello, Daniel, *Technophobia!: Science Fiction Visions of Posthumanity* (Austin, TX: University of Texas Press, 2005).
Drees, Willem B., "'Playing God? Yes!': Religion in the Light of Technology," *Zygon*, 37/3 (2002): 643–54.
Dvorsky, George, "All Together Now: Developmental and Ethical Considerations for Biologically Uplifting Nonhuman Animals," *Journal of Evolution and Technology*, 18/1 (2008): 129–42.
Eiesland, Nancy, *The Disabled God: Toward a Liberatory Theology of Disability* (Nashville, TN: Abingdon Press, 1994).
Eiesland, Nancy, "What Is Disability," *Stimulus*, 6 (1998): 24–30.
Elizondo, Virgilio, *The Future Is Mestizo: Life Where Cultures Meet* (New York: Crossroad, 1992).
Firestone, Shulamith, *The Dialectic of Sex: The Case for Feminist Revolution* (New York: Farrar, Straus and Giroux, 1970).

Fukuyama, Francis, *Our Posthuman Future: Consequences of the Biotechnology Revolution* (New York: Farrar, Straus and Giroux, 2002).

Gaine, Vincent M., "The Emergence of Feminine Humanity from a Technologised Masculinity in the Films of James Cameron," *Journal of Technology, Theology & Religion*, 2/4 (2011): www.techandreligion.com/Resources/Gaine%20JTTR.pdf, 1–41.

Gane, N., and D. Haraway, "When We Have Never Been Human, What Is to Be Done? Interview with Donna Haraway," *Theory Culture & Society*, 23/7–8 (2006): 135–58.

Garner, Stephen, "Transhumanism and Christian Social Concern," *Journal of Evolution and Technology*, 14/2 (2005): 89–103.

Garner, Stephen, "Transhumanism and the *Imago Dei*: Narratives of Apprehension and Hope," PhD Dissertation (The University of Auckland, 2006).

Garner, Stephen, "The Hopeful Cyborg," in Ron Cole-Turner (ed.), *Transhumanism and Transcendence: Christian Hope in an Age of Technological Enhancement* (Washington, DC: Georgetown University Press, 2011).

Geraci, Robert M., "Apocalyptic A.I: Religion and the Promise of Artificial Intelligence," *Journal of the American Academy of Religion*, 76/1 (2008): 138–66.

Goizueta, Roberto S., *Caminemos Con Jesús: Toward a Hispanic/Latino Theology of Accompaniment* (Maryknoll, NY: Orbis Books, 1995).

Graham, Elaine, "Words Made Flesh: Women, Embodiment, and Practical Theology," *Feminist Theology*, 21 (1999): 109–21.

Graham, Elaine, "'Nietzsche Gets a Modem': Transhumanism and the Technological Sublime," *Literature & Theology*, 16/1 (2002): 65.

Graham, Elaine, *Representations of the Post/Human: Monsters, Aliens and Others in Popular Culture* (New Brunswick, NJ: Rutgers University Press, 2002).

Graham, Elaine, "In Whose Image? Representations of Technology and the 'Ends' of Humanity," *Ecotheology*, 11/2 (2006): 159–82.

Graham, Kevin M., "The Political Significance of Social Identity: A Critique of Rawl's Theory of Agency," *Social Theory & Practice*, 26/2 (2000): 201–22.

Gray, Chris H., "Medical Cyborgs: Artificial Organs and the Quest for the Posthuman," in Chris H. Gray (ed.), *Technohistory* (Malabar, FL: Krieger Publishing Company, 1996), 141–78.

Grosz, Elizabeth, *Volatile Bodies: Toward a Corporeal Feminism* (Bloomington, IN: Indiana University Press, 1994).

Habermas, Jürgen, *Die Zukunft der Menschlichen Natur: Auf dem Weg zu einer liberalen Eugenik?* (Frankfurt am Main: Suhrkamp, 2001).

Hanson, Robin, "Enhancing Our Truth Orientation," in Julian Savulescu and Nick Bostrom (eds), *Human Enhancement* (London: Oxford, 2009), 357–72.

Haraway, Donna J., "Living Images: Conversations with Lynn Randolph," www.lynnrandolph.com/essays.haraway-2.html, date accessed August 22, 2009.

Haraway, Donna J., "Monkeys, Aliens, and Women: Love, Science and Politics at the Intersection of Feminist Theory and Colonial Discourse," *Women's Studies International Forum*, 12/3 (1989): 295–312.

Haraway, Donna J., "A Cyborg Manifesto: Science, Technology and Socialist-Feminism in the Late Twentieth Century," in *Simians, Cyborgs and Women: The Reinvention of Nature* (New York: Routledge, 1991), 149–81.

Haraway, Donna J., "Cyborgs at Large: Interview with Donna Haraway," in A. Penley and C. Ross (eds), *Technoculture* (Minneapolis, MN: University of Minnesota, 1991), 1–20.

Haraway, Donna J., "Introduction," in *Simians, Cyborgs and Women: The Reinvention of Nature* (New York: Routledge, 1991), 1–4.

Haraway, Donna J., "Situated Knowledges: The Science Question in Feminism and the Privilege of Partial Perspective," in *Simians, Cyborgs and Women: The Reinvention of Nature* (New York: Routledge, 1991), 183–201.

Haraway, Donna J., "Ecce Homo, Ain't (Ar'n't) I a Woman, and Inappropriate/D Others: The Human in a Post-Humanist Landscape," in Judith Butler and Joan W. Scott (eds), *Feminists Theorize the Political* (New York: Routledge, 1992), 86–100.

Haraway, Donna J., "The Promises of Monsters: A Regenerative Politics for Inappropriate/D Others," in Lawrence Grossberg, Cary Nelson, and Paula Treichler (eds), *Cultural Studies* (New York: Routledge, 1992), 295–337.

Haraway, Donna J., "When Man Is on the Menu," in Jonathan Crary and Sanford Kwinter (eds), *Incorporations* (New York: Zone, 1992), 39–43.

Haraway, Donna J., "A Game of Cat's Cradle: Science Studies, Feminist Theory, Cultural Studies," *Configurations*, 2/1 (1994): 59–71.

Haraway, Donna J., "Femaleman©_Meets_Oncomouse™. Mice into Wormholes: A Technoscience Fugue in Two Parts," in *Modest_Witness@Second_Millennium. Femaleman©_Meets_Oncomouse™: Feminism and Technoscience* (New York: Routledge, 1997), 49–118.

Haraway, Donna J., "Fetus: The Virtual Speculum in the New World Order," in *Modest_Witness@Second_Millennium.Femaleman©_Meets_Oncomouse™: Feminism and Technoscience* (New York: Routledge, 1997), 173–212.

Haraway, Donna J., "Modest_Witness@Second_Millenium," in *Modest_ Witness@Second_Millennium.Femaleman©_Meets_Oncomouse™: Feminism and Technoscience* (New York: Routledge, 1997), 23–45.

Haraway, Donna J., *Modest_Witness@Second_Millennium.Femaleman©_Meets_ Oncomouse™: Feminism and Technoscience* (New York: Routledge, 1997).

Haraway, Donna J., *How Like a Leaf: An Interview with Thyza Nichols Goodeve* (New York: Routledge, 1998).

Haraway, Donna J., "Cyborgs, Dogs and Companion Species" (video lecture, 2000): www.youtube.com/view_play_list?p=C017E496EEE63132, date accessed December 14, 2010.

Haraway, Donna J., *The Haraway Reader* (New York: Routledge, 2004).

Haraway, Donna J., *When Species Meet*. Edited by Cary Wolfe, Posthumanities (Minneapolis: University of Minnesota, 2008).

Hauskeller, Michael, "Nietzsche, the Overhuman and the Posthuman: A Reply to Stefan Sorgner," *Journal of Evolution and Technology*, 21/1 (2010): 5–8.

Hayles, N.K., *How We Became Posthuman: Virtual Bodies in Cybernetics, Literature, and Informatics* (Chicago, IL: University of Chicago Press, 1999).

Hayles, N.K., "Refiguring the Posthuman," *Comparative Literature Studies*, 41/3 (2004): 311–16.

Hayles, N.K., "Wrestling with Transhumanism," *The Global Spiral*, 9/3 (June 2008): http://metanexus.net/magazine/tabid/68/id/10543/Default.aspx, date accessed March 1, 2009.

Hector, Kevin, "Actualism and Incarnation: The High Christology of Friedrich Schleiermacher," *International Journal of Systematic Theology*, 8/3 (2006): 307–22.

Hefner, Philip, *The Human Factor: Evolution, Culture, and Religion* (Minneapolis, MN: Fortress Press, 1993).

Hefner, Philip, *Technology and Human Becoming* (Minneapolis, MN: Fortress Press, 2003).

Hefner, Philip, "The Animal That Aspires to Be an Angel: The Challenge of Transhumanism," *Dialog: A Journal of Theology*, 48/2 (2009): 158–67.

Herzfeld, Noreen, "Cybernetic Immortality Versus Christian Resurrection," in Ted Peters, Robert J. Russell, and Michael Welker (eds), *Resurrection: Theological and Scientific Assessments* (Grand Rapids, MI: Eerdmans, 2002), 192–201.

Herzfeld, Noreen, *In Our Image: Artificial Intelligence and the Human Spirit* (Minneapolis, MN: Fortress Press, 2002).

Hibbard, Bill, "Nietzsche's Overhuman Is an Ideal Whereas Posthumans Will Be Real," *Journal of Early Christian Studies*, 21/1 (2010): 9–12.

Hochberg, Leigh R., Mijail D. Serruya, Gerhard M. Fries, Jon A. Mukand, Maryam Saleh, Abraham H. Caplan, Almut Branner, David Chen, Richard D. Penn, and John P. Donahue, "Neuronal Ensemble Control of Prosthetic Devices by a Human with Tetraplegia," *Nature*, 442 (2006): 164–71.

Hopkins, Patrick D., "Transcending the Animal: How Transhumanism and Religion Are and Are Not Alike," *Journal of Evolution and Technology*, 14/2 (2005): 11–26.

Hughes, James, "Democratic Transhumanism 2.0," www.changesurfer.com/Acad/DemocraticTranshumanism.htm, date accessed March 11, 2008.

Hughes, James, "Problems of Transhumanism: The Unsustainable Autonomy of Reason," Institute for Ethics and Emerging Technologies, http://ieet.org/index.php/IEET/more/hughes20100108/, date accessed January 15, 2010.

Hughes, James, *Citizen Cyborg: Why Democratic Societies Must Respond to the Redesigned Human of the Future* (Cambridge, MA: Westview Press, 2004).

Hughes, James, "The Compatibility of Religious and Transhumanist Views of Metaphysics, Suffering, Virtue and Transcendence in an Enhanced Future,"

*The Global Spiral*, 8/2 (2007): www.metanexus.net/magazine/tabid/68/id/9930/Default.aspx, date accessed October 8, 2008.

Hughes, James, and George Dvorsky, "Postgenderism: Beyond the Gender Binary," *IEET Monograph Series* (2008): http://ieet.org/archive/IEET-03-PostGender.pdf, date accessed January 26, 2009.

"Humanity+ Goals," Humanity+, http://humanityplus.org/projects/goals/, date accessed November 8, 2010.

Isherwood, Lisa, and Elizabeth Stuart, *Introducing Body Theology* (Sheffield: Sheffield Academic Press, 1998).

Johnson, William Stacy, *A Time to Embrace: Same-Gender Relationships in Religion, Law and Politics* (Grand Rapids, MI: Eerdmans, 2006).

Kass, Leon, "The Wisdom of Repugnance," *New Republic*, 216/22 (1997): 17–26.

Kass, Leon, *Life, Liberty and the Defense of Dignity: The Challenge for Bioethics* (San Francisco, CA: Encounter Books, 2002).

Krueger, Oliver, "Gnosis in Cyberspace? Body, Mind and Progress in Posthumanism," *Journal of Evolution and Technology*, 14/2 (2005): 55–67.

Kull, Anne, "A Theology of Technonature Based on Donna Haraway and Paul Tillich," PhD Dissertation (Lutheran School of Theology, 2000).

Kull, Anne, "Cyborg Embodiment and the Incarnation," *Currents in Theology and Mission*, 28/3–4 (2001): 279–84.

Kull, Anne, "Mutations of Nature, Technology, and the Western Sacred," *Zygon*, 41/4 (2006): 785–92.

Kurzweil, Ray, *The Singularity Is Near: When Humans Transcend Biology* (New York: Penguin Books, 2005).

Kwok, Pui-lan, *Postcolonial Imagination & Feminist Theology* (Louisville, KY: Westminster John Knox, 2005).

LaTorra, Michael, "Trans-Spirit: Religion, Spirituality and Transhumanism," *Journal of Evolution and Technology*, 14/2 (2005): 39–53.

Lee, Jung Y., *Marginality: The Key to Multicultural Theology* (Minneapolis, MN: Fortress Press, 1995).

Lester, Rita, "Ecofeminism and the Cyborg," *Feminist Theology: The Journal of the Britain & Ireland School of Feminist Theology*, 19 (1998): 11.

Lomeña, Andrés, "Interview with Nick Bostrom and David Pearce," The Hedonistic Imperative (December 2007): www.hedweb.com/transhumanism/index.html, date accessed October 7, 2008.

Longman, Jeré, "An Amputee Sprinter: Is He Disabled or Too-Abled?" *The New York Times* (May 15, 2007).

Mantin, Ruth, "Can Goddesses Travel with Nomads and Cyborgs? Feminist Thealogies in a Postmodern Context," *Feminist Theology*, 26 (2001): 21–43.

McKenny, Gerald P., "Technologies of Desire: Theology, Ethics, and the Enhancement of Human Traits," *Theology Today*, 59/1 (2002): 90–103.

Mercedes, Anna, and Jennifer Thweatt-Bates, "Bound in the Spiral Dance: Spirituality and Technology in the Third Wave," in Chris Klassen (ed.),

*Feminist Spirituality: The Next Generation* (Lanham, MD: Lexington Books, 2009), 63–83.
Mohanty, Chandra T., *Feminism without Borders: Decolonizing Theory, Practicing Solidarity* (Durham, NC: Duke University Press, 2003).
Mohanty, Chandra T., and M. Jacqui Alexander (eds), *Feminist Genealogies, Colonial Legacies, Democratic Futures* (New York: Routledge, 1997).
Moltmann-Wendel, Elizabeth, *I Am My Body: New Ways of Embodiment* (London: SCM Press Ltd., 1994).
Monáe, Janelle, "Many Moons" (music video, 2010): www.jmonae.com/video/many-moons-official-video/, date accessed April 19, 2011.
More, Max, "Transhumanism: A Futurist Philosophy" (1990): www.maxmore.com/transhum.htm, date accessed April 18, 2010.
More, Max, "A Letter to Mother Nature" (1999): www.maxmore.com/mother.htm, date accessed April 18, 2010.
More, Max, "Principles of Extropy Version 3.11," Extropy Institute (2003): www.extropy.org/principles.htm, date accessed May 21, 2008.
More, Max, "The Overhuman in the Transhuman," *Journal of Evolution and Technology*, 21/1 (2010): 1–4.
Morriss, Peter, "Blurred Boundaries," *Inquiry*, 40/3 (1997): 259–90.
Mullins, Aimee. "Prosthetic Power," *The Utne Reader*, July–August 2009, pp. 54–5.
Nelson, James, *Body Theology* (Louisville, KY: Westminster/John Knox Press, 1992).
Niebuhr, Reinhold, *The Nature and Destiny of Man*. 2 vols. Vol. 2 (New York: Charles Scribner's Sons, 1941–2).
Norris, Richard A. (ed.), *The Christological Controversy*, Sources of Early Christian Thought, ed. William G. Rusch (Philadelphia, PA: Fortress Press, 1980).
O'Brien, Kevin J., "An Ethics of Natureculture and Creation: Donna Haraway's Cyborg Ethics as a Resource for Ecotheology," *Ecotheology: Journal of Religion, Nature & the Environment*, 9/3 (2004): 295–314.
Olson, Nikki, and Hank Pellisier, "Artificial Wombs Will Spawn New Freedoms," Institute for Ethics and Emerging Technologies (2011): http://ieet.org/index.php/IEET/more/olson20110526, date accessed June 27, 2011.
"Overview of Biopolitics," Institute of Ethics and Emerging Technologies, http://ieet.org/index.php/IEET/biopolitics, date accessed May 19, 2011.
Pasnau, Robert, "Introduction," in *The Treatise on Human Nature: Summa Theologicae 1a, 75-89* (Indianapolis, IN: Hackett Publication Company, 2002), xii–xxi.
Pearce, David, "The Abolitionist Project," The Hedonistic Imperative, www.hedweb.com/abolitionist-project/index.html, date accessed August 22, 2009.
Pearce, David, "The Hedonistic Imperative," The Hedonistic Imperative, www.hedweb.com/hedab.htm, date accessed October 10, 2008.

Pederson, Ann M., "A Christian Theological Response to Aubrey De Grey's Prospects for the Biomedical Postponement of Aging, or What Does It Mean to Love Long and Prosper?" in James Haag, Michael L. Spezio, and Gregory R. Peterson (eds), *Routledge Companion to Religion and Science* (New York: Routledge, 2011), 558–65.

Peters, Ted, *Anticipating Omega: Science, Faith and Our Ultimate Future* (Göttingen: Vandenhoeck & Ruprecht, 2006).

Peters, Ted, "Transhumanism and the Posthuman Future: Will Technological Progress Get Us There?" *The Global Spiral*, 9/3 (2008): http://metanexus.net/magazine/tabid/68/id/10546/Default.aspx, date accessed March 1, 2009.

Peterson, Gregory R., *Minding God: Theology and the Cognitive Sciences* (Minneapolis, MN: Fortress Press, 2003).

Plaskow, Judith, and Elizabeth S. Fiorenza, "Women with Disabilities: A Challenge to Feminist Theology," *Journal of Feminist Studies in Religion*, 10 (1994): 99–134.

Prins, Baukje, "The Ethics of Hybrid Subjects: Feminist Constructivism According to Donna Haraway," *Science, Technology, & Human Values*, 20/3 (1995): 352–67.

Privett, Katharyn, "Sacred Cyborgs and 21st Century Goddesses," *Reconstruction*, 7/4 ( December 31, 2007): http://reconstruction.eserver.org/074/privett.shtml

Pullin, Graham, "Design Meets Disability," *The Utne Reader*, July–August 2009, pp. 48–51.

Regis, Ed, *Great Mambo Chicken and the Transhuman Condition: Science Slightly over the Edge* (New York: Perseus Books, 1990).

Robinson, Kim S., *Forty Signs of Rain* (New York: Random House, 2004).

Robinson, Kim S., *Fifty Degrees Below* (New York: Random House, 2005).

Robinson, Kim S., *Sixty Days and Counting* (New York: Random House, 2007).

Roden, David, "Deconstruction and Excision in Philosophical Posthumanism," *Journal of Evolution and Technology*, 21/1 (2010): 27–36.

Rose, Nikolas, *The Politics of Life Itself: Biomedicine, Power, and Subjectivity in the Twenty-First Century* (Princeton, NJ: Princeton University Press, 2007).

Rowlands, Mark, "Extended Cognition and the Mark of the Cognitive," *Philosophical Psychology*, 22/1 (2009): 1–19.

Rowlands, Mark, "The Extended Mind," *Zygon*, 44/3 (2009): 629–41.

Ruether, Rosemary R., *Sexism and God-Talk: Toward a Feminist Theology* (Boston, MA: Beacon Press, 1983).

Ruether, Rosemary R., "Imago Dei: Christian Tradition and Feminist Hermeneutics," in Ted K.E. Børresen (ed.), *The Image of God: Gender Models in Judaeo-Christian Tradition* (Minneapolis, MN: Fortress, 1991), 282–3.

Sawyer, Robert, *Mindscan* (New York: Tor Books, 2005).

Schneider, Joseph, *Donna Haraway: Live Theory* (New York: Continuum, 2005).

Schrag, Calvin, *The Resources of Rationality: A Response to the Postmodern Challenge* (Bloomington, IN: Indiana University Press, 1992).

Schueller, Malini J., "Analogy and (White) Feminist Theory: Thinking Race and the Color of the Cyborg Body," *Signs: Journal of Women in Culture & Society*, 31/1 (2005): 63–92.

Schwarz, Alan, "An Injured Soldier Re-Emerges as a Sprinter," *The New York Times* (August 13, 2009).

Scott, Peter M., "We Have Never Been Gods: Transcendence, Contingency and the Affirmation of Hybridity," *Ecotheology*, 9/2 (2004): 199–220.

Shults, F. LeRon, *Reforming Theological Anthropology: After the Philosophical Turn to Relationality* (Grand Rapids, MI: Eerdmans, 2003).

Shults, F. LeRon, *Christology and Science* (Grand Rapids, MI: Eerdmans, 2008).

"The Singularity FAQ," The Singularity Institute for Artificial Intelligence, http://singinst.org/singularityfaq#WhatIsTheSingularity, date accessed May 16, 2011.

Sorgner, Stefan Lorenz, "Beyond Humanism: Reflections on Trans- and Posthumanism," *Journal of Evolution and Technology*, 21/2 (2010): 1–19.

Sorgner, Stefan L., "Nietzsche, the Overhuman and the Transhuman," *Journal of Evolution and Technology*, 20/1 (2009): 29–42.

Soskice, Janet M., "The Ends of Man and the Future of God," in John Polkinghorne and Michael Welker (eds), *The End of the World and the Ends of God* (Harrisburg, PA: Trinity Press International, 2000), 78–88.

Stenmark, Mikael, *Rationality in Science, Religion and Everyday Life: A Critical Evaluation of Four Models of Rationality* (Notre Dame, IN: University of Notre Dame Press, 1995).

Stenmark, Mikael, *How to Relate Science and Religion: A Multidimensional Model* (Grand Rapids, MI: Eerdmans, 2004).

Stephenson, Lisa P., "Directed, Ordered and Related: The Male and Female Interpersonal Relation in Karl Barth's Church Dogmatics," *Scottish Journal of Theology*, 61/4 (2008): 435–49.

Stock, Gregory, *Redesigning Humans: Choosing Our Genes, Changing Our Future* (New York: Mariner Books, 2002).

Stout, Jeffrey, *Ethics after Babel: The Languages of Morals and Their Discontents* (Boston, MA: Beacon Press, 1988).

Thweatt-Bates, J. Jeanine, "Artificial Wombs and Cyborg Births: Postgenderism and Theology," in Ron Cole-Turner (ed.), *Transhumanism and Transcendence: Christian Hope in an Age of Technological Enhancement* (Washington, DC: Georgetown University Press, 2011), 101–14.

Thweatt-Bates, J. Jeanine, "Feminism, Religion and Science," in James Haag, Michael L. Spezio, and Gregory R. Peterson (eds), *The Routledge Companion for Religion and Science* (New York: Routledge, 2011), 69–78.

Tobler, Judy, "Beyond a Patriarchal God: Bringing the Transcendent Back to the Body," *Journal of Theology for Southern Africa*, 106 (2000): 35–50.

"The Transhumanist Declaration," World Transhumanist Association, http://transhumanism.org/index.php/WTA/declaration/, date accessed November 12, 2008.

van Huyssteen, J. Wentzel, "Postfoundationalism in Theology and Science," in J. Wentzel van Huyssteen and Niels H. Gregerson (eds), *Rethinking Theology and Science: Six Models for the Current Dialogue* (Grand Rapids, MI: Eerdmans, 1998), 13–49.

van Huyssteen, J. Wentzel, *The Shaping of Rationality: Toward Interdisciplinarity in Theology and Science* (Grand Rapids, MI: Eerdmans, 1999).

van Huyssteen, J. Wentzel, *Alone in the World? Human Uniqueness in Science and Theology*, The Gifford Lectures (Grand Rapids, MI: Eerdmans, 2006).

Vinge, Vernor, "The Coming Technological Singularity," *Whole Earth Review* (1993): www.ugcs.caltech.edu/~phoenix/vinge/vinge-sing.html, date accessed July 20, 2010.

Vita-More, Natasha, "Next Steps," The Extropy Institute, www.extropy.org/future.htm, date accessed April 15, 2008.

Waters, Brent, *From Human to Posthuman: Christian Theology and Technology in a Postmodern World* (Burlington, VT: Ashgate, 2006).

Weatherson, Brian, "Are You a Sim?," *Philosophical Quarterly*, 53/212 (2003): 425–31.

Wildman, Wesley J., "Distributed Identity: Human Beings as Walking, Thinking Ecologies in the Microbial World," in Nancey Murphy and Christopher C. Knight (eds), *Human Identity at the Intersection of Science, Technology and Religion* (Burlington, VT: Ashgate Publishing Company, 2010), 165–78.

Wolfe, Cary, *What Is Posthumanism?* (Minneapolis, MN: University of Minnesota Press, 2010).

Young, Simon, *Designer Evolution: A Transhumanist Manifesto* (Amherst, NY: Prometheus Books, 2006).

Yudkowsky, Eliezer, "The Singularitarian Principles," http://yudkowsky.net/sing/principles.ext.html#desc, date accessed May 22, 2008.

Yudkowsky, Eliezer, "Twelve Virtues of Epistemology," http://yudkowsky.net/rational/virtues, date accessed June 2, 2011.

Yudkowsky, Eliezer, "What Is the Singularity?," The Singularity Institute for Artificial Intelligence, www.singinst.org/overview/whatisthesingularity, date accessed May 22, 2008.

Yudkowsky, Eliezer, "An Intuitive Explanation of Bayesian Reasoning," Less Wrong (2003): http://yudkowsky.net/rational/bayes, date accessed January 20, 2011.

Yudkowsky, Eliezer, "What Do We Mean by Rationality?" Less Wrong (2009): http://lesswrong.com/lw/31/what_do_we_mean_by_rationality/, date accessed January 20, 2011.

# Index

57821/Cindi Mayweather (character) 26

"A Cyborg Manifesto"
   *Designer Evolution: A Transhumanist Manifesto* 41
   Enlightenment anthropology 96
   feminist posthuman construction 5, 15, 88
   Genesis 82
   goddess and feminism 161
   nonhuman animals 104–5
   technological analysis 38
   transhumanism 67
"A Letter to Mother Nature" 56–7
"abstract masculinity" 97
Adam and Garden of Eden 172
aging research 77–8
AI, *see* artificial intelligence
Akeley, Carl 27
Alexander, M. Jacqui 166
Alone in the world?
   at home in TechnoNature 123–5
   dominion and ontological disjunction 120–3
Althaus-Reid, Marcella 161–4, 167, 187
   Am I my sister's keeper?
   abolitionist project and uplifting 100–4
   human, nonhuman and posthuman kinship 104–7
ambivalent cyborgs 132–3
Andrews, Lori 78
Anissimov, M. 52, 53
*Anticipating Omega* 126
Antiochene school of Christology 177–9, 189–90
Apollinaris of Laodicea 177, 188
Aquinas, Thomas 112
ArchAndroid project 25–6
Artificial Intelligence (AI) 8, 52–3, 137

Asimov, Isaac 25
*Astronautics* (journal) 18
at home in TechnoNature 123–5
Athanasius (Bishop of Alexandria) 177
Augustine of Hippo 111

Bacon, Francis 92
Barth, Karl 115–16
Bastian, Michelle 37–8, 133, 136
*Battlestar Galactica* 53
Bernal, J.D. 44
"better than well" (WTA) 42–3
"Bi/Christ" 185
"bioLuddites" 63–4
biopolitics and bioLuddites 61–5
body as property
   all heart, cyborgs and hybrid bodies 80–1
   femaleman 84–92
   introduction 80
   posthumans without a soul 81–4
"body theology" 149, 152, 160
Boethius and human person definition 112
book structure 12–13
"Borg" (character) 5, 23–4
Bostrom, Nick 8, 41, 43, 47, 49–50, 73–5, 92, 139
Brasher, Brenda 119, 180
"breached boundaries" 16, 21
Bresnahan, David 58
Bush, George W. 63
Butler, Octavia E. 25

Cameron, James 24
Campbell, Heidi 8–9, 59
"*capax dei*" 144
Captain Picard (character) 23
Castree, Noel 4
Cayenne (dog) 170

Chalcedon Council  175, 178–80, 184, 188, 190
Chalmers, David  147
chimera (mythical beasts)  16–17
Chisenko, Alexander  20
Christian theology  149, 158–9, 164, 165, 168
    Christology and the posthuman cyborg Christ  176–81
    introduction  175–6
    Jesus as trickster figure  181–3
    posthuman subjectivity and mind of Christ  187–90
    quest for the hybridized Jesus  183–7
    ultimate human  191–2
Clark, Andy  18, 20–1, 38, 42, 147
Clynes, Manfred  18, 23, 38
coalition cyborg  37–8
Cockburn, Cynthia  38
"coded devices"  18
Coyle, Fiona  122
Coyote Trickster metaphor  104
Creator God concept  127
*Cronopsis* (magazine)  73
"cybernetic postman"  67, 69–70
"cyborg anthropology"  39
cyborg Christ concept  13, 175, 176–81, 188–90, 192
"cyborg citizenship concept  62
"Cyborg Embodiment and the Incarnation"  175, 187
    cyborg manifesto
    death of God/Goddess  30–6
    earthly survival  36–40
    introduction  15
    (mother?) nature  26–30
    neither fish nor fowl  16–26
    *see also* Haraway, Donna
"cyborg ontology"  37
"cyborg" term  18
cyborg/transhumanism comparison  68
Cyril of Alexandria  178

"Daedalus: Science and the Future"  44
Daly, Mary  185
Darwin, Charles  161
Darwin, Hetty  161
de Grey, Aubrey  77–8

"democratic transhumanism"  48
democratic transhumanism/technoprogressivism  48–50
*Designer Evolution: A Transhumanist Manifesto*  41
"designer revolution"  56
deterred subjects and extended selves  142–9
DeVries, Diane  154
Diaz, Miguel H.  116, 165
Dinello, Daniel  25
dinosaur comics  2, 21
disability theologies as cyborg  152–61
Douglas, Mary  55
Dvorsky, George  85–8, 91–2, 101–4

e-mail to mother nature  55–8
*Ecco Homo*  192
ECMO (extracorporeal membrane oxygenation)  17
Eiesland, Nancy  153–4, 157–60
Elizondo, Virgilio  164–6, 185
embodiment  81, 151, 161, 175
    Enlightenment
    aging  78
    cultural/scientific progress  131
    epistemology and anthropology  96
    humanism  44
    posthumans without a soul  81
    rational humanism  43, 101
    scientific objectivism  135–6
    transhumanism  58
    universal Man  183
*Epic of Gilgamesh*  43
Esfandiary, F.M. (FM-2030)  4
Ethics After Babel  22
eugenics  44–5
Eve and Garden of Eden  172
*Exogenesis*  25
"extended minds" concept  21, 147
"Extropian Principles"  48, 52
"extropianism"  47–50
*Extropy Magazine*  47

FemaleMan concept
    beyond gender "as we know it"  90–2
    psychological androgyny and artificial wombs  85–90

*The Female Man* 25, 91, 186
"Femaleman Meets Oncomouse" 98, 104–5
feminist science fiction narratives 25
Firestone, Shulamith 89
Formula of Reunion (AD 433) 178
Foucault, Michel 96
Fukuyama, F. 63
fyborg (functional cyborg) 20, 38

Gaine, Vincent 24
Gane, Nicholas 104
Garden of Eden 172
Garland-Thomson, Rosemarie 169
    Garner, Stephen
    ecotheological interpretation of cyborgs 167
    functional interpretations 113
    hybridity in Christology 180–1
    Hefner, Philip 144
    "hopeful posthuman" 141–2
    "narratives of apprehension" 5
    posthuman discourse 23, 128–9, 136–8, 143
Genesis 82, 109–10, 133, 172
Gilkey, Langdon 131
    glorified bodies
    disability theologies as cyborg 152–61
    postcolonial theologies as cyborg 164–8
    queer theologies as cyborg 161–4
God
    humanity 128–9
    Old Testament 109–11
    plastic images 109–117
    transhumanism 58–9
God-man concept 185
    God/Goddess
    death 30–6
    Haraway, Donna 82–3
"Godwin's Law" 44
Goizueta, Roberto S. 116
Graham, Elaine
    bodies of human beings and cyborgs 152
    Borg (character) 23
    cyborgs
        description 168

    ecotheological interpretation 167
    hybridity 125
    disability 157
    Haraway, Donna
        cyborgs 141
        God/Goddess 82–3
        techno-optimism 132–3
    *homo sapiens/techno sapiens* 142
    "hopeful posthuman" 138
    human uniqueness 168
    posthuman discourse 124, 145, 192
    *Star Trek: The Next Generation* 24
    theology and cyborgs 12, 142
    transcendance 139
    transhumanism 140–1
Gray, Chris H. 18, 155–6
Great Ape Project 62–3, 70

Habermas, Jurgen 63
Haldane, J.B.S. 44
Ham (chimpanzee) 39
Hampson, Daphne 185
Hanson, Robin 93
Haraway, Donna
    animals 104
    anthropological dualism 72
    "breached boundaries" 16, 21
    "Catholic sacramentalism" 30
    "Catholic sentimentality" 82
    Cayenne (dog) 170
    Christian theology 164
    Christianity 30–2, 34
    Coyote Trickster 104, 182
    cyborg discourse
        Crucified Jesus 159
        description 11–13, 40, 80–4, 96
        disability 159, 161
        earthly survival 36–7
        feminism 15, 27, 35, 89, 122, 135, 151, 154, 162, 167
        gender 166
        Hughes, James 106
        human/animal boundary 104
        hybridity 120, 125
        imagery 90
        "Man and Machine" 151
        "man in space" 133
        "needy of connection" 144

politics/economics 158
politics/ethics 123
re-invention 132
"world without gender" 163
eating 118, 171
*Ecco Homo* 192
essentialism 84
"Femaleman Meets Oncomouse" 98, 104–5
"figuration" 34
Garner, Stephen 137
god/goddess 82–3
Graham, Elaine 82–3, 124, 141
"heteroglossia" 36
human bodies 164
hybridity 81
instrumentality 170–1
Jesus
    as Christ 33–4
    as "trickster figure" 178, 181–4
machines and technologies 19
materialism 72, 80, 90
"modern medicine" 17
*Modest Witness* 32
"Nature" concept 15, 28–9
"nature of no nature" 28
"Oncomouse" 82, 104
personhood 106
"possible liveable worlds" 190
postgenderism 88
posthuman discourse 25, 67, 70, 80–1, 89, 99, 104, 192
*Primate Visions* 27
"sacramental consciousness" 34
scientific revolution 148
"Second Millenium" 30
"Situated Knowledges"... 11, 97–8, 104
Sojourner Truth 181–3
species boundaries 169
technoscience 32, 36–7
*The Female Man* 91
"The Laboratory/The Passion of the OncoMouse" 32–3
transhumanism 88, 99, 137
Waters, Brent 136
Western technoscience 141
*When Species Meet* 33, 82

*see also* "A Cyborg Manifesto"
Hartsock, Nancy 97
Hauskeller, Michael 71
Hayek, Friedrich 48
Hayles, N. Katherine
    autonomous self 18
    "cybernetic postman" 67, 69–70
    cyborgs and feminism 122
    *How We Became Posthuman* 67, 72
    "kinder gentler transhumanism" 137
    "liberal Humanist subject" 78
    personhood 138
    posthuman discourse 6, 11, 20–1, 42, 68–9, 71, 144, 146, 151, 192
    transhumanism 72, 137
heart and soul
    all heart? transhumanists on embodiment 71–2
    uploads, sins and virtual embodiment 72–7
*hedonistic transhumanism* 50–1
Hefner, Philip 114, 117, 124–7, 133, 138, 143–4, 168
Hehn, Johannes 113
Herzfeld, Noreen 76, 109–10, 115–16
*Homo faber* 20, 126
*Homo sapiens* 21, 56–7, 73, 103, 142, 170, 173, 177
hope without techno-optimism 126–32
hopeful cyborg 138–42
"hopeful posthuman" 137, 138, 141
*How We Became Posthuman* 67, 72
Hughes, James
    body description 78–9
    cultural taboo/boundary transgression 55–6
    cyborgs 58
    extropianism 48
    Haraway, Donna, androgyny of cyborgs 89
    "libertarian transhumanism" 48
    "morphological freedom" 79
    "personal/human" comparison 101
    personhood 101, 106
    postgenderism 85–8, 91–2
    rationality 95
    religion/transhumanism 82
    religious faith 57

transhumanism 41, 43–4, 48–9, 57, 60, 62
Western democracy 62
World Transhumanist Association 51
"human racism" 56
human/animal boundary 16–17
Humanity+ (WTA) 62, 70
humanity, plus 41–7
Huxley, Julian 44
   hybridity
   Chalcedon 180
   Christology 175
   cyborgs 120, 125, 142, 151, 159–60, 164, 168, 180–1
   Garner, Stephen and Christology 180–1
   Jesus 179, 181, 184–6
   location 165
   posthuman discourse 81
   theology 180

Institute for Ethics and Emerging Technologies (IEET) 49, 62, 70, 85, 88, 95
Isherwood, Lisa 150, 162–3

Jake (character) 55
Jantzen, Grace 140
Jesus
   Chalcedon Council 179
   Haraway, Donna 181–2
   and humanity 177
   hybridity 179, 181, 184–6
   New Testament 176
   socio-cultural identity 187
   trickster figure 178, 181–4
   Waters, Brent 180
*Journal of Evolution and Technology* 60

Kass, Leon 22–3, 63
Kaufert, Joseph 156–7
Kilner, John 59
Kline, Nathan 18, 23, 38
know thyself
   rational humanists and Bayesian reasoners 92–6
   situated knowledges 96–9
Krueger, Oliver 4

Kull, Anne
Christ 187
cyborg
   discourse 12, 123–5, 148
   nature and culture 123, 132, 141–2
"Cyborg Embodiment and the Incarnation" 175, 180–1, 187
"hopeful posthuman" 138
human uniqueness 168
Jesus as hybrid creature 179, 181
posthuman discourse 192
Kurzweil, Ray 4, 25–6, 46, 51, 53–4, 56, 73–7, 80
Kwok Pui-Lan 164–8, 180, 183–6, 190

Lang, Fritz 25
Lee, Jung Young 164–6
Less Wrong (community blog) 93, 95–6
LGBTQ rights activism 79
"libertarian humanism" 48
limited dominion and ontological disjunction 120–3
Locker, David 156–7
Logos theology 176–7
Logos-*anthropos* Christology 190
Logos-*sarx* Christology 177, 188, 190
Logos-theology 176
Luhman, Niklas 99

McCollum, Adele 154–6
Mckenny, Gerald 126
"Man and Machine" 18, 151
"man in space cyborg" 39
Mantin, Ruth 162–3
"Many Moons" (video) 26
Mary Magdalene 90
"materialistic anthropology" 136
"medical cyborg" 19, 152, 161
*Metropolis* 25
*Mindscan* 55, 74
Minsky, Marvin 4
Mitchell, C. Ben 59
*Modest Witness* 32
Mohanty, Chandra Talpade 166
Moltmann-Wendel, Elizabeth 149–50, 152–3, 157
Monáe, Janelle 25–6
Moravec, Hans 4, 51, 72

More, Max 41, 45–8, 53, 56–7, 96
Morriss, Peter 21
Morrow, Tom 47
Mullins, Aimee 155

Nash, Catherine 4
*Natural-Born Cyborgs* 20, 147
Nelson, James 149–50, 152–3, 157
Nestorius 178
New Testament and God 110–11
Niebuhr, Reinhold 131
Nietzsche 45–6, 121, 135
Noble, David 140
Norris, Richard A. 178–9, 188–9

O'Brien, Kevin J. 168–9
Olson, Nikki 88
organism/machine boundary 17
    original, technological sin
        ambivalent cyborgs 132–3
        hope without techno-optimism 126–32
*Our Posthuman Future: Consequences of the Biotechnology Revolution* 63
"Overview of Biopolitics" (IEET) 62

"patternism" concept 76
Paul of Samosata 177–8
Pearce, David 41, 50–1, 100–2
Pellisier, Hank 88
Peters, Ted 76–7, 129–32, 138–9
plastic images of God
    functional interpretations 113–14
    introduction 109–11
    relational interpretations 114–17
    substantive interpretations 111–13
playing god 58–61
post-anthropologies
    am I my sister's keeper? 100–7
    body as property 77–84
    heart and soul 71–7
    introduction 67–70
    know thyself 92–9
"postcolonial" term 164
postcolonial theologies as cyborg 164–8
"postfoundationalism" 6, 11–12
postgenderism 85–8, 90–1
posthuman discourse
    "A Cyborg Manifesto" 5

definition 1–3, 77
femaleman 84
introduction 1
representation 23–5
terminal(ogical) confusion 3–6
transversing
    cyborgs 11–12
    introduction 6–8
    transhumanists 8–11
*see also* Haraway, Donna
posthuman subjectivity and mind of Christ 187–90
"posthuman" term 4–5, 41, 67, 104, 191
"posthuman*ism*" term 4
Prabhu, George Soares 184
Prins, Baukje 98
psychological androgyny and artificial wombs 85–90
Psychophysiological Aspects of Space Flight Symposium 18

queer theologies as cyborg 161–4
quest for the hybridized Jesus 183–7

Rand, Ayn 48
Randolph, Lynn 31–2, 34–5, 171
rational humanism
    Bayesian reasoners 92–6
    Enlightenment 43
rationality 93–5
Rawls, J. 102
Regis, Ed 139
*Religion Without Revelation* 44
Robinson, Kim S. 57
*Robocop* 18, 68, 132
Rose, Nikolas 44, 149, 157, 160
"Rose" (rat-pump system) 38–9
Ruether, Rosemary Radford 185
Russ, Joanna 25, 91, 186

Sawyer, Robert 55, 74
Schneider, Joseph 30, 133
Schrag, Calvin 7, 145
Schueller, Malini J. 37
Schwarzenegger, Arnold 5
*Science in the Capital* 57
Scrabble 147

Shults, F. LeRon 111, 115, 148, 179, 187, 191
singularitarianism 51–3
Singularity Institute for Artificial Intelligence (SAIA)... 52, 93
"Situated Knowledges: The Science Question in Feminism" 11, 97–8, 104
Smuts, Barbara 33
Sojourner Truth 181–3
Sorgner, Stefan 45
*Star Trek: The Next Generation* 5, 23–4
Stenmark, Mikael 94–5
Stiteler, Valerie 154–5
Stout, Jeffrey 22
Stuart, Elizabeth 150
*Summa Theologica* 112

T-rex 1, 20
*techno sapiens* 142
*Technology and Human Becoming* 124
"technoprogressivism" 48
*Terminator* 5, 53, 132
Tetris (computer game) 147
*The Female Man* 25, 91, 186
*The Future is Mestivo* 185
"*The Laboratory/The Passion of the OncoMouse*" (painting) 31–3, 39
*The Passion of the OncoMouse* 171
"The Second Christian Millenium" 82
*The Singularity is Near* 25
*The Socialist Review* 5
"The World, the Flesh and the Devil" 44
Theodore of Mopsuestia 178, 189–90
theological anthropologies
    alone in the world? 117–25
    functional interpretations 113–14
    limited dominion and ontological disjunction 120–3
    original, technological sin 126–33
    plastic images of God 109–11
    relational interpretations 114–17
    substantive interpretations 111–13
theological post-anthropology
    cyborgs in the garden 172–3
    deterred subjects and extended selves 142–9
    glorified bodies 149–68

hopeful cyborg 138–42
introduction 135–8
when species meet 168–72
Tillich, Paul 123
"transhuman" term 4
"transhumanism" term 4, 41
transhumanism
    "A Cyborg Manifesto" 67
    anthropology 71
    Christian theology 8
    description 10–11
    Enlightenment 9, 58
    eugenics 44
    goals 77
    Haraway, Donna 88, 99, 137
    Hayles N. Katherine 72, 137
    "materialistic anthropology" 136–7
    popularizing 9
    postgenderism 85–8
    posthuman definition 77
    posthumanism 3–4
    technology 77
transhumanism/cyborg comparison 68
"Transhumanist Declaration" (WTA) 61
"Transhumanist FAQ" 41–2, 52–3, 56, 62, 64, 73
transhumanist manifesto
    biopolitics and bioLuddites 61–5
    democratic transhumanism/ technoprogressivism 48–50
    e-mail to mother nature 55–8
    extropianism 47–50
    hedonistic transhumanism 50–1
    humanity, plus 41–7
    playing god 58–61
    singularitarianism 51–3
    upload scenario 53–5
    Young, Simon 84
"transitional human" term 4
"Twelve Virtues of Rationality" 94

ultimate human 191–2
"uplifting" concept 101–4
Utahraptor 1, 20

van Huyssteen, J. Wentzel
    Alone in the world? 117–19
    cyborgs 11

Genesis 110, 133
human uniqueness 125, 169
interdisciplinary public theology 9–10, 12
"postfoundationalism" 6, 11–12
rationality of theology 10
transversality metaphor 7
Vinge, Vernor 51
von Rad, Gerhard 113

Walker, Mark 8–9
"walking, thinking ecologies" 146
Waters, Brent
    Christ 191
    cyborg hybridity 125
    Hefner, Philip and anthropology 126–7
    *imago dei* 143
    Jesus 180
    limited dominion and ontological disjunction 120–2
    posthuman discourse 1, 129–30, 135–6, 143, 191–2
*When Species Meet* 33
Wiener, Norbert 69
Wildman, Wesley 145–6
"wisdom of repugnance" 22
Wolfe, Cary
    "animal studies" 105
        disability, animals and posthuman 169

Garland-Thomson, Rosemarie 169–70
humanism 100
"posthuman"/posthumanism 4, 105
posthumanism 92, 99, 145
"shared finitude" 160
transhumanism 67
World Transhumanist Association (WTA)
    "better than well" 42–3
    Bostrom, Nick 8, 50
    survey of members (2006) 58, 60, 100
    "Transhumanist Declaration" 61
    "Transhumanist FAQ" 41
    *see also* Humanity+

Yerkes, Robert 27
Young, Simon
    Cartesian dualism 73
    *Designer Evolution: A Transhumanist Manifesto* 41–2
    eugenics 44–5
    God 58–9
    Nature 57
    "new scientism" 93
    Transhumanist Manifesto 84, 140
Yudkovsky, Eliezer 53, 93–6
Yuval-Davis, Nira 38